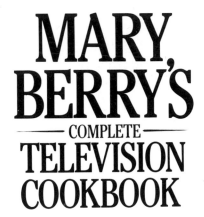

MARY, BERRY'S
—— COMPLETE ——
TELEVISION COOKBOOK

Erratum

Page 126: Traditional Christmas Cake

The list of ingredients should include
4 eggs.

MARY, BERRY'S

COMPLETE

TELEVISION

COOKBOOK

THAMES MACDONALD

Managing Editor
Robin Cross

Design
Jerry Goldie/Grub Street

Production
John Moulder

Picture Research
Jenny de Gex
Tony Satin

Food Photography
John Lee
Martin Brigdale
Peter Myers
Paul Kemp

Additional Illustrations
Zefa (p8)
Alan Hutchinson (pp 14-15)
Peter Myers (p 20)
Chris Drake (pp 22, 25)
Jenny de Gex (pp 21, 26, 27)
**National, Federation of Women's
Institutes** (pp 149, 150)

A THAMES MACDONALD BOOK

This edition first published 1983
Macdonald & Co (Publishers) Ltd
Maxwell House
Worship Street
London EC2A 2EN

ISBN 0 356 07548 6 (PB)
    0 356 09756 0 (HB)

CONTENTS

THE KITCHEN

PLANNING YOUR KITCHEN

If you are lucky enough to be able to plan your kitchen from scratch, decide first what activities other than cooking you will need it for. Will the washing and ironing be done there too? Do you want to eat there? My family has always loved the cosy atmosphere of the kitchen and my own kitchen is large enough to accommodate a sizeable dining table. Kitchen/diners are very popular and convenient if you have the space. For informal eating with friends or family, they are the ideal, no long trek away from the kitchen to the dining room with the food growing colder as you go. If you do not have enough space for a permanent dining table, you could have a breakfast bar or a fold-away or pull-out table. I have a separate laundry room which houses my washing machine etc., so that the kitchen is devoted solely to cooking and eating. It is the centre of my house and as I spend a lot of time there, I took great care in planning it. Make sure you do the same.

One of the main things to bear in mind when planning a kitchen is what the experts call the 'work triangle'. This triangle consists of storage, preparation and cooking areas, i.e., the refrigerator, sink and cooker. These three areas are the ones that are most constantly in use, so it makes sense to keep them all within easy reach of each other – this is where the triangle comes in. The total length of its three sides should not be more than 6.6. metres (22 feet) or less than 3.6 metres (12 feet). Try not to position the cooker too near a door or under a window. There are two principal reasons for this: first, you are likely to have people coming in and out of the kitchen and there is a risk of collision when you are carrying something hot and heavy; and second, if you have gas the flame can get blown out by the breeze. It is also likely that a curtain could catch fire if it is directly above the cooker.

Next, the shape of the kitchen should be decided upon. To a large extent this will depend on the size and the dimensions of the room. It is simplest to have everything along one wall. This takes up very little space and is particularly suitable for a long, narrow kitchen. The other shapes usually found are the L-shape (two adjacent walls used), the U-shape (three walls used) and the galley kitchen (two parallel walls used). Whatever the shape, it is best to have a worktop on both sides of the cooker so there is plenty of room to put down hot pans.

Work surfaces should be heat-proof and easily cleaned. The most popular surface is probably laminate, with wood and ceramic tiles next on the list. You could include a marble worktop which is ideal for pastry-making.

Heating is often not considered in a kitchen. If you do a lot of cooking and baking, you will not need the heating on very often. Heaters should be wall-mounted and not free-standing, as the latter are obviously a hazard.

Ventilation is very important because condensation caused by steam from cooking can ruin your decoration. Cooking smells are also unpleasant and tend to waft through to the rest of the house. The two main ways of ventilating are by use of an extractor fan, or a cooker hood.

When lighting a kitchen, make sure that you will not be standing in the way of the light and are therefore working in shadow. If you have wall units or shelves above the worktops, you can fix small fluorescent tubes to the underside which will light the surface underneath. Spotlights can be fitted on the ceiling and then angled to direct light wherever you need it.

Some ways to avoid accidents in the kitchen have already been mentioned – keeping the cooker away from a door and having adjacent work surfaces on either side of it, for example. The position of the cooker controls are also important if you have small children. They should not be able to reach them. Do not keep poisonous things like bleach and cleaning fluids where children can get their hands on them – under the sink is a favourite place for most of us – in a wall unit, or even locked away is much better.

Once you have your kitchen planned and built you can have fun filling it with all the utensils you will need. Here is a suggested list of the pots and pans you should have in a well-stocked kitchen: 3 saucepans with lids, 2 casseroles with lids, 2 frying pans, 2 pie dishes, 1 omelette pan, 1 colander, 1 soufflé dish, 1 roasting tin, 1 non-stick milk pan and 1 deep-frying pan and basket. Optional extras are: sauté pans, cocottes, gratin dish, oval terrine and a double boiler. You may also find a pressure cooker and a slow cooker useful.

Good knives and chopping boards are just as important as good pots and pans. Try to have a few cook's knives ranging from 9 in (22 cm) long to 5 in (12 cm), a good meat knife, a bread knife and a steel for sharpening. You should also have a wooden chopping board, a small bread board and perhaps a marble slab for pastry-making if you have not incorporated one as a worktop. Baking tins come in all shapes and sizes, but the most useful will be an 8-in (20 cm) cake tin, 7- and 8-in sponge tins, loaf tins, flat baking sheets, jam tart tins and biscuit cutters. You will also need a variety of bowls, wooden spoons, a rolling pin, spatula, fish slice, egg whisk, tin opener, corkscrew, bottle opener, soup ladle, grater, masher, pastry brush, perforated spoon, sieve, kitchen scissors, skewers, vegetable scraper, mandoline for slicing, mincer, lemon squeezer, measuring jug, scales, pestle and mortar, piping bag, nutcrackers, kettle and teapot.

Before you buy anything – from flooring to cutlery – take a good look at what is available in the shops and compare prices and qualities. Get all the leaflets you can and study them at home. Remember that if you choose wisely you may never have to buy replacements, so that a little extra initial outlay, if you can afford it, is often a saving in the long run.

KITCHEN UNITS

The best are those which need the least maintenance. Laminates look well but need constant polishing. I have chosen sealed dark oak which occasionally needs wiping down with a cloth. Wooden units should always be sealed otherwise they will absorb fat, which makes them unsightly as well as unhygienic. Avoid those wooden units which have an intricate pattern. They may look attractive but they trap dirt and are difficult to clean. You can buy units ready made which can probably be installed for you by the manufacturer. You can also buy units for self-assembly. They will virtually all comprise base units and wall units, and the variations on these themes are almost endless, from sink and hob units to broom cupboards and corner carousel units. There are many styles, everything from streamlined ultra-modern to the rustic charm of wood.

Floor-standing units incorporate drawers of various depths. First you must decide what kitchen equipment you require and where you are going to put it. This concerns not only large items such as washing machines and freezers but also pans and crockery. You must ask yourself, 'How much do I need and where am I going to store it?'

Top: Kitchen in a top-floor flat, making full use of a limited amount of space – an ideal 'galley' kitchen. Above: An elegant combination of wood and tiles.

Don't forget equipment like floor mops and carpet sweepers. Once you have made up your mind, you can determine which units will be most suitable for your needs.

Keep everything as near as possible to where you are going to need it. Shallow adjustable shelves are better than deep ones for most types of storage. China can be stacked on shelves the width of a dinner plate so that nothing gets hidden at the back of the cupboard.

If you don't like the sight of dishes on the draining board have a louvred-doored cupboard fitted with plastic plate racks and a tray to catch the drips underneath. Wire racks are also useful in cupboards and in drawers to carry pans.

To avoid clutter on the window sill put the washing-up mops, cloths and brushes with the cleaning agents in plastic racks fitted to the door below the sink.

Vertical storage for baking trays, meat tins, Swiss roll tins, chopping and bread boards, cooling racks and bun tins take up less room. Any small spaces left between the floor units are useful for this.

STORE CUPBOARDS
I am a great believer in having a well-stocked store cupboard. It's never a good idea to run out of staple foods that you use all the time, and it's often handy to have in a good supply of basic foods for those days when you just don't feel like menu-planning.

The cupboard should be cool and well ventilated. If space will allow it, choose shallow shelves for preference, so that things don't get hidden out of reach. Keep tall packets and jars at the back and smaller ones in front so that you can see what is there at a glance. If you don't have a special rack or cupboard for herbs and spices, these can be kept together in trays or shallow tins to stop them falling over. You can then lift the whole tray out of the cupboard when you need it.

Keep in the store cupboard or larder everything that is not stored in the fridge. If it is well ventilated, it will be ideal for vegetables, fruit and cooked meats, as well as flour, sugar, dried fruit and biscuit tins. The store cupboard or larder should be as near as possible to the food preparation area.

It is important to have a well-organized store cupboard. It is all too easy to run out of essentials without realizing it. Here are some of the items you should keep in stock.

Flavourings and seasonings:
Herbs
Spices
Stock cubes
Salt
Breadcrumbs
Mustard (powder and ready-made)
Tomato purée (in cans or tubes)
Olives
Gravy browning
Worcester sauce

Cake-making ingredients:
Sugar (granulated, caster, brown and icing)
Flour (plain and self-raising)
Dried fruits (apricots, currants, raisins, sultanas, dates and prunes)
Arrowroot
Cornflour
Baking powder
Custard powder
Essences (vanilla and almond)
Nuts (almonds and walnuts)
Glacé cherries, candied peel, angelica
Dried and evaporated milk.

Staple foods:
Rice (short and long-grained)
Pasta (spaghetti, macaroni or any one of the many varieties of pasta).
Dried vegetables (lentils, haricots, kidney beans, onions, peas).

Canned foods:
Fish (tuna, anchovies, salmon, sardines, prawns).
Meat (chopped ham, corned beef, pâté)
Soup (consommé and tomato are particularly useful).
Vegetables (pimentos, sweetcorn, new potatoes, tomatoes).

PLANNING YOUR KITCHEN

Fruit (blackcurrants, cherries, pineapple and raspberries are particularly useful).
Various biscuits (sweet and savoury)
Coffee, tea, chocolate and cocoa

Jams and preserves
Oil (salad and cooking)
Tomato juice
Vinegar (malt and wine)
Wine for cooking (keep in small bottles and refill when necessary).

FLOORING

Ease of cleaning is the first consideration when choosing a material for the kitchen floor. Because of this, it is rare to find carpet (even a washable, bathroom type) in a kitchen. Materials like rush matting are not suitable for the same reason. Many people choose vinyl, because the variety of colour and effects is enormous. It is available in sheet form, which is reasonably easy to lay, non-slip and quickly washed clean. It is also quite cheap. Sheet-cushioned vinyl has the same advantages, although it's more expensive. However, it is softer underfoot. Some of the most popular designs are imitations of other floor surfaces – tiles, brick, marble, parquet, etc. Vinyl tiles are easier to handle than the sheets and there is less wastage if you are covering a small area. They are also easier to cut when fitting, and can be individually replaced if and when necessary. It is possible to invent your own patterns, like a checkerboard effect, or a colourful border, by using different coloured plain tiles.

Wooden floorboards, if they are carefully sealed, can look very attractive, giving a pleasant rustic effect. Cork tiles also benefit from good sealing when they are used on the floor. There are some available which have a vinyl skin, which makes them tougher. Linoleum has gone out of fashion rather, to be replaced by vinyl. However, heavy-duty linoleum which is laid by an expert is still very hard-wearing and quiet underfoot, although the choice of colour and design is limited. Ceramic tiles look lovely on a floor, especially in interesting patterns like herring

bone or basketweave, but you can't really do it yourself properly. They are rather expensive, but are very hard-wearing.

My first choice will always be for mottled ceramic tiles. Don't be put off if people tell you they're hard on the feet and cold into the bargain – it simply isn't true. The Italian who laid my tiles told me that his 84-year-old mother had been on the tiles all her life and never complained. It's always a good idea to put one row of tiles round the wall instead of a skirting board under your units. This helps with the cleaning and means you don't get the woodwork or wallpaper wet when mopping the floor. You don't need to polish ceramic tiles.

If they are outside your price range, consider Amtico tiles or sheet flooring as a very good second choice. Buy a little bit extra to put behind work surfaces so that your wallpaper doesn't get splashed. It is better not to choose a plain colour for flooring – it will show every smear, no matter how careful you are to keep it clean.

WALLS

Paint is the simplest wall covering for a kitchen. Gloss paint is easily washed, but you must make sure that you have no condensation – it looks particularly unattractive on gloss paint. This and vinyl emulsion paint are easier to clean than water-based paints. Whichever you use should be applied to a good, even surface with no cracks or bumps.

Wallpaper is also suitable, but it is better not to have it round the cooker and sink areas where there is a lot of steam. Vinyl-coated wallpaper is more expensive but can easily just be wiped clean.

Wood panelling, in the form of tongued and grooved boarding, is attractive and practical, as long as it is sealed properly. It gives a warm and homely atmosphere.

Ceramic tiles are a favourite and the best wall covering for areas where it will be wet – behind the sink and draining board – and also behind the cooker where splashes of fat might appear.

If you have the room, it's nice to make

—The microwave—

the kitchen feel more homely with the addition of a few pictures. If, as I do, you like the warm glow of red brick in the kitchen, make sure it is sealed with several coats of sealant. This prevents the bricks from marking and shedding dust.

THE COOKER
Many people still prefer the all-in-one, free-standing cooker to the split-level hob and oven. Free-standing cookers come in an amazing range of sizes – from those with four burners, double oven, grill, griddle and storage drawers, to those with only a single oven. There are also some small cookers which you can stand on a work surface.

The split-level cooker enables you to have different fuels for the hob (even to the extent of having two gas rings and two electric plates) and the oven. It also gives you more scope in the design of your kitchen, aided by the fact that there is more choice in the available colours and styles.

The type of fuel you use is a matter of preference. Gas cookers are easier to regulate, but some people prefer the simplicity of electricity. Ceramic hobs are cleaned with a wipe, and are now available in white, brown and black. Electric fan ovens make sure that the temperature is the same on every shelf and many cookers now have stay-clean sides, though you will still have to use a bit of elbow-grease on the floor of the oven. It is a good idea to have both the oven and the fridge built into the wall and raised off the floor so that you don't have to bend every time you want to use them.

Solid fuel cookers are regaining their former popularity. They are ideal in a large country kitchen where they give a real welcoming warmth when you come down-stairs first thing on a winter's morning. They are not so suited to small kitchens, and especially not in summer.

Microwave ovens are a luxury, but if you can run to one you will find it marvellously useful. I use mine quite frequently when entertaining. I might cook a selection of vegetables like new potatoes, baby carrots, early peas and broad beans in parsley

PLANNING YOUR KITCHEN

sauce in the afternoon, and reheat them in the evening. This way you can be sure they're cooked to perfection (just slightly underdone), arrive on the table piping hot, and save you cluttering up the kitchen with steaming pans. Serve them attractively arranged on the dish you heated them up in.

Microwaves are also excellent for defrosting joints taken from the freezer, and for cooking fish and some sauces. When time is short they are a real boon. A child coming in for tea craving a baked potato can have one in front of him in just four minutes (four potatoes, on the other hand, take six minutes). You can buy ovens which have both a microwave and a conventional oven in the same unit.

As mentioned earlier, having a hood over your hob is a good idea, as it will get rid of smells and steam. Two types are available – one is ducted to an outside wall where the air escapes, the other is a recirculation model which passes the air through a filter (made from carbon, charcoal, plastic foam or aluminium) to extract the grease, smells and steam before returning it to the room.

The use of the micro-processor, or the 'chip', has improved cooker design. It not only gives accurate time and temperature control, but a better scope for pre-programming. It will be able to memorize a variety of cooking sequences; for example, heat up to boiling point, simmer for a specific time and then turn off. Thermostatic sensors can keep the temperature stable at any given setting.

THE FRIDGE
The first thing you need to decide upon is how much freezer space and how much refrigerator space you need. If you have a separate, large freezer, you will probably not need a separate freezer compartment in your fridge. Do ensure that you are making full use of your freezer. There is no point in having one which you do not use to its capacity.

Fridges are now available that have a chiller or cellar compartment – ideal for storing wine, cheese, butter, eggs, fruit and vegetables. Their temperature range is between 7° and 12°C, with the temperature in the fridge being below 7°C. Also available is a unit known as a cold storage centre, which consists of a freezer, fridge and chiller.

The ideal refrigerator is wide and shallow, so that even the things at the back are easily accessible. But in a small kitchen it is best to choose one that is tall and takes up less floor space. Make sure you don't buy too small a fridge. A rough guide, is at least one cubic foot for each member of the family.

Star markings on the frozen food compartment show the length of time food may be stored. One star means that frozen food can be stored up to a week, two stars for a month and three stars for up to three months.

When you are choosing a fridge you should consider buying one which automatically defrosts. Defrosting is a chore that most people don't do often enough, with the result that the fridge works less efficiently.

RUBBISH
If you have a garden it is a good idea to start a compost heap. Any vegetable waste from the kitchen can be disposed of on it. An electric waste disposal unit fitted into the sink will deal with most of other food refuse – but beware of it eating your teaspoons! Anything that is left, should go into an upright plastic rubbish bin fitted with a binliner. Be careful to empty the bin regularly and keep it, and the floor it stands on, scrupulously clean, especially in summer.

More simply, you can instal a waste chute in the wall or worktop, which leads straight to a sealed bin outside. There are also incinerators available which will burn waste down to a fine ash.

DISHWASHER
The dishwasher is still considered a luxury, but they are worth the money if you have a large family and little time or inclination to be up to your elbows in suds all day.

ELECTRIC FOOD PROCESSORS
There are some wonderful food processors

on the market today that will do almost any job in the kitchen. Use them to purée cooked vegetables, chop and slice raw vegetables, chop meat for pâtés, or make pastry, bread and cakes. The three main types are food mixers, food processors and blenders.

The food mixer, either hand-held or the table top variety, often comes with a small blender attachment. If you do not do a large amount of cooking, and are not cooking for a large family, the food mixer should be sufficient. The hand-held mixer's capacity is fairly small, but the table mixer's can cope with up to 6 lb (2.72 kg) of cake or pudding mixture or 4½ lb (2.42 kg) of dough. Some of the better table mixer models have a wider choice of accessories, like a liquidizer, slicer/shredder, juice extractor, mincer and even a sausage maker.

An alternative appliance to a food mixer is a food processor. The basis of this machine is an electric motor which turns a very sharp double-bladed knife. The motor only comes into action when the lid of the plastic bowl is set firmly in place. The lid has a funnel through which you can drop food while the blade is turning. The blades go round at an amazing speed – up to 3,000

rpm. This means that chopping can take only 10 seconds; mincing can take 15 seconds; and food can be reduced to a paste in about 30 seconds. Most food processors are relatively small – they can hold about a pint and a half of liquid, or about one pound of cake mixture. This is not a big disadvantage, however, because the machines work very quickly. Some models have what is called continuous feed – a dispenser allows the mixed food to be transferred to a separate bowl, while you can be using the funnel to put in more food. In this way you can process large amounts of food without stopping the motor. However, food processors cannot whip up egg whites or thicken up double cream. If you like making soufflés and mousses, you will probably benefit from a mixer.

The last type of machine is the blender or liquidizer. It functions in a similar fashion to the food processor, with a high-speed blade chopping the food. Blenders are ideal for making things like soups, purées, sauces and food for babies. They come in various sizes: the large, two-pint model is suitable for families, while the smaller one-pint model is better for one or two people. Like the food processor it has a funnel through which you can pour or add food while the machine is running – especially useful when making mayonnaise. You should only fill it to two-thirds full, as the contents expand when the motor is switched on. The drawback with blenders is that they can only be run for a short time, as the motor becomes over-heated.

THE SINK
For preference choose a double sink, so that you can use the smaller of the two for soaking, rinsing or draining. A good surface for sinks and worktops is the American synthetic marble Corian. This is exceedingly tough, cool and easy to clean. It will withstand bleach and abrasives. Stainless steel would be my second choice for sinks, and for work surfaces a very acceptable alternative is a durable laminate. Enamel sinks are available in some attractive

–A liquidizer, ideal for soups and purées–

colours, but are not always big enough. If you are going to hand-wash clothes in a sink, it should be at least 10 in (25 cm) deep. Otherwise the depth should be 7-8 in (17.5-20 cm). Make sure the sink is wide enough to take the largest item you need to wash — in most cases this will be an oven shelf. If you have two sinks, one of them can contain a waste disposal unit.

MEAT

The meat we eat in Britain comes mostly from three animals: cattle, sheep and pigs. Deer are now being farmed like cattle, on a small scale, to increase the amount of venison we eat.

BEEF

The more expensive cuts are fore rib, sirloin, rump and fillet. Topside and silverside are also quite expensive nowadays. Brisket, shin, neck and flank are more economical. Skirt, a thin lean steak from inside the animal, is excellent value and goes well in pies, puddings and stews. Sirloin can be roasted whole on the bone or with the fillet removed, or used for grilled and fried steaks. For the best results, sirloin should not weigh less than 2 lb (900 g). Fore rib can be roasted on the bone or boned and rolled. Alternatively they can be pot roasted braised or boiled. Topside, which has no bone, gives good value for money. It can be slow or medium roasted with added fat, but braising and pot roasting are also recommended. Silverside is a popular joint for salting and making the traditional 'boiled beef and carrots'. It can also be boiled or braised, but it does need long, slow cooking. Brisket can also be salted. When fresh it may be slow-roasted, pot roasted, braised or boiled. Once again long slow, cooking is required. Shin is the fore leg of the animal (leg is the hind leg). A coarse cut, it is excellent for stewing, giving delicious gravy.

How to recognize good quality beef

1.   The meat should be firm to the touch.
2.   The lean should have a bright red colour with just a brownish tinge. If the appearance is very dark and dry this is a good indication that the meat has been cut and exposed to the air for some time, or that it has been taken from an inferior

3. The flesh should contain small flecks of fat, an effect known as 'marbling', which keeps the lean meat moist during cooking.
4. The fat should be creamy in colour — although the colour of the fat is governed by particular types of breeding and feeding.
5. The amount of gristle which is visible will vary with the cut, but prime cuts should contain very little.

LAMB

Leg, loin and shoulder are the most popular cuts. Breast, scrag and middle neck, chops and cutlets are also available. With the exception of scrag and middle necks, all cuts are suitable for roasting, with saddle, leg, shoulder and loin gaining pride of place. Breast, scrag or neck — well trimmed of excess fat — are ideal for stews and casseroles.

How to recognize good quality lamb

1. The flesh will vary in colour from the light pink of a very young lamb to a dark red, depending on the age and type of sheep.
2. It is easy to distinguish between the fat of home-produced and imported lamb. The former should be creamy white, the latter white and firm.
3. Avoid brittle white and yellowish fat as the former is a good indication of an overlong stay in the freezer and the latter is a giveaway for elderly meat. Joints with these characteristics require longer and slower cooking methods.
4. Look for plumpness and a good layer of covering fat in legs and shoulders. Blue-tinged knuckle bones indicate a young animal.

PORK

Now that cold storage is universal pork can safely be bought and eaten at any time of year. However, in hot weather be wary of pork displayed in an unrefrigerated window. Pork is the fattiest of meats. Both the leg and the loin cuts are best roasted. Belly, hand and spring, chops and spare ribs can be roasted, fried, grilled or casseroled.

How to recognize good quality pork

1. The meat should be firm and smooth, with very little gristle or no gristle. The more gristle there is, the older the pig. An older animal will also display dark and coarse-grained flesh, contrasting with the pink or rose colour of a younger animal.
2. Small flecks of fat in the flesh — known as 'marbling' — increases both tenderness and flavour.
3. A well-fed animal will have firm white fat in a thick outside layer. Grey, soft or oily looking fat is a sign of poor quality.
4. Cut surfaces of the meat should be slightly moist to the touch but not wet with fluid.

VEAL

There are two distinct types of veal. The first is from calves fed on milk and fatty foods. The second from calves fed on grass. The former is very tender and also very expensive, much of it coming from Holland and France. Although grass-fed veal is less tender, many consider it has more flavour. Veal does not keep well and should be consumed within three or four days of slaughtering. This is perhaps the reason why many butchers are reluctant to keep veal if they feel that the demand is not constant. The higher priced cuts are fillet (from the top of the leg), loin (a large joint from the back) and leg. All three are suitable for roasting although fillet may be bought in slices, as medaillons, and loin is often cut into chops. Best end of neck is often sold boned, stuffed and rolled for roasting, but can also be bought on the bone in a piece or as cutlets. Middle neck, a cheaper cut, is ideal for braising and stewing and making pies. Knuckle, an economical cut from the lower part of the leg, is also good for braising and stewing. The shin is often cut into pieces 2-3 in (5-8 cm) long and, cooked with tomatoes, herbs and onions, is transformed into the celebrated Italian dish Osso Bucco.

How to recognize good quality veal

1. The flesh should be moist and soft, but not over-wet and flabby.
2. The flesh should have a fine texture. Milk-fed veal should be very pale pink or off white in colour; grass-fed will be pale pink. Avoid meat with a bluish tinge or mottled flesh, both indications of staleness.
3. The bones are pinkish white and soft. When boiled they produce a considerable amount of jelly.
4. There should be very little fat except around the kidneys. This fat should be very white. The colour of the external fat will vary from a pinkish white to a slightly yellow tinge. The fat should be firm.

BACON, GAMMON AND HAM

Bacon, gammon and ham are pork joints which have been dry salted, brined or smoked. They combine good flavour with value for money. Bacon is divided into cuts that come as joints, such as forehock and collar, or sliced in rashers like streaky, oyster and back. The forehock or foreleg can be cooked whole and is one of the cheaper bacon joints. It can also be divided into three. The collar, divided into prime and end, is a good boiling joint cut from the neck. Streaky is the cured equivalent of belly of pork and is usually fried or grilled. Back bacon makes lean rashers and is sold as long back, short back, back and ribs and top back.

Gammon is a more expensive cut usually sold in 4 joints: slipper, hock, middle gammon and corner gammon. Hock and slipper are good for boiling, middle and corner can be boiled or cut into grilling rashers. Ham is the hind leg of the pig, cut while it is still fresh pork and cured much more slowly than gammon or bacon. If a ham is cut square it is known as a short cut ham.

How to recognize good quality bacon, gammon and ham

1. 'Green' bacon, just taken out of the brine should have a delicate flavour, pleasant smell and pink flesh. Smoked bacon is darker in colour.
2. The lean meat should be firm and deep pink without any yellow or green stains. A very dark, dry appearance indicates that it has been cut and exposed to the air for some time.
3. The fat should be firm and white, not soft, oily or have yellow or green stains.
4. The rind should be thin, smooth and elastic.
5. In the case of ham, a well-matured, dry cured ham develops a bluish-green mould on the lean which is a sign of good quality.

OFFAL

Offal are the parts which remain after the slaughtered animal has been dressed. Liver and kidney are by far the most popular, but all are highly nutritious.

LIVER

Calf's liver: The most expensive and the best liver. It is best fried, grilled or used in a pâté. Avoid over-cooking, which produces hard, dry results.

Lamb's liver: Cheaper than calf's liver, and more popular. Suitable for grilling, frying, braising. Avoid over-cooking.

Pig's liver: Cheaper than lamb's liver and with a slightly stronger flavour. I like to make it milder by soaking slighty in milk for a couple of hours before cooking. Not to everyone's taste when grilled or fried, but excellent in pâtés and stews.

Ox liver: The cheapest liver, coarse in texture and often varying between strong flavour and lack of flavour. Unsuitable for grilling and frying, but it can be stewed alone or with steak. It can also be braised.

KIDNEYS

Ox kidney: The cheapest kidney, with a tendency to toughness. Long, slow cooking for stews, steak and kidney pies and puddings. One kidney usually weighs about 1½ lb (680 g). Since we joined the Common Market, the suet surrounding the kidney is not available. Much of it is used in meat product manufacture.

Calf's kidney: The most tender kidney, but not always easy to obtain.

Lamb's kidney: Excellent for grilling and frying, they are smaller than calf's kidney. The skin — which is removed before cooking — should look slippery and the kidneys should be firm and light brown.

Pig's kidney: Larger and flatter than lamb's kidney. Cut right through them for grilling or chop for risottos and stews.

HEART

Ox heart: The largest heart, with thick strong muscle that requires long careful cooking to avoid toughness and dryness. Heart is often parboiled and then roasted. It requires robust flavourings, such as plenty of onions or well-seasoned stuffings. An economical buy. usually weighing about 4 lb (1.8 kg), which will be enough for about 5 portions.

Calf's heart: Much smaller than ox heart, usually enough for 2 portions. More tender than ox heart, but it still needs careful cooking.

Lamb's heart: The smallest heart, enough for only one person. It is excellent stuffed and then roasted or braised.

HEAD

Ox cheek: Good for stews and brawn. A very economical buy.

Calf's head: Sold whole or in halves, it is usually boiled and served with sauces, or made into brawn. A whole head weighs 8-10 lb (3.63-4.54 kg) and will have enough meat for eight portions.

Sheep's head: Usually split in half and boiled for broth, with the meat being served as a separate dish with a sauce made from the broth.

Pig's head: Fresh or boned, boiled for brawn. The cheek can be brined, boned and boiled to produce Bath Chap, which is sliced and fried or eaten cold with salad. It is essential that heads be thoroughly cleaned and blanched before cooking.

TONGUE

Ox Tongue: Full of flavour and with a velvety texture. Ox tongues average 4-6 lb (1.8-2.72 kg) and are mostly cooked after salting.

Calf's Tongue: Delicate in texture and flavour, weighing 1-2 lb (450-900 g). It can be salted like ox tongue but is generally cooked unsalted.

Lamb's Tongue: The smallest tongue, weighing 8-12 oz (227-340 g). Excellent boiled or braised and served hot with parsley sauce.

FEET

Calf's feet: The basis of the celebrated calf's foot jelly which is traditionally served to invalids. They can be cooked with other meats to make brawn or a gelatinous stock.

Pig's trotters: Ideal for making stock. They may also be boned. They can be boiled, boned and stuffed and then grilled or fried.

SWEETBREADS

These are the pancreas and the thymus glands. They should be bought only when fresh and cooked quickly. One pound (450 g) of sweetbreads will be sufficient for 3-4 portions.

Ox sweetbreads: The cheapest, needing long, slow cooking.

Calf's sweetbreads: More expensive and more tender.

Lamb's sweetbreads: The most expensive, tender and flavoursome. Allow one pair per portion and soak for at least 4 hrs in cold water, which should be changed several times. Put them in cold, salted water and bring to the boil. Remove the veins and skin, place the blanched sweetbreads between two plates to flatten them and allow to cool. They can then be coated with egg and breadcrumbs and sautéed in butter.

TRIPE

Tripe is the lining of an ox's stomach. Tripe from the first stomach is known as 'blanket' and that from the second stomach is known as 'honeycomb'. Tripe can be stewed in milk and deep fried. Tripe in a butcher's shop has already been parboiled, so consult the butcher about the length of cooking time.

OXTAIL

Ideal for soups and stews. Oxtail should be lean and deep red in colour. Look out for an even ratio of meat to bone. Ask your butcher to skin and joint the oxtail. It needs long slow cooking, best done the day before. Allow the oxtail to get cold then remove the fat on top. Reheat and if liked top with dumplings.

BRAINS

Like sweetbreads, brains should be bought when very fresh and used up quickly.

Calf's brains: Prepare by soaking for about two hours in cold, lightly salted water. Simmer gently for about 20 minutes and then press them as they cool. They can then be sliced, coated in flour and fried in butter.

Lamb's brains: Frequently cooked with the head for stews and broth. They can also be cooked in the same way as calf's brains.

GAME

This category covers all wild animals which are protected by law and may therefore be shot only at certain times of the year. However, nowadays frozen game of many kinds is easily obtained out of season.

FEATHERED GAME AND WILDFOWL

GROUSE: Average size about 1¼ lb (566 g). In season from 12 August ('the glorious twelfth') to 10 December. Grouse are usually roasted.

PARTRIDGE: In season from 1 September to 1 February. A small, plump bird ideal for roasting.

PHEASANT: In season from 1 October to 1 February. Hens, distinguishable by their shorter tails and duller plumage, are considered preferable to cocks. Pheasant can be roasted or cooked in game pie.

PIGEON: These are not classed as game, so there is no close season. Both domestic and wood pigeon are eaten, the latter being smaller. Roast young pigeons; casserole older birds. They can take as long as 4 hours.

PTARMIGAN: In season from 12 August to 10 December. A small version of grouse and cooked in the same way.

QUAIL: Available in the summer months (farmed or frozen all year round). It can be roasted, split open and grilled, or, more adventurously, roasted wrapped in vine leaves.

SNIPE: In season from 12 August to 31 January. Usually roasted.

WILD DUCK: Three varieties are common in Great Britain – teal, mallard and widgeon – and all of them are in season from 1 September to 31 January. If the duck is a mallard, allow one bird for 2 people.

WOODCOCK: In season from 1 October to 31 January. Delicious roasted and served as a savoury.

FURRED GAME

HARE: In season from September to February. Young hares (leverets) and young females (does) are more tender then males (bucks), and can be roasted. Older, tougher hares are best cooked in stews or jugged. A young hare should have soft, pliable ears, a smooth coat and slender paws. The preparation of hare (and rabbit) – skinning, paunching and catching the blood – is not a task relished by the squeamish, and it is best to let your butcher handle this work.

I discard the blood as so often it makes the sauce curdle.

RABBIT: In season from September to February. Tame and imported rabbits are available throughout the year. Their flesh is softer and whiter than that of wild rabbit. Sold whole, they can be roasted. Joints can be grilled, braised or casseroled. Older rabbit should be cooked as hare. You can now buy boneless rabbit meat, which is good value.

VENISON: The flesh of deer, principally red deer, roebuck and fallow deer. Venison is in season during the autumn. Frozen venison is available at all other times throughout the year. Prime cuts are the leg and loin, which together make a haunch, a very large joint for roasting. Venison cutlets or sticks can be grilled or fried, the meat from the shoulder is excellent stewed. Good venison should display dark, fine-grained lean meat with thick, firm white fat. Venison, being a totally lean meat, is greatly improved by being soaked in a marinade of wine, onion and oil for a few days in the fridge.

HANGING GAME

All game, with the exception of rabbit, should be hung if the flesh is to be tender. If you order your game well in advance, a butcher will do it for you. For those who hang their game at home, the length of hanging will depend on the weather and personal taste. In cold weather, for example, pheasant should be hung in a cool place – preferably with a draught – for about a fortnight. At the start of the shooting season in early October, when the weather can be muggy, seven days is a more appropriate time. In cold weather hare should be hung for about ten days. Some people who like their game to be very 'high' will leave a pheasant hanging for a month, though the results will not be guaranteed to suit everybody's palate.

Left to right: capon, wild duck, domestic duck, guinea fowl, turkey, boiling fowl, single and double poussins, roasting chicken.

POULTRY
Fresh or frozen, poultry of good quality is available throughout the year from supermarkets and butchers. Poultry is defined as a bird bred for the table: chicken, boiling fowl, duck, goose and turkey fall into this category, as does guinea fowl, which used to be a game bird.

CHICKEN
Poussins: These are young chicken, about six to eight weeks old. They weigh about 1-2 lb (450-900 g) and will serve one or two people. They are usually grilled or fried in halves and occasionally roasted.
Roasting chicken: A bird of 4-5 lb (1.8-2.3 kg) should serve six people. Portions of small roasting chicken are usually tender enough for grilling or frying.
Broilers: Twelve-week old chicken weighing from 2½-3 lb (1.1-1.4 kg), enough to feed three or four people.
Boiling fowls: Older birds up to 18 months old, which require long, slow cooking. Cook with wine, cider, stock, with vegetables, herbs and spices. Simmer on top of the stove or in the oven.
Capon: These are young cocks, 10-12 weeks old, which have been castrated and fed a special diet to produce a large amount of flesh. They usually weigh 6-8 lb (2.7-3.6 kg) and are ideal for roasting.
GUINEA FOWL: Weighs about 2½-3 lb (1.1-1.4 kg), providing enough for three or four portions. Roast as chicken.
DUCK: 4-6 lb (1.8-2.7 kg), serving three to four people. Fresh duck are usually sold with their heads and feet on. Bright yellow feet indicate that the bird is young and suitable for roasting. Small birds under 3½ lb can be snipped in half with kitchen scissors or game shears after roasting to serve two.
GOOSE: A goose will usually weigh about 6-12 lb (2.7-5.5 kg) and will feed about eight people. They are usually stuffed and roasted. Young geese have pliable under-bills.
TURKEY: Look for a 10-14 lb (4.5-6.3 kg) bird for about twelve servings. Fresh young turkeys have smooth black legs. Most turkeys sold are frozen.
FROZEN POULTRY
When you buy frozen poultry, ensure that it is completely thawed out before cooking.

Thawing times:
Chicken: Whole chicken about 24 hrs in a refrigerator or 3 hrs per lb at room temperature. Once thawed, remember to remove the bag of giblets, rinsing the inside of the bird by holding it under a running tap and allowing the water to run through. Then dry the bird carefully, inside and out, with kitchen paper. Once thawed, keep in the fridge. Cook within 12 hours of thawing.
Turkey: About 4-5 hrs per lb in a refrigerator, or 1 hr per lb at room temperature. Observe the same procedure for frozen geese.

FISH

Although Britain is surrounded by waters which are extensively fished, it is sometimes difficult to buy fresh fish in some parts of the country. Nevertheless, fish which has been commercially frozen is of good quality, as it is frozen soon after being caught and its flavour is not drastically impaired. Keep it in its pack and store in the freezing compartment of your refrigerator for the recommended length of time. Once thawed, do not refreeze. If you live near a good fishmonger, make full use of his skills. Although it is not difficult to gut and fillet fish yourself, the fishmonger possesses the equipment and skills to perform a neat professional job. Remember that fish does not keep very well, so try to cook and eat on the day you buy it. Always store fresh fish in the refrigerator, keeping it covered so that the smell does not affect other foods.

When buying fresh fish, look for brightness. The eyes should be prominent, the gills red and the scales sparkling. The body should be firm and there should be a fresh smell.

White and oily fish are both rich in protein and oily fish contain vitamin D which encourages good teeth and strong bones.

Fish is quick to cook, so useful when you are in a hurry. White fish (low in calories and an invaluable part of any diet) will start off almost transparent, but turns white when cooked. The most popular methods of cooking are poaching (remember not to boil the fish or it will disintegrate), steaming (traditionally good for invalids), grilling, frying, or deep-frying in batter. If in doubt about which method to use for the

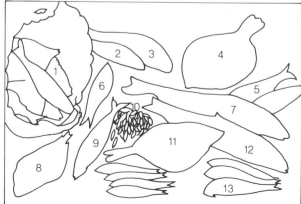

In the fish basket 1 skate. On the slab from left to right 2 rainbow trout 3 haddock 4 brill 5 smoked mackerel 6 herring 7 cod 8 Dover sole 9 mackerel 10 whitebait 11 plaice 12 sea trout 13 red mullet 14 sardines

type of fish you have chosen, ask your fishmonger. He will also advise you on bargain buys. One of my own favourite fish buys is lemon sole. It is good value, has a lovely texture and looks attractive served up with a wedge of lemon and a sprig of parsley.

WHITE FISH
BASS A round fish with delicate flesh. Bake or poach a large fish; grill or fry smaller ones.
BREAM Sea bream is a round fish, with coarse scales. Its flesh is sweet and tender. Bake larger fish with a stuffing; grill or fry smaller fish.
BRILL A firm white, flat fish which looks like a turbot and has a similar but less succulent taste. Bake, grill or poach.

COD A round fish with close, white flesh and a mild flavour. It is usually bought in steaks or as fillets. Grill, bake or fry.

COLEY Is always sold filleted. When raw, the flesh is greyish, but becomes white after cooking. Because cod has become expensive, coley is often used as a substitute. You can fry, grill or bake it.

DAB AND FLOUNDER Part of the plaice family, with soft, white sweet flesh. Grill, fry or bake.

DOGFISH Also called flake, huss and rig, this is a firm-fleshed member of the shark family. It used to be known, incorrectly, as 'rock salmon'. Use it in casseroles, soups and fish stocks.

HADDOCK A member of the cod family. Buy it whole, or in cuts or fillets. It has firm fine-textured white flesh. Bake, grill or fry.

HAKE A member of the cod family. Cook as for cod and enhance its taste with a well-flavoured sauce.

HALIBUT A large, flat fish, usually sold in cutlets. Bake whole, with a stuffing; fry, grill or poach. Mock halibut is smaller.

MONKFISH: An ugly fish, very firm in texture, excellent for Bouillabaise and for stews. Also good treated as scampi.

PLAICE Has a greyish upper side with bright orange spots and a white underside. Its flesh is soft and sweet. Use it whole, fried or grilled, or filleted. You may use plaice in recipes which call for the more expensive sole.

ROCKFISH Also known as cat-fish. Look for firm, pinkish coloured flesh; use for fish stews and soups.

SKATE A flat fish with large 'wings' – the part we eat. The sweet flesh comes away from the bones easily; grill or fry in butter.

SOLE Dover sole is often thought to be the best of all white fish. Its flavour is delicate but not insipid; its flesh firm but creamy. Grilled, fried on the bone, or filleted, sole is often served with a sauce. Dover sole is oval, its upper side is brownish, with irregular black markings on the rough skin; its underside is white. Ask your fishmonger to skin it. Lemon and witch soles are cheaper. Their flavour is not quite as good but they are excellent value; fry, grill or poach them. Serve with a sauce.

TURBOT A large flat fish, with a creamy flavour; cook as for halibut, preferably whole. Expensive.

WHITING A round fish part of the cod family. Whiting is bony, but has soft, flaky flesh and a delicate flavour. Bake, fry or poach it.

OILY FISH
CARP A freshwater fish which sometimes tastes muddy. To prevent this, soak for about three hours beforehand in salted water. Especially good stuffed and baked.

CONGER EEL A saltwater fish with a greyish black skin. It has a distinctive flavour and is excellent in stews, soups and fish kebabs.

HERRING A small, oily fish with creamy-coloured flesh. Bought whole, it is often brushed with melted butter, seasoned, sprinkled with oatmeal and grilled or fried.

MACKEREL A cheap, tasty saltwater fish. It is round, with a silvery underside and a blue and green striped upperside. It is usually grilled, but you can stuff and bake it. Cut its slightly oily flavour with a gooseberry or apple sauce.

MULLET (GREY) This is a large estuary fish with firm flesh. Small grey mullet are best grilled and served with savoury butter; larger ones are excellent stuffed and baked.

MULLET (RED) A uniquely flavoured red-skinned saltwater fish, delicious grilled or baked and served with butter, lemon and seasoning.

PERCH Requires careful cleaning. Remove hard scales by plunging into boiling water. Best grilled and served with melted butter.

PIKE A large fish with very coarse flesh and masses of bones. Prepare by soaking and then boil, or bake with a stuffing. Pike is traditionally used in quenelles.

PILCHARD Large sardine, often sold in cans. Pilchards make very economical fish dishes.

SALMON A freshwater fish, sold as steaks or whole. Excellent poached and garnished with cucumber, sprigs of parsley and lemon wedges. Delicious served cold with mayonnaise. Fresh Scotch farmed salmon has brought the price down considerably – it's delicious and well worth trying.

SARDINE Sardines are young pilchards which are usually bought canned in oil or tomato sauce, but may also be bought fresh. If canned, serve cold or grilled on toast.

SPRATS Small fish similar to herrings, but silver-skinned. Young sprats, known as brislings, are canned in oil or tomato sauce. If you buy them fresh, flour, deep fry and sprinkle with lemon juice and black pepper.

TROUT (rainbow) This is the most common. It has creamy flesh and is best grilled and served with *maitre d'hôtel* butter, or fried and served with almonds. Farmed trout is readily available and inexpensive in sizes from 6 oz (175 g) upwards.

TROUT (river or brown) Distinguished from rainbow trout by its darker skin.

TROUT (sea or salmon) A pink-fleshed fish, salmon-like in flavour. Cook as rainbow.

WHITEBAIT Very small herring or sprat, about 1½ in (4 cm) in length and silver-skinned. Especially good coated in flour and deep fried until crisp, served with lemon juice, salt and pepper.

SHELLFISH

Shellfish are divided into molluscs, such as mussels and oysters, winkles, whelks and cockles, and crustaceans such as shrimps, prawns, crabs and lobsters. With the exception of oysters and mussels, shellfish are usually sold boiled. The live fish are thrown into boiling water. When buying, always choose shellfish that are fresh and clean; in the case of molluscs, the shells should be tightly closed and then open when cooking. Frozen shellfish should be allowed to thaw completely and then be used as soon as possible.

CRABS: The best crabs to buy are those that are medium sized, some 6-10 inches (15-25 cm) across. The claws should be stiff, the shell rough and brightly coloured and the crab should be heavy in proportion to its size. You can ask the fishmonger to prepare (dress) it for you. If you wish to do it yourself, pull off the claws, crack them and pick out the meat. Turn the crab over and divide the two halves of the shell, removing the small pointed piece known as the 'apron' at the base of the shell. The gills, stomach and green intestine should be removed. If it is a live crab, put it in a pan of cold water, bring to the boil and cook for about 15-20 minutes.

LOBSTER: A good lobster should be heavy and the tail should be springy if pulled back. To prepare, break off the claws and crack, remove any spawn under the tail and remove the intestinal vein running down the centre of the tail. Cut the body lengthwise and discard stomach, green liver and gills. If it is live, and it must be alive when cooked, tie the tail in a curled position and plunge head first into boiling water and cook for 15-20 minutes. This can be a little off-putting to the squeamish, so it is better to buy a ready-cooked one.

PRAWNS AND SHRIMPS: Make sure these are really fresh. They have a sweet smell if fresh but if stale give off a pungent odour, are pale in colour and have limp tails. They are brownish when live. To shell, hold the head and body with a thumb and forefinger. With the other hand grasp the joints of the tail and bend back. Then pull the end of the tail and the tail shell should come off. Twist off the head and peel away the rest. To cook put into boiling water for 5 minutes (shrimps) and 15-20 minutes (Dublin Bay prawns or scampi).

MUSSELS: These are always sold live. The shells should be tightly closed, discard any that are not. Wash the mussels several times, removing as much sand as possible. To make the shells open, put them into a pan with a little water and cook quickly, covered until the shells open – about 5 minutes. Any shells that are still closed after cooking should be thrown away.

OYSTERS: Oysters when fresh should be hard to open and should close firmly on the knife when it is inserted. Wash and scrub well. They are usually eaten raw. To open, hold in a cloth with the larger, deeper half of the shell underneath to catch the juice. Slide the knife in with a see-saw movement.

COCKLES, WHELKS AND WINKLES: These are usually sold cooked and served cold with a dressing of vinegar, salt and pepper. A pin is needed to prise out the winkles from their shells.

CLAMS: These can be served raw or cooked in the same way as mussels.

SCALLOPS: These are usually sold opened or on the half-shell. They must be very fresh, look for a bright orange roe surrounded by plump, creamy white flesh. Cut off the beards and intestinal threads. Ease the white parts from the shells, slice and poach for 10 minutes, adding the orange roe after 5 minutes.

VEGETABLES

The place of the vegetable in English cooking has long been neglected. All too often the only time the family eat vegetables is as an over-cooked accompaniment to meat. Vegetables are nourishing and infinite in their variety; their flavours change constantly with the seasons, and they can often be eaten raw as well as making the basis for delicious salads, soups and flans. Even the choicest of vegetables can prove cheaper than the cheapest cuts of meat, and this in itself should be an encouragement to be more adventurous in your shopping and cooking.

There are two important points to remember when buying vegetables. Only buy what is fresh and crisp. Limp, soggy or off-colour produce will have lost its true flavour. And, unless you are really splashing out, only buy what is in season. If you are making a salad in winter time,

don't spend a lot on a floppy forced lettuce – buy a white cabbage or even a Savoy, and shred it. A cabbage salad chilled for an hour or so in the refrigerator before serving is beautifully refreshing. Similarly, don't feel that tomatoes are compulsory in a salad. If they are very expensive, why not try a red pepper (one will stretch to two salads) to add flecks of colour and a different flavour? Finely chopped leeks can be used in place of spring onions, and shredded sprouts and spinach are also good.

Salads can be eaten cheaply all the year round, as long as you use the ingredients which are in season at the time. Naturally, in spring and summer it is easier as there is a greater variety of vegetables on sale and they are much cheaper. But you can still be adventurous and try mixing fruit with vegetables (especially apples). In the winter, rice or beans (kidney and haricot) can provide a good base, as well as white cabbage,

carrots, chicory, celery and potatoes. Don't be too rigid in your choice of ingredients, it is often rewarding to experiment with whatever is available in the fridge. The important thing to remember is that salads should be appealing to the eye and interesting in texture. Choose colours which combine attractively. An unusual combination which looks good is yellow and green peppers with celery, apple and sunflower seeds. Sunflower seeds are very inexpensive. They can be bought from health food shops and are absolutely delicious in salads.

When you are preparing a salad, put the dressing in the bowl first with the flavouring (garlic, onion, chives, shallots, herbs etc.) Remember to choose a very large bowl so that when you toss the salad your guests don't get showered in dressing. Next, add firm vegetables that won't become limp like cucumber, celery and peppers. Avocado and apple should also be added at this stage as the acid in the vinegar will stop them discolouring. Put leafy vegetables on top ready to toss later. Delicate squashy things like the egg in Salade Niçoise should be left till after tossing.

I am always being asked the best way to keep a lettuce fresh. When you get the lettuce home wash it carefully and discard the outer leaves. Use a spinner to remove excess water, but don't break it up before serving. Bruising will impair both appearance and flavour. Store it in a large earthenware pot or saucepan with a well-fitting lid in the fridge – or in a cool part of the kitchen.

To store watercress, trim off the parts you won't eat, invert in a jug of water so that the leaves are submerged and the stalks in the air, and keep in the fridge.

Other additions to salads which can be kept on hand in the fridge are hard-boiled eggs (in their shells they keep perfectly well for a week) and dressing. Make a large bottle of it and add different flavourings when you are ready to dress the salad.

Remember that salads make slimming packed lunches. Try taking crudités to work as a change. Take a dip along too. Interesting ones can be made with yoghurt or cottage cheese as a base.

Introduce the more exotic vegetables to the

perfected the art of cooking vegetables and always serve them piping hot but still crisp, so as to retain all the flavour. It is worth taking a tip from them and learning never to overcook your vegetables – there is nothing less appetizing, and if boiled for too long they lose their flavour, texture and all their goodness.

If you are preparing root vegetables for a dinner party you can get them ready in advance and store them in the fridge covered with water. Don't keep them longer than two days, and change the water every 24 hours. Green vegetables can be prepared a day ahead and kept in the refrigerator in bags. Don't discard the outer leaves, they can always be used in a soup if they are clean.

When you are ready to serve them, try not to keep them hot for too long. Toss them in butter rather than leave them sitting. Remember that appearance is part of the pleasure of eating and never serve white vegetables with white potatoes. Julienne strips of carrot look good tossed in butter and garnished with parsley, and for a change why not mash carrot and swede together? It tastes delicious and looks pretty as well as being very economical.

It is always useful to keep a quantity of vegetables in store as a standby. Frozen vegetables are a good alternative to fresh ones out of season. I am not personally as keen on the tinned variety, though I would never be without a good supply of tinned tomatoes and I like to use tinned baby onions occasionally as a garnish. Tinned celery hearts are also handy in emergencies and taste wonderful in a good brown sauce.

Dried vegetables such as onions can be handy when you have no fresh ones available, but add them sparingly and remember that they need lots of cooking time (about an hour) unless you reconstitute them in water first. Another invaluable addition to the larder is a selection of dried pulses. These can make meals in themselves and are a rich source of protein, or they can be added to meat dishes to make them go further.

family gradually as a second choice. When you find that they like them, you may want to spin out the more expensive ones, like courgettes, by adding them to frozen peas or cauliflower in season. Another way of making vegetables go further is by adding rice and stir-frying them.

Frozen stir-fry vegetables are now available, and I find them very good, though my own family is invariably so hungry that I always add a few more of my own. Almost any green vegetable can be stir-fried. Shred leaf vegetables very finely with a good sharp kitchen knife and toss in a Chinese wok or large shallow pan over a high heat for a few minutes. The Chinese add soy sauce and cornflour slaked with stock, water or sherry for extra taste. They have

FREEZING FOOD

The freezer is an invaluable labour-saving device, and particularly useful if you have a large family or live a long way from the shops. By freezing vegetables in season and taking advantage of special offers at the butcher's, you can save money and enjoy top-quality fresh food all year round. If you use your freezer economically by keeping it fairly full (top it up with fresh bread if you are between shopping sprees), you will find you have plenty of scope for varied menu-planning. Keep a surplus of pre-cooked dishes in your freezer and you will never be caught out in emergencies.

A freezer is easy to use, but for the best results you need to know how to prepare, package and store your food properly. It is as well to bear in mind when you are making a pie filling, a soup, casserole or sauce that you could just as easily double the quantity and put half in the freezer for another day. This saves time as well as money on fuel bills. If you have just served a roast chicken, but have no time to make a stock from the carcass, don't throw it away – wrap it up and put it in the freezer to use later.

Freezers come in two forms – the chest and the upright. The upright usually has an interior of drawers of differing depths, which makes it easier to retrieve food rather than rooting about in the bottom of a chest freezer. An upright freezer also takes up less floor space. A chest freezer is better for holding large joints of meat, and if you are well organized you will be able to pack a lot into it. It is also cheaper to run.

PACKAGING FOOD FOR THE FREEZER

It is important to package your food correctly to stop it losing its flavour and nutritional value through dehydration. A tidy freezer full of well-labelled packages will also save you time and frustration.

Specially made polythene freezer bags are ideal methods of storage and will even take liquids. Seal them with twist ties. If you find you are always losing the ties that come with the bags, you can buy a twist-tie dispenser. The wire comes in a reel and you cut off the length required. Thin polythene bags are not suitable for freezing as they split at very low temperatures. Don't re-use old bags or bags which have contained clothes in case of contamination. It's a very good idea to have boil-in bags handy in the kitchen. Use them for storing sauces, such as bolognaise sauce, which can then be heated straight from frozen without any mess in a pan of boiling water.

Foil cases can be bought in a variety of shapes and sizes and are useful for storing pies, flans and casseroles. Don't throw away containers which held take-away meals, but do make sure you sterilize them before use. Margarine, yoghurt and ice-cream cartons can be thoroughly washed and lined with new plastic bags. The smaller ones are just the right size for holding puréed baby and toddler meals.

Rigid plastic containers, for use in the larder or fridge, can also be bought specially for the freezer and are ideal for stacking. They should come with lids which seal perfectly. As an alternative to these lids you can use freezer-wrap, but it should be sealed with freezer tape – normal adhesive tape will not stick at low temperatures.

ORGANIZING THE FREEZER

It is fatal to put anything in the freezer without labelling it. Food changes its colour and appearance drastically once frozen, and of course entirely loses it smell. By the time you have thawed something out it will be too late and your surprised guests may find themselves with meatballs for dessert instead of raspberries! Self-adhesive labels and a special freezer-proof pen will save you no end of time and bother, especially if you note down the date by which you must eat the food and the number of people it will serve.

Other methods of recognizing your food parcels are grouping and colour-coding. It is a good idea to keep the different categories of food, meat, fish, vegetables, fruit, etc., separate in the freezer in their own compartments. Stacking and hanging baskets are available from freezer manufactur-ers, and will help you do this. Or you can buy coloured freezer bags with twist ties and use one colour for each category.

Whether you adopt these methods or not, it is vital that you keep a record of what is in the freezer and note the quantity of food and the date you put it in. This way you won't leave food too long, or forget the variety available when it comes to menu-planning. Keep your exercise book and pen near to the freezer and remember to cross items off as you use them.

For compact packing and to avoid uneconomical air spaces between your packages, try to freeze items into cubes or 'briquettes'. Before you pour a liquid into a freezer bag, put it inside a square freezer-proof container. When the contents of the bag are frozen, the container can be removed. When freezing liquids you must allow room for expansion, at least ½ inch (1 cm). Casseroles can be frozen in polythene or foil inside the dish in which they were cooked. When the food is frozen, the dish can be returned to the kitchen. Use it again when you are ready to thaw the casserole.

FREEZING FOOD
Always make sure you only freeze food which is perfectly fresh – do not freeze inferior products.

To make extra sure that cooked food does not get contaminated before you put it in the freezer, cool it quickly. This will also stop ice crystals forming in the food and spoiling its texture.

When you are packing food, remove as much air as possible from the bag by smoothing it out with your fingers. Make sure that the seal is airtight. Use shallow containers for preference so that freezing is rapid and even.

Many freezers have fast-freezing switches which override the normal temper-ature of the freezer. Some have fast-freezing compartments. These are useful because even dishes at room temperature will raise the temperature of the foods they come into contact with. For this reason you should turn

to fast-freezer about three hours before adding to your store of frozen food, and never try to freeze too much at once – not more than 10 per cent of the freezer's capacity in a 24-hour period. Keep the fast-freeze switch on for a couple of hours after you have added the unfrozen items.

OPEN FREEZING
This method of freezing prevents individual items like cakes, meatballs, fruit and vegetables from sticking together, thus making it easier to remove and prepare only the quantity you need. To open freeze, lay the items on a sheet of tin foil on a baking tray and put in the freezer until frozen. Then pack in bags in the normal way. If you have a family, it is a good idea to build up a store of frozen meals for the school holidays.

FREEZING VEGETABLES
Always choose fresh young vegetables for freezing. Wash them thoroughly and pre-pare them as you would if you were going to use them immediately.

BLANCHING TIMES	minutes
Asparagus	2-4
Aubergines	4
Broad beans	2
Whole or thickly cut French bean	2
Coarsely sliced runner beans	1
Broccoli	3-4
Brussels sprouts	3
Carrots	3-5
Cauliflower	3
Celeriac	4
Corn-on-the-cob	4-8
Courgettes	1
Leeks	2-4
Onions	2
Parsnips	2
Peas	1
Spinach	2
Swedes	3
Turnips	2

NB: To freeze mushrooms, sauté in butter, drain and cool.

FREEZING FOOD

For the best results, vegetables should always be blanched before freezing. If you have a large quantity of vegetables and no time, it is possible to freeze them as they are, but they must then be eaten within two months.

To blanch vegetables, immerse them in a wire basket in a pan of boiling water for the time given. Only blanch small quantities at a time, after which they should be rapidly cooled, either by putting them in a colander under running water, or by plunging the blanching basket into a bowl of cold water filled with ice cubes. The cooling time should be the same as the blanching time. Blanching is measured from the moment the water gets back to the boil.

FREEZING FRUIT

A very useful way of freezing some fruits is to purée them first. The results can be used as baby food, in mousses or ice creams, and has the added advantage of being handy to store. It is also the only way of storing fruit that is over-ripe. Otherwise, you should choose fruit that is in the peak of condition, and open freeze or freeze in bulk. Another way of freezing fruit is to prepare it with sugar or syrup. Add ascorbic acid (Vitamin C) to fruits such as peaches, apricots and pears, which are prone to discolouration. Use a quarter teaspoon of ascorbic acid to a pint (600 ml) of syrup.

Here is a suggestion of when to freeze certain fruit and vegetable produce:

January   broccoli, celery, cooking apples, cranberries, horseradish, Seville oranges

February   avocados, beetroot, broccoli, cooking and eating apples, cabbage, celery, horseradish, parsnips, old potatoes, spring greens, swedes, turnips, Seville oranges, grapefruit

March   horseradish, parsnips, pineapple

April   carrots, cauliflower, spinach, rhubarb

May   broccoli, carrots, cauliflower, green peppers, spinach, rhubarb

June   broccoli, carrots, cauliflower, courgettes, peas, peppers, new potatoes, spinach, tomatoes, rhubarb, strawberries, cherries

July   French and broad beans, broccoli, cauliflower, courgettes, peas, peppers, new potatoes, spinach, tomatoes, apricots, black-currants, cherries, goose-berries, grapes, peaches, raspberries, strawberries

August   French, broad and runner beans, cabbage, marrow, peas, peppers, spinach, tomatoes, blackberries, blackcurrants, redcurrants, cherries, gooseberries, grapes, greengages, peaches, plums, raspberries, strawberries

September   runner beans, red cabbage, marrow, peas, peppers, spinach, tomatoes, cooking apples, blackberries, damsons, greengages, melons, pears, plums

October   beetroot, brussels sprouts, celery, chestnuts, horseradish, leeks, marrow, spinach, swedes, tomatoes, cooking and eating apples, damsons, melons, plums, pumpkins, pears

November   broccoli, brussels sprouts, celery, leeks, swedes, cranberries, mandarins, pears, tangerines

December   avocados, broccoli, brussels sprouts, celery, parsnips, swedes, cranberries, apricots

THAWING

Frozen vegetables taste fresher if plunged into boiling water straight from the freezer, but as a general rule it is better to thaw most food before cooking – it also saves fuel! The best place to thaw food is overnight in the refrigerator. *Never* cook poultry straight from its frozen state. Complete thawing before cooking ensures that all harmful bacteria which may be present in poultry are destroyed.

Do not allow fruit such as strawberries and raspberries to thaw too long before eating, as they tend to go mushy. Bread can be wrapped in foil and warmed through in the oven, and bread slices can be toasted frozen.

PITFALLS TO AVOID

Cream and cream cheese containing less than 40 per cent butter fat tend to separate when frozen. Whip double or whipping cream before freezing. Yoghurt also separates when frozen although commercially frozen yoghurt contains a stabilizer. If you want to freeze plain yoghurt, you can mix in a teaspoon of honey. Custards separate, and so should be frozen before they are cooked.

Mayonnaise curdles on thawing and whole eggs break. If they are hard-boiled they become rubbery. If you want to store eggs in the freezer, beat them first. You can also freeze eggs when the yolk is separated from the white – ice cube trays are useful for this. A pinch of salt or sugar added to a beaten egg yolk gives the best result.

Salad vegetables get limp after they have been frozen. They should only be put into the freezer in soups. Tomatoes can be frozen, but will not be suitable for use in salads afterwards.

Whole boiled potatoes and spaghetti become soft after being frozen. Roast potatoes and mashed potato toppings freeze well.

Dishes which contain garlic should be frozen for a short time, otherwise they taste slightly musty. Do not freeze previously frozen food, unless it is to be used in a cooked dish which you wish to freeze. The reason for this is that the flavour and texture of food which has been refrozen deteriorates more quickly, although there will still be no risk to health.

STORAGE TIMES	
Most vegetables	12 months
Raw mushrooms	1 month
Cooked mushrooms	3 months
Onions	3-6 months
Most fruit	12 months
Unstoned fruit	3 months
Fruit pies	6 months
Uncooked meats:	
lamb	6 months
pork	3 months
beef	8 months
mince, offal, tripe	3 months
vacuum-packed bacon	3 months
smoked bacon joints	2 months
unsmoked bacon joints	4 weeks
sausages	2 months
Poultry:	
chicken	12 months
duck	6 months
giblets	2 months
game	6 months
Fish:	
white	3 months
oily	2 months
Cooked dishes:	
pies, casseroles etc.	3 months
Cakes, bread, pastry	6 months
Sandwiches, scones	2 months
Crispbread and rolls	1 week
Enriched bread, soft rolls	4 months
Breadcrumbs, croûtons	6 months
Risen dough	2 weeks
Unrisen dough	1 month
Yeast	1 month
Dairy produce:	
clotted cream	12 months
cream	3 months
eggs, unsalted butter	6 months
salted butter, hard cheese, cream with more than 35% butter fat content	3 months
cream cheese	6 weeks
Camembert, Brie	3 months
Nuts – well wrapped	5 years

Tools of the trade

This is a list of some of the smaller items of kitchen equipment you will need. Buy the best you can afford, starting with the essentials and build up your collection.

A

Aluminium foil: I like to have two widths. Because I do a lot of cooking I buy them in economy length rolls in wall dispensers.
Apple Corer
Aprons

B

Baking tins: Two baking sheets
One bun tin
One Yorkshire pudding tin
One meat loaf tin
Two sponge sandwich tins
One cake tin
One plain flan tin
One roasting tin for oven
Two pie plates
One Swiss roll tray
One cooling tray
Boiling bags: Made of heat-proof plastic. Useful for freezer-to-table meals.
Bottle opener
Bowls
One 12 in (30 cm) mixing bowl
Two 1½ pt (852 ml) pudding basins
One ½ pt (284 ml) pudding basin
One 1 pt (586 ml) pudding basin
One 1 pt (586 ml) pie dish
It is essential to have several different sized bowls. You will often be using several at one time with differing amounts of ingredients in each.
Breadbin: A metal one is best. Bread tends to go mouldy in a plastic bin.
Breadboard: Can also be used as a chopping board.

Bun trays: One 9-hole and one 12-hole.

C

Cake tins: For storing cakes
Cake tins: 6 inch (15 cm), 7 inch (17 cm) and 8 inch (20 cm) are the standard. Also you could gradually collect a selection of special cake tins, e.g. Savarin mould, baba mould, spring-sided cake tin, charlotte mould, brioche mould, moule à manqué (shallow tin with sloping sides) and tartlet tins.
Can opener: A stainless steel wall-mounted opener is ideal. Place it near the rubbish bin.
Casseroles: You will need at least two: a large one and one with a capacity of about 2 pints (1.2 l). These can be of heat resisting glass or china, earthenware, enamel, aluminium or steel. Enamelled cast iron is the best and most durable. Lids should fit well and can be used sometimes separately as baking dishes. The most useful casseroles are those that can be used on top of the stove as well as in the oven and can also be brought to the table.
Chopping board
Cling film: This is invaluable for keeping foods fresh in the fridge and you can see what's in the packet without opening it. Also very good for wrapping sandwiches.
Colander: Choose one with two handles. Aluminium or stainless steel will last longest.
Conical strainer
Corkscrew: If you are not very strong the best type to get is a stainless steel one with two 'arms', which works on the lever principle.

D

Decorating and icing pipes

Dishes: Various sizes of dish will be needed. The most useful are those that are oven proof and can be taken to the table.
Gratin dishes
Medium and large soufflé dishes
Invidividual soufflé dishes
Pie-dishes
Dishcloth: The disposable ones are good for emergencies, but for every day use I prefer a boilable dish cloth.

E

Egg poacher: Eggs can be poached quite successfully in a shallow pan of water but many people find the non-stick poachers unbeatable.
Egg whisk
Electric kettle: The fastest way of boiling water.

F

Fish slice
Floorcloths: There's nothing like old nappies for cleaning the floor.
Flour dredger
Fondue set: A fondue makes a marvellous entertainment. Choose a set with a cast iron burner which can be cleaned in warm soapy water. The copper burners are very difficult to clean and never look as good. The best pans are also cast iron. The shallower pans are ideal for cheese fondue and the deeper ones for meat.
Forcing bags
Forks: Carving fork
Cook's fork
Salad server.
Funnel
Freezer bags: These are made of specially toughened plastic. The most useful are the ones with a white area on them for writing with a waterproof pen.

G

Garlic press
Grater: Stainless steel grater.
Greaseproof paper: Useful for lining cake tins.

I

Ice cream scoop
Icing tubes

J

Jugs: Have handy measuring jugs of 2 sizes with both metric and imperial measures marked.
Jelly bag: For straining jellies.
Jelly mould

K

Kitchen roll: On a dispenser.
Kitchen scissors
Kitchen tool set: Can be mounted on the wall and should include a ladle, palette knife, fish slice and large slotted spoon.
Knives: Carving set of knife, fork and sharpening steel
Serrated bread knife
Chopping knives
Small vegetable knife
Small palette knife
Grapefruit knife
Boning knife
Potato peeler
French cooks' knives – usually Sabatier – are best.
Electric carving knives are very efficient for cutting boneless meat, though they are best used away from the dining table. I always prefer a really sharp steel knife.

L

Lemon squeezer: A plastic one which catches the juice is ideal.

M

Meat mincer: This can be useful, though you can always ask the butcher to do it for you and some processors chop meat very efficiently for pâtés.
Melon baller
Meringue tubes
Mills: For sea-salt and pepper. There is nothing to compare with freshly ground black pepper.

N

Nutcrackers

P

Pastry brush
Pastry cutters: Both fluted and plain.
Pestle and mortar
Pie funnel
Pinger timer: For up to four hours. Useful if your oven doesn't have its own timer.
Plastic bags: Various sizes.
Plastic containers: For fridge and freezer.
Potato peeler
Potato masher
Preserving pan
Pressure cooker: These are very useful for making ham and speeding up things that are best cooked slowly, like casseroles, stews and stock. They are also good for cooking pulses (dried vegetables). They are invaluable fuel and timesavers.

R

Rolling pin
Ruler: It's always useful to have a ruler handy in the kitchen for checking tin sizes – often they aren't marked on the bottom, and using the wrong tin when baking can give very disappointing results.

S

Salad shaker
Saucepans: Frying pan (non-stick)
Cast iron frying pan
Omelette pan/pancake pan
Grill pan (normally supplied)
Milk pan (non-stick)
Deep fat pan with basket
Egg poacher
Double boiler with lid
Three saucepans (one shallow) all with lids, and insulated handles so that they do not get too hot.
The best pans you can buy are the heavy cast-iron Le Creuset. These will last you a lifetime. Good stainless steel or aluminium pans are also made to last. Buying thin pans is a waste of time.
Scales
Scissors: Keep a pair of scissors which you do not use for anything else in the kitchen.
Scoops: for creamed potatoes or ice cream.
Scourers: Make sure you don't use them on non-stick pans.
Sieves: One large, one small. Use stainless steel for preference, as this will not rust or melt.
Silicon paper: Non-stick paper available from stationers in rolls or sheets. This is particularly useful for cooking meringues or anything sugary – and you can use it again.
Silver cloth: A blue long-life silver cloth from Goddards is invaluable. Rub the silver with the cloth as you put it away in the drawer and you will never have to clean it.
Skewers
Spice rack: This can be attached to the wall and should contain small jars of essential herbs and spices, clearly labelled.
Spoons: Perforated spoon
Spatula
Soup ladle

TOOLS OF THE TRADE

Measuring spoons
Three wooden spoons, one bowl-shaped and one straight-ended for stirring mixtures right in the corners of saucepans.

Steamer: This should have a lid and should fit into several different sized saucepans. It is invaluable for cooking crisp vegetables.

Storage jars: For dry goods and spices. Also Kilner jars which are especially airtight and are used for bottling and preserving.

Strainers: Nylon mesh ones, small and medium.

Sugar dredgers: For icing and caster sugar.

T

Tea towels: Buy towelling ones for drying heavy equipment and linen ones for glassware. Also useful are paper kitchen towels on a wall dispenser.

Thermometer: A thermometer is a great help in jam making and an oven thermometer will check the temperature of the oven.

Time-savers: These are slightly more expensive items, but which in the long run will save you a lot of time. Two or three specialist machines might be better than a large one which is never fully used:
Electric Beaters
Mixers
Blenders
Processors
Sieves
Juice extractors
Coffee grinders
Shredders
Trussing needle

V

Vegetable slicer or mandolin

W

Washing-up brush: You'll need one for getting into the corners.
Wire cooling racks
Whisks: A rotary stainless whisk and a small wire balloon whisk for making sauces.

CARE OF COOKING UTENSILS:

1. Always wash and rinse well. Put utensils to soak immediately after use. Those with flour mixtures, fish, egg and milk should be soaked in cold water.
2. If food sticks or burns, soak dishes well. Then use fine steel wool or a nylon pot scraper.
3. Never pour cold liquid into a hot dish, it may crack.
4. Rub an omelette or pan-cake pan with cooking salt and a piece of paper to get a smooth surface.

CLEANING DIFFERENT MATERIALS:

Glass, china, earthenware: Soak until food can be removed with ease. Avoid pouring cold water onto the hot dish.

Wood: Scour with steel wool and make sure the bowl is thoroughly dry. Scrub chopping boards in the direction of the grain. Do not soak or dry near heat or they may warp. Wipe teak salad bowls with cooking oil to preserve the wood.

Non-stick surfaces: Do not scratch the coating. Always use a washing-up brush or gently scour with a nylon pad if the food is really stuck.

Aluminium: Fine steel wool is best and avoid using strong washing powders if you are putting these in a washing-up machine. Discoloured pans benefit from water boiled up with some vinegar.

Copper: Avoid harsh abrasives as these might wear away the surface. Do not use unlined copper — it develops verdigris which is poisonous.

Steel: Avoid scratching and dry well.

Tin: Avoid harsh scouring. Dry well and stand in a warm place.

Cutlery: Acids mark cutlery so do not leave vinegar or lemon juice on too long unwashed. Egg and salt also leave marks. Cooking knives may not be stainless and will need cleaning with steel wool pads.

SOUPS AND STARTERS

Soups have a tremendous range – from clear consommé to thick and nourishing Scotch broths and American chowders. Starters are equally varied, and this section provides a combination of the two which will meet all the requirements of economical family cooking or more sophisticated home entertaining.

SOUPS

A selection of soups for both warm and cold weather. In the depths of winter keep out the cold with lentil soup or gulasch soup, virtually a meal in itself. In the grip of high summer heatwaves delight your dinner party guests with iced Spanish soup or the unusual and original curried apple soup.

—Frugal Soup—

FRUGAL SOUP

8 oz (225 g) sprouts and trimmings
1 leek
1 oz (25 g) butter
¾ pint (450 ml) water
1 chicken stock cube
1 oz (25 g) flour
½ pint (300 ml) milk
Large pinch grated nutmeg
Salt and pepper

Wash and roughly chop the sprouts and trimmings, thoroughly wash the leek and cut in slices.

Melt the butter in a pan and add the leek, cover and cook gently for 5 minutes, add the water, stock cube and sprouts and bring to the boil. Simmer uncovered for 15 minutes or until tender, then sieve or purée in the blender.

Blend the flour with a little of the milk, then stir in the remainder. Return the soup to the pan and stir in the milk and flour. Bring to the boil, stirring until thickened, season with nutmeg and salt and pepper. If the soup should be a little too thick thin down with stock or milk. Serves 4.

COOK'S TIP. Cut down on waste by using the outside leaves of sprouts for this soup. They do not detract from its beautiful flavour.

SOUP À LA REINE

3 oz (75 g) butter
4 oz (100 g) onion, chopped
1 large parsnip, cubed
1 clove garlic, crushed
1 oz (25 g) flour
1 rounded teaspoon curry powder
2 pints (1.1 l) beef stock
Salt and pepper
¼ pint (150 ml) single cream
Snipped chives or chopped parsley

Melt the butter in a large pan and add the onion, parsnip and garlic and fry gently for 10 minutes. Stir in the flour and curry powder and cook for a minute, then add the stock and seasoning and bring to the boil, stirring. Cover and simmer gently for 20 to 30 minutes or until the parsnip is tender.

Sieve or purée the soup in an electric blender. Rinse out the pan and return the soup. Reheat and taste and check seasoning and when ready to serve, remove from the heat and stir in the cream. Pour into a tureen and sprinkle with chives or parsley. Serves 6.

COOK'S TIP. The large parsnip should be about 1 lb (450 g) in weight. This is a superb soup, and no one would guess it was based on the humble parsnip.

OLD-FASHIONED LENTIL SOUP

8 oz (225 g) lentils (orange or brown)
1 large onion
2 sticks celery
2 potatoes
1 oz (25 g) bacon fat
2 pints (1 l) chicken stock
Bacon or ham bone if available
About 1 teaspoon salt
Ground black pepper

COOK'S TIP. A nutritious warming soup. It works well with split peas instead of lentils.

Wash the lentils, put in a bowl and cover with cold water. Leave to soak overnight.

Drain the lentils and discard the water. Chop the onions, slice the celery and cube potatoes. Melt the fat in a large saucepan and add vegetables. Sauté gently for 10 minutes, without browning. Add lentils, stock, ham bone and seasoning, and bring to the boil. Cover the saucepan and simmer for one hour or until lentils are tender.

Lift out ham bone and purée the soup in a blender, taste and check seasoning. Rinse out the saucepan, return soup and reheat. Serve piping hot. Serves 6.

— French Onion Soup and Tomato Soup —

QUICK CREAM OF TOMATO SOUP

2 oz (50 g) butter
1 large onion, finely chopped
2 oz (50 g) flour
1 pint (600 ml) water
1 pint (600 ml) milk
5 oz (150 g) can tomato purée
2 teaspoons caster sugar
Salt and ground pepper
Chopped parsley

Melt the butter in a saucepan. Add the onion and fry, stirring occasionally for 5 minutes or until soft but not brown. Stir in the flour and cook for a minute.

Remove the pan from the heat and gradually add the water, return to the heat and bring to the boil, then blend in the milk stirring constantly. Add the purée, sugar and seasoning and simmer the soup for 15 to 20 minutes or until the onion is tender.

Taste and check seasoning and serve hot sprinkled with parsley. Serves 4.

FRENCH ONION SOUP

2 oz (50 g) good dripping
1 lb (450 g) onions, finely chopped
1 oz (25 g) flour
1½ pints (900 ml) good beef stock
Salt and pepper
Gravy browning
2 oz (50 g) Cheddar cheese, grated

Melt the dripping in a large pan and add the onion and fry gently stirring occasionally until it begins to brown. Stir in the flour and cook stirring constantly until the mixture is browned. Gradually add the stock and bring to the boil, stirring all the time. Add the seasoning and a little gravy browning to give a good colour.

Cover the pan and simmer for 40 minutes, taste and check seasoning and serve hot sprinkled with the cheese. Serves 4

—Dutch Pea Soup—

DUTCH PEA SOUP

A thick tasty warming soup that makes a nice light lunch in winter. It is delicious served with crispy bread and followed by Dutch cheese.

1 lb (450 g) green split peas
1 lb (450 g) gammon knuckle or 2 pig's trotters
4 pints (2.3 l) water
8 oz (225 g) onions, chopped
4 sticks celery, chopped
4 potatoes, diced
2 leeks, sliced
1 tablespoon chopped parsley
Salt and pepper
1 oz (25 g) unsalted butter

Soak the peas and knuckle or trotters overnight in enough cold water to cover.

Drain in a colander and place peas and knuckle or trotters in a pan with water. Simmer uncovered for an hour. Add the vegetables, except the leeks, cover and simmer for 2½ hours.

Take the knuckle or trotters from the pan, remove the meat from the bones and return to the pan. Add leek, parsley and seasoning with the butter, bring back to the boil before serving. Serves 6 to 8.

FRESH LEEK SOUP

2 oz (50 g) butter
1½ lb (675 g) leeks, cleaned and finely chopped
1 oz (25 g) flour
1 pint (600 ml) home-made stock or 2 chicken stock cubes dissolved in 1 pint (600 ml) water
Salt and pepper
½ pint (300 ml) milk
A little single cream if liked

COOK'S TIP. Add single cream before serving for special occasions, about ¼ pint (150 ml) is plenty.

Melt the butter in a large saucepan. Add the leeks and fry gently stirring occasionally without browning for 5 minutes. Stir in the flour and cook for 2 minutes.

Gradually add the stock, stirring continually. Add seasoning and milk, bring to the boil and simmer for 40 minutes. Taste and check seasoning and if liked add a little cream. Serves 4.

CREAM OF SPINACH SOUP

2 oz (50 g) butter
1 medium onion, chopped
1 large clove garlic, crushed
1 lb (450 g) fresh spinach
2 chicken stock cubes
1½ pints (900 ml) hot water
1 level teaspoon salt
Freshly ground black pepper
Juice of ½ lemon
A little ground nutmeg
¼ pint (150 ml) single cream

Melt the butter in a saucepan, add the onion and garlic and fry for 5 minutes until soft. Wash the spinach very well in several lots of fresh water and remove all the stalks.

Dissolve the stock cubes in the hot water and add to the saucepan with the spinach, seasoning, lemon juice and nutmeg and bring to the boil, stirring. Cover the pan and simmer for 15 to 20 minutes.

Purée the spinach in an electric blender or sieve and pour into a clean bowl.

Rinse out the saucepan and return the soup to it. Bring back to the boil. Taste and check seasoning and just before serving, stir in the cream but do not allow to boil. Serves 6.

COOK'S TIP. Tastes best with fresh spinach but if none is available substitute an 8 oz (225 g) pack of frozen leaf spinach.

MINESTRONE

1 oz (25 g) bacon fat
1 large onion, finely chopped
3 carrots, finely diced
2 sticks celery, finely chopped
1 leek, thinly sliced
2½ pints (1.4 l) beef or chicken stock
2 level tablespoons tomato purée
1 level teaspoon salt
Black pepper to taste
3 oz (75 g) spaghetti broken into 1½ inch (3.75 cm) lengths
¼ small cabbage, finely shredded

COOK'S TIP. A good main meal soup. Sprinkle with Parmesan cheese if liked and serve hot with brown rolls and butter.

If making your own stock, strip any pieces of meat from the bones and chop them up. Put on one side to add to the soup.

Melt the bacon fat in a saucepan and fry the onion until it begins to colour. Add the carrots, celery and leek and fry gently for 8-10 minutes, stirring frequently. Add the stock, tomato purée, salt and pepper and bring to the boil. Cover and simmer for 30 minutes until all the vegetables are tender. Add any chicken meat or small pieces of beef with the spaghetti and cabbage and cook for a further 10 minutes, stirring occasionally.

Taste and check seasoning. Serves 6.

GOOD CARROT SOUP

1 lb (450 g) carrots
1 small onion
1 oz (25 g) butter
1¼ pints (750 ml) chicken stock or
   1¼ pints (750 ml) water and 2
   chicken stock cubes
3 strips of orange peel
1 bay leaf
Salt and pepper

Peel and slice the carrots and onions. Melt the butter in a pan and add the vegetables, cover and cook gently for 5 to 10 minutes. Pour on the stock or water and stock cubes and add the strips of orange peel (take the peel from the orange with a potato peeler). Add bay-leaf and seasoning and bring to the boil. Cover and simmer for about 15 minutes or until the carrots are tender.

   Remove the bay-leaf then sieve or liquidize the soup in a blender. Taste and check seasoning and if the soup should be too thick, thin down with a little extra stock. Serves 4.

COOK'S TIP. For special occasions add swirls of cream or yoghurt to the soup before serving.

ICED SPANISH SOUP

COOK'S TIP. A soup for a summer's day. Serve ice cold with side dishes of cubed cucumber, cubed red and green pepper, and diced onion. You could add fried croutons of bread too.

2 x 14 oz (397 g) cans tomatoes
1 large onion, peeled
1 large green pepper, seeds and
   pith removed
Half a cucumber, peeled
3 small cloves garlic, peeled
2 tablespoons chopped parsley
2 slices white bread without the
   crusts
Salt and freshly ground black
   pepper
3 tablespoons (45 ml) wine
   vinegar
3 tablespoons oil
A few drops of Tabasco sauce
½ pint (300 ml) iced water

Place all the ingredients together and purée in an electric blender in two or three batches until smooth. Turn into a bowl and mix well. Chill in the refrigerator for 2 to 3 hours. Check seasoning. Serve the soup very cold with an ice cube in each bowl and the side dishes suggested above. Serves 6.

—Iced Spanish Soup—

GAME SOUP

The basis of any good soup is the stock, so for a really good game soup, put bones and carcass in a large saucepan with onion, herbs and seasoning, cover with cold water and bring to the boil. Simmer very gently for an hour, then strain off the stock and if there is any meat on the bones this may be kept to add to the soup.

2 oz (50 g) dripping or bacon fat
2 onions, roughly chopped
2 large carrots, roughly chopped
2 sticks celery, sliced
2 oz (50 g) flour
2½ pints (1.4 lt) good game stock
Salt
Freshly ground black pepper
A little sherry or port (optional)

Melt the dripping or bacon fat in a large saucepan and add the vegetables. Cover and cook gently for 10 minutes. Stir in the flour and cook for 2 to 3 minutes to brown lightly. Blend in the stock and bring the soup to the boil, stirring. Season well and cover and cook gently for about 30 minutes or until the vegetables are cooked.

   Remove from the heat and purée in a blender for processor.

   Rinse out the saucepan and return the soup to it. Bring to the boil and taste and check seasoning, if liked stir in a little sherry or port before service.

   Serve very hot. Serves 6 to 8.

CORN CHOWDER

5 rashers streaky bacon
1 oz (25 g) butter
1 large onion, sliced
12 oz (340 g) can corn niblets,
   drained
8 oz (225 g) cooked potato, finely
   diced
10.2 oz (290 g) can mushroom
   soup
1 pint (600 ml) milk
1 level teaspoon salt
Freshly ground black pepper

—Curried Apple Soup

A quick soup to make and deliciously different.

Remove the rind and bone from the bacon and cut into strips, place in a large saucepan with the butter and fry gently until the fat has run out and the bacon is golden brown and crisp. Lift out with a slotted spoon and put on one side.

Add the onion to the fat remaining in the pan and fry gently for 5 to 10 minutes until soft but not brown. Add the rest of the ingredients to the saucepan and bring to the boil, stirring, then reduce the heat and simmer for 10 minutes.

Taste and check seasoning and serve in bowls with the bacon sprinkled on top. Serves 6 to 8.

CURRIED APPLE SOUP

A really unusual soup that also tastes delicious served chilled.

1 oz (25 g) butter
1 onion, finely chopped
1 1/2 oz (40 g) flour
1 level tablespoon curry powder
1 1/2 pints (900 ml) water
2 chicken stock cubes
1 1/2 lb (675 g) cooking apples,
    peeled and roughly chopped
2 tablespoons redcurrant jelly
Juice of 1/2 lemon
Salt and pepper
1/4 pint (150 ml) single cream

Melt the butter in a large saucepan, add the onion and fry slowly with the lid on for 10 minutes or until soft. Stir in the flour and curry powder and cook for a minute.

Add water, stock cubes, apples, redcurrant jelly, lemon juice and seasoning and bring to the boil, stirring. Simmer for 15 minutes. Leave the soup to cool slightly and then sieve or purée in a blender.

Rinse out the saucepan, return the soup to it and bring to the boil. Taste to check seasoning. If necessary, add a little extra stock to thin down the soup. Pour a little cream on top of each bowl of soup as it is served. Serves 6.

GOULASH SOUP

A filling soup that is full of meat and vegetables, best eaten in a bowl or dish.

1 lb (450 g) stewing steak
2 oz (50 g) dripping
1 lb (450 g) onions
1 level tablespoon paprika pepper
14 oz (397 g) can peeled tomatoes
2 beef stock cubes
1 1/2 pints (900 ml) water
1 lb (450 g) potatoes, diced
2 green peppers, chopped
1-2 teaspoons salt
Pepper

Cut the meat into very small cubes. Melt the dripping in a large saucepan and fry the beef and onions for 10 minutes to lightly brown. Stir in the paprika pepper, tomatoes, stock cubes and water and bring to the boil, stirring.

Cover the pan and simmer for an hour, then add the potatoes and green pepper and continue cooking for a further 30 minutes or until the meat and vegetables are tender. Taste and check seasoning.

Serve very hot. Serves 6.

STARTERS

Nowadays starters have become more imaginative and sophisticated. This section takes on something of an international flavour with guacomola from Mexico, hummus from Greece and tagliatelle with garlic cream sauce, a great favourite in Italy. Try easy-to-make potter's pâté, always a success at picnics. If guests arrive unexpectedly, then hot grapefruit, our first recipe, will prove a useful standby.

HOT GRAPEFRUIT

2 large grapefruit
4 tablespoons light soft brown
  sugar
1/2 level teaspoon ground ginger
  or cinnamon
Large knob of butter

Cut the grapefruit in half and cut around each half to loosen the flesh. Cut between the segments and remove pith and white skin.

Mix the sugar with the ginger or cinnamon and sprinkle over the grapefruit, then dot with butter.

Place under a moderate grill and grill lightly until the sugar has melted and the grapefruit are hot through. Serve at once.

COOK'S TIP. This starter is quick to prepare and makes a useful standby if guests arrive unexpectedly.

GARLIC MUSHROOMS WITH CREAM

12 oz (350 g) small button
  mushrooms
1 1/2 oz (40 g) butter
1 clove garlic, crushed
Salt
Freshly ground black pepper
1/4 pint (150 ml) double cream

Wash the mushrooms and trim the ends of the stalks. Melt the butter in a saucepan, add the garlic and mushrooms and cook for 5 minutes. Season well, stir in the cream and simmer gently for a further 5 minutes or until the mushrooms are tender. Serve hot with cheese bread rolls. Garnish with parsley. Serves 4.

COOK'S TIP. Extremely delicious if you use really fresh snow white button mushrooms.

–Garlic Mushrooms and Melon and Tomato in Mint Dressing–

MELON AND TOMATO IN MINT DRESSING

COOK'S TIP. Sometimes I use mint jelly instead of mint sauce to flavour this dish, in which case I decrease the sugar and mash the jelly with a fork to blend it with the other dressing ingredients.

1 Honeydew or Galia melon
¾ lb (350 g) firm tomatoes
1 cucumber

MINT DRESSING:
about 10 sprigs of mint or 2 teaspoons bought mint sauce concentrate
3 tablespoons caster sugar
2 tablespoons wine vinegar
Salt
Ground black pepper
6 tablespoons oil

Cut the melon in half and remove the seeds. Either scoop the melon flesh out using a melon baller or cut in wedges and then cut the flesh into cubes. Skin and quarter the tomatoes. Remove the seeds and put on one side (these can be used up in soup or added to a casserole). If the tomatoes are large cut each quarter in half. Peel the cucumber with a potato peeler and cut into neat dice and then put in a large bowl with the melon and tomatoes and mix well together.

To make the dressing: Chop the mint very finely with the sugar and place in a screw top jar with the vinegar, salt, pepper and oil and shake well. Pour over the fruit and vegetables and cover and leave in the refrigerator for about 5 hours. Taste and check seasoning and then spoon into 6 glasses and garnish with a sprig of mint. Serve very cold with hot garlic roll or bread. Serves 6.

MELON AND PRAWNS IN SOUR CREAM

1 small melon
A little shredded lettuce
4 oz (100 g) frozen prawns, thawed
5 fl oz (150 ml) carton soured cream, chilled
1 rounded teaspoon chopped mint
Small sprigs of mint

Cut the melon in half and remove all the seeds. Scoop out the flesh into balls and leave to chill in the refrigerator.

Place a little shredded lettuce in the bottom of 6 glasses.

Thoroughly dry the prawns on kitchen paper. Put (drained) melon balls and prawns in a bowl with the cream and chopped mint and blend lightly. Divide between the glasses, garnish each with a small sprig of mint and serve at once. Serves 6.

COOK'S TIP. I often do this easy first course when melons are reasonably priced. Serve a non-fruity dessert to follow. Take care to thaw the prawns slowly in the fridge and dab off every drop of liquid before blending with the cream.

AVOCADO MOUSSE

A splendid first course to serve at a special dinner or luncheon.

½ oz (12.5 g) gelatine
4 tablespoons cold water
¼ pint (150 ml) boiling water
1 chicken stock cube
2 large avocado pears
1 level teaspoon salt
½ level teaspoon ground black pepper
Piece of onion the size of a walnut, crushed in a garlic press
1 tablespoon lemon juice
½ pint (300 ml) mayonnaise
¼ pint (150 ml) double cream, lightly whipped
Prawns for decoration

Place the gelatine and cold water in a small bowl. Stand for 3 minutes until consistency is spongy, then stand the bowl in a pan of simmering water and allow the gelatine to dissolve. Stir boiling water and stock cube together until cube has dissolved. Stir in the gelatine.

Peel and quarter the avocados, removing the stones, and crush with a fork or potato masher, stir in stock, salt, pepper and onion and lemon juice. Alternatively, process in a blender. Leave to become quite cold and then fold in the mayonnaise and cream.

Pour into a 2 pint (a good litre) ring mould and leave in the refrigerator to set. Turn out and decorate with prawns. Serves 4 for lunch or 6 as a starter.

GUACOMOLA

1 level teaspoon salt
¼ level teaspoon freshly ground black pepper
1 level teaspoon made mustard
2 level teaspoons caster sugar
6 tablespoons salad oil
2 tablespoons lemon juice
2 ripe avocado pears
2 tomatoes, skinned, seeded and chopped
4 spring onions, chopped

Put the salt, pepper, mustard and sugar into a small bowl. Blend in the oil a little at a time, then blend in the lemon juice.

Cut the avocado pears in half, remove the stones and scoop out the flesh into another bowl. Mash with a fork until quite smooth.

Blend in the dressing slowly and then finally fold in the tomato and spring onion.

Turn the guacomola into a dish and serve with chilli con carne or as a dip with crisp raw vegetables.

COOK'S TIP. If you have to leave your avocados once mashed, put the stones back into the flesh to stop it discolouring.

– Salade Niçoise –

MOULES MARINÈRES

6 pints (3.4 l) fresh mussels
1 oz (25 g) butter
1 large onion, chopped
4 stalks parsley
2 sprigs fresh thyme
1 bayleaf
Freshly ground black pepper
½ pint (300 ml) dry white wine or
* cider*
Salt
Chopped parsley

BEURRE MANIÉ:
1 oz (25 g) creamed soft butter
½ oz (12.5 g) flour

COOK'S TIP. Discard any mussels which are badly chipped or cracked or that do not close tightly. Those which remain open are dead and should not be used.

Scrape and clean each mussel with a strong knife, removing every trace of seaweed, mud and beard. Wash in several changes of water. Drain in a colander.

Melt the butter in a large pan over a low heat. Add the onion to the pan and fry until soft but not coloured. Add the herbs, pepper, wine, salt and mussels, cover with a tightly fitting lid and cook quickly, shaking the pan constantly until the mussels open. This takes about 5 or 6 minutes. Lift the mussels out, discard the empty half of the shell and keep hot in a covered dish. Boil the cooking liquor to reduce to about ½ pint (300 ml), remove the herbs.

Blend the butter and flour together to a smooth paste. Drop into the simmering stock a teaspoonful at a time and whisk until the stock is smooth and has thickened. Taste and check seasoning and then pour over the mussels and sprinkle with plenty of chopped parsley.

Serve with French bread and butter. Finger bowls are a help, and you will need a dish for the empty shells. Serves 6.

SALADE NIÇOISE

4 tomatoes
8 oz (225 g) French beans, cooked
1 crisp lettuce heart
⅛ pint (75 ml) French dressing
1 clove garlic, crushed
7 oz (200 g) can tuna fish
2 oz (50 g) can anchovy fillets
8 black olives
1 onion, finely sliced
2 hard-boiled eggs, quartered

COOK'S TIP. Cos or Webb's lettuce are perfect for this. Don't use a flabby round lettuce as it doesn't have the crispness.

Plunge the tomatoes in boiling water for a few minutes, then drain and skin, cut in quarters and remove all the seeds.

Cut the French beans into short even lengths.

Wash the lettuce and tear into strips and place in a salad bowl with the beans.

Flavour the French dressing with the garlic and add half to the salad bowl, tossing with the lettuce and beans.

Drain and flake the tuna and arrange with the drained anchovy fillets, olives and onion rings on top of the lettuce and beans.

Decorate the salad bowl with the quartered tomatoes and eggs and sprinkle over the remaining French dressing. Serves 4.

BISMARK HERRINGS

A useful dish for entertaining because it is prepared in advance. Leaves you more time to enjoy your guests!

6 small herrings
About 1 pint (600 ml) vinegar
Salt
Cayenne pepper
2 onions, very finely sliced

Scale and clean the herrings and wash under plenty of cold running water. Lay them in a dish and pour over the vinegar, adding a little extra vinegar if necessary to cover the fish. Cover and leave in a cool place for 24 hours.

Lift the herrings from the vinegar and remove the heads and backbone. Cut each herring into two fillets and arrange in a serving dish, sprinkle with salt and cayenne pepper and thinly sliced onions. Cover and leave again for another 24 hours in a cool place before serving. Serves 6.

TARAMASALATA

A pretty pink spread that makes a delightful summer starter

8 oz (225 g) smoked cod's roe
   (can be bought in a jar)
2 small slices white bread, with
   crusts removed
2 tablespoons milk
1 clove garlic, crushed (optional)
1/4 pint (150 ml) less 2 tablespoons
   oil
2 tablespoons lemon juice
Salt and pepper
2 bayleaves to garnish

Remove the skin from the cod's roe. Reduce to a paste in a blender or processor or place in a mortar and pound it with a pestle until smooth.

Soak the bread in the milk, then squeeze out as much milk as possible. Add the bread to the roe and blend or mash again with the

— Moules Marinières —

garlic, if used. Add the oil one teaspoon at a time until all has been absorbed. Stir in the lemon juice and seasoning.

Turn into a small dish and chill well. When ready to serve, garnish the dish with bayleaves. Serve with hot buttered toast. Serves 4.

HUMMUS

This is delicious eaten with warm pitta bread

8 oz (225 g) dried chick peas
1 1/2 teaspoons salt
3 cloves garlic, crushed
6 tablespoons lemon juice
5 oz (125 g) tahina paste
Cayenne pepper

Put the peas in a bowl after rinsing them, cover with cold water and leave to soak for at least 12 hours.

Drain the peas and put them in a saucepan. Add the salt and enough water to cover them, bring to the boil and simmer for 2-3 hours until they are very tender. Drain the peas and reserve the cooking water.

Mash the peas to a smooth purée with the garlic and 6 tablespoons of cooking water (or use a blender). Add the lemon juice a little at a time, beating continually with a large spoon. Add the tahina paste, and beat until smooth.

Turn into a bowl and sprinkle with cayenne pepper. Serves 4.

TAGLIATELLE WITH GARLIC CREAM SAUCE

8 oz (225 g) tagliatelle
A good knob of butter
Large clove garlic, crushed
¼ pint (150 ml) double cream
1 rounded tablespoon chopped
  parsley
Salt and freshly ground black
  pepper

Cook the tagliatelle in plenty of fast boiling salted water until just soft as directed on the packet. Drain very well and rinse in warm water and then drain again.

Rinse out the saucepan, melt the butter, add the garlic and fry for 2-3 minutes. Stir the cream into the pan with the parsley and then add the tagliatelle and toss well until coated with the sauce. Taste and add salt and plenty of ground black pepper. Turn into a warm dish and serve. Serves 4 for a first course.

CURRIED EGG MAYONNAISE

COOK'S TIP. If you boil the eggs for only 9 or 10 minutes and then cool them quickly under running water until absolutely cold, you will avoid an unsightly black ring around the edge of the yolk.

6 hard-boiled eggs
6 tablespoons home-made
  mayonnaise
3 teaspoons lemon juice
2 tablespoons mango chutney
  juice
1 teaspoon curry powder
Salt and pepper
Sprigs of cress

Cut the hard-boiled eggs in half lengthways and set out on a serving dish. Make the mayonnaise and blend it with the lemon juice, chutney juice, curry powder and salt and pepper. Spoon the mixture over the eggs and decorate with sprigs of cress. Serves 6.

Above Tagliatelle   Right Cheese Soufflé

CHEESE SOUFFLÉ

1½ oz (40 g) butter
1½ oz (40 g) flour
½ pint (300 ml) hot milk
Salt and pepper
1 level teaspoon made mustard
4 oz (100 g) strong Cheddar
  cheese, grated
4 large eggs

Heat the oven to 375 deg.F, 190 deg.C, gas mark 5 and place a baking sheet in it. Melt the butter in a pan, stir in the flour and cook for 2 minutes without browning. Remove the pan from the heat and stir in the hot milk. Return to the heat and bring to the boil, stirring until thickened, then add the seasoning and mustard and leave to cool.

Stir in the cheese. If preferred use 3 oz (75 g) strong Cheddar cheese and 1 oz (25 g) grated Parmesan. Separate the eggs and beat the yolks one at a time into the cheese sauce. Whisk the egg whites with a rotary hand or electric whisk until stiff, but not dry. Stir one heaped tablespoonful into the cheese sauce and then carefully fold in the remainder.

Pour into a buttered 2 pint (a good litre) soufflé dish, run a teaspoon around the edge of the dish and bake on a hot baking sheet in the centre of the oven for about 40 minutes until well risen and golden brown. Serve at once. Serves 3 to 4.

VARIATIONS:
Choose any flavouring and add to the mixture before the egg yolks.
Ham: add 4 to 6 oz (100 to 175 g) ham or boiled bacon, finely chopped.
Fish: add 4 to 6 oz (100 to 175 g) finely flaked cooked smoked haddock.
Shellfish: add 4 oz (100 g) peeled prawns or shrimps.
Mushroom: add 8 oz (225 g) finely chopped mushrooms, cooked in 1 oz (25 g) butter.
Spinach: add 1 lb (450 g) cooked

finely chopped spinach with a pinch of nutmeg and topped with a little grated cheese.

COOK'S TIP. This makes a delicious light lunch, but if you prefer, serve it as a first course baked in small ramekins. In smaller dishes the soufflé will only take about 20 minutes to cook.

CHEESE AIGRETTES

Serve as a savoury first course or as a snack with drinks.

1 oz (25 g) butter
1/4 pint (150 ml) water
2 oz (50 g) self-raising flour
1 egg yolk
1 egg
2 oz (50 g) Cheddar cheese,
    grated
Salt
Cayenne pepper

Put the butter and water in a small saucepan and bring to the boil. Remove from the heat and add the flour, beating well until the mixture is glossy and leaves the sides of the pan clean. Cool slightly.

Lightly mix the yolk and the egg together and beat into the mixture a little at a time. Stir in the cheese, salt and a pinch of cayenne pepper. Check seasoning.

When required, drop the mixture in heaped teaspoonfuls into hot deep fat and fry gently until golden brown, turning once. Lift out and drain on kitchen paper. Serve at once. Makes about 16.

–Bitterballen–

BITTERBALLEN

Delicious served hot with a mild mustard. Eat with drinks.

2 level teaspoons powdered
    gelatine
1/2 pint (300 ml) chicken stock
1 oz (25 g) butter
1 oz (25 g) flour
6 oz (175 g) cooked ham and veal,
    coarsely chopped
1 teaspoon chopped parsley
Salt and pepper
2 oz (50 g) flour for coating
1 egg, beaten
3 oz (75 g) browned breadcrumbs
Deep fat or oil for frying

Put the gelatine with the chicken stock in a small saucepan and leave to soak for 2 minutes, then put over a gentle heat until the gelatine dissolves.

Melt the butter and stir in the flour and cook for a minute. Stir in the stock, bring to the boil, stirring, then simmer for 2 minutes. Stir in the meat and parsley and taste and check seasoning.

Wrap the mixture in a piece of foil and chill until firm.

Roll into small balls, dip in flour, then into the beaten egg and breadcrumbs. Fry in hot deep fat or oil until golden brown. Drain on kitchen paper. Makes about 30.

PÂTÉS AND MOUSSES

It is always difficult to tell whether you have seasoned a pâté to your liking. This is what to do: when the pâté is made and ready to go into the dish, take a spoonful of the mixture and fry it gently in butter for 5 minutes or so, turning in the pan, then taste this sample and adjust seasoning by adding a bit more salt, pepper and herbs.

COUNTRY PÂTÉ

1 egg
¼ lb (100 g) salt belly of pork
¾ lb (350 g) green bacon pieces
¾ lb (350 g) pig's liver
2 shallots or 1 onion
2 oz (50 g) lard
1 oz (25 g) flour
2 cloves garlic, crushed
Plenty of ground black pepper
4 tablespoons sherry or port
1 level tablespoon freshly
    chopped mixed herbs
6 crushed juniper berries
To garnish: 2 bay leaves

Check with the butcher if the belly of pork has been salted and if it has soak overnight before using.

Skin and bone the belly and roughly cut up. Remove the rind and bone from the bacon and trim the liver. Peel and roughly chop the shallots and fry in the lard for 4 to 5 minutes.

Mince the pork, bacon, liver and shallots, add the remaining ingredients and mix well. Pour the mixture into a greased 2 pint (a good litre) dish, lay the bay leaves on top, cover with a piece of foil and stand in a dish of hot water and cook at 325 deg.F, 170 deg.C, gas mark 3 for 1½ to 2 hours.

Remove from the oven. The pâté is cooked if when the centre is pierced the juices that run out are clear and it has shrunk slightly from the edges of the dish.

Lightly weight the pâté with weights, tins or a piece of foil-covered wood and leave to become quite cold.

Serve sliced with French bread or hot toast. Serves 10.

LEMONS FILLED WITH SARDINE PÂTÉ

COOK'S TIP. This makes an inexpensive starter and looks very pretty with each lemon garnished with a fresh bay leaf.

4 small lemons
2 oz (50 g) butter, softened
2 oz (50 g) cream cheese
4½ oz (125 g) can sardines in oil
Ground black pepper

Cut a thin slice from the base of each lemon so that they stand flat, then cut a larger slice from the top of each lemon and scoop out the insides using a grapefruit or serrated knife and strain through a sieve.

Cream the butter and cheese together. Drain the sardines, mash with a fork, and beat into the butter with 2 tablespoons (30 ml) of the strained lemon juice and plenty of black pepper.

Pile the mixture into the lemon shells, top each with a lid and serve on individual plates.
Serves 4.

—Sardine Pâté—

KIPPER PÂTÉ

COOK'S TIP. In the unlikely event that you have any leftovers of this delicious pâté you will find that children love it as a sandwich filling.

10 oz (300 g) frozen kipper fillets, thawed
1/4 pint (150 ml) double cream
Pinch cayenne pepper
Sprig parsley

Cook kipper fillets according to the directions on packet. When they are cooked, remove them from bag. Pour the butter into a mixing bowl and set aside.

Remove all dark skin and any bones from kipper fillets. Add kipper fillets to bowl with cream and cayenne. Mash ingredients together with a fork until smooth. Alternatively, mix all the ingredients together in an electric blender. Spoon pâté into a serving dish and smooth the top. Chill for at least 2 hours. Garnish with parsley and serve with hot toast and butter. Serves 4.

SMOKED MACKEREL PÂTÉ

For a milder flavour make this pâté using smoked trout.

2 smoked mackerel
10 oz (275 g) butter, melted but not hot
4 oz (100 g) cream cheese
Juice of 1/2 lemon
Small sprigs of parsley

Remove the skin and bones from the mackerel and put the fillets with 8 oz (225 g) of the butter, the cream cheese and the lemon juice in the blender in two batches and blend until smooth.

Divide the pâté between 6 individual serving dishes and smooth the tops or put in a small loaf-shaped tureen or dish, about 1 pint (600 ml) size. Spoon on a little of the remaining butter, remelted so that it pours on top of each dish and leave in a cool place until set.

Serve garnished with small sprigs of parsley and with hot toast and butter. Serves 6.

POTTER'S PÂTÉ

COOK'S TIP. Surprisingly easy to make – a very good all-purpose pâté. Ideal for a first course, equally delicious for a picnic.

1 large onion
8 oz (225 g) chicken livers
8 oz (225 g) pork sausagemeat
1 heaped tablespoon chopped parsley
1 level teaspoon salt
Pinch ground black pepper
2 cloves garlic, crushed
About 5 rashers streaky bacon

Peel and quarter the onion and pass through the mincer with the chicken livers or put in the blender and purée. Turn into a large bowl with the sausagemeat, parsley, seasoning and garlic, mix well together.

Remove the rind and bone from the bacon, place on a board and spread flat with the back of a knife. Line the bottom and sides of a 1 lb or 1 1/2 pint (450 g or 900 ml) loaf tin, with the bacon rashers, put in the meat mixture and spread flat.

Cover the tin with a piece of foil, place in a roasting tin half filled with hot water, and cook at 325 deg.F, 170 deg.C, gas mark 3 for 1 1/2 hours.

The pâté is cooked if, when the centre is pierced with a skewer, the juices that run out are clear and it has slightly shrunk from the edges of the tin.

Lightly weight the pâté with weights, or tins on top of a piece of wood covered with foil and leave to become quite cold. Serve sliced with hot toast and butter. Serves 6.

—Smoked Mackerel Pâté and Potter's Pâté—

—Salmon Mousse—

SALMON MOUSSE

1 rounded tablespoon gelatine
4 tablespoons cold water
10½ oz (298 g) condensed
    consommé soup
½ pint (300 ml) double cream,
    whisked until just thick
¾ pint (450 ml) good mayonnaise
Juice of 1 lemon
12 oz (350 g) cooked flaked
    salmon
Salt and black pepper
1 tablespoon chopped parsley

To cook the salmon, cover with water, add a slice of lemon, salt and pepper and bring to the boil slowly. Simmer for 4 minutes and then leave to cool in the water preferably overnight.

Put the gelatine in a small bowl or cup with the water and leave to soak for 5 minutes to form a sponge. Stand in a pan of simmering water and stir until dissolved and the gelatine is clear.

Put the undiluted consommé in a bowl and stir in the gelatine. Blend the cream, mayonnaise and lemon juice together in another bowl, then fold in the flaked salmon and three quarters of the consommé, taste and check seasoning.

Pour into a 2½-3 pint (1.4-1.7 l) dish and leave to set. Stir the parsley into the remaining consommé and carefully spoon over the mousse. It may be necessary to warm the consommé slightly if it has set.

Return to the refrigerator and chill until required. If frozen, thaw for six hours. Serves 10 as a first course.

COOK'S TIP. This makes a little salmon go a long way. You could use pink trout instead.

SMOKED HADDOCK MOUSSE

COOK'S TIP. Make either as one large mousse or in individual ramekin dishes. Serve with a tossed green salad and thin brown bread and butter.

1 lb (450 g) smoked haddock
½ pint (300 ml) milk
Freshly ground black pepper
1 oz (25 g) butter
¾ oz (19 g) flour
½ oz (12.5 g) powdered gelatine
    (1 packet)
2 tablespoons (30 ml) water
Scant ½ pint (300 ml) home-made
    or good bought mayonnaise
Juice of 1 lemon
¼ pint (150 ml) double cream,
    whipped
2 hard-boiled eggs, finely
    chopped
Small sprigs parsley or watercress

Place the fish in a shallow pan, pour over the milk and season with pepper. Poach gently for about 10 minutes or until the fish flakes easily. Drain the fish, reserving the milk, and flake, removing all the skin and bones.

Melt the butter in a small saucepan and stir in the flour, cook for a minute, add the milk and bring to the boil, stirring until thickened.

Place the gelatine in a small bowl with the water and leave to soak for a few minutes, then add to the sauce and stir until dissolved. Put the white sauce and flaked fish in a blender and purée until smooth. Turn into a large bowl and leave to cool.

Add the mayonnaise and lemon juice to the sauce and fold in the whipped cream and hard-boiled eggs. Taste and check the seasoning and either turn into a 2 pint (1 l) dish or into 6 – 8 individual ramekins.

Chill until firm and set, and garnish each ramekin or the large dish with small sprigs of parsley or watercress. Serves 6 to 8.

MAINCOURSES

This part of the book ranges far and wide, from the hearty eating provided by steak and kidney pudding to the subtle oriental delights of the famous Japanese dish Sukiyaki. There are recipes for nourishing family meals, more sophisticated entertain- ing at home and quick, economical suppers. There is also a section on cooking vegetables and accompaniments and a useful guide to the many superb varieties of French cheese which are now available in shops and supermarkets.

CASSEROLES

In these cost-conscious times, it has become increasingly important to cook imaginatively with the meat we can afford. The traditional British roast is not yet a thing of the past, but nowadays we have to learn to use cheaper cuts of meat in casseroles, making less go further. Remember that a casserole is always improved by a good stock, a supply of which can be stored in your freezer. Don't stint on herbs, either. Fresh herbs can be chopped up and frozen in ice cubes or small butter pots.

FRENCH COUNTRY CASSEROLE OR PIE

1 oz (25 g) dripping
6 oz (175 g) streaky bacon, rinded and cut in strips
1 1/2 lb (675 g) thin flank cut in 1 inch cubes
1 oz (25 g) flour
1/2 pint (300 ml) stock
1/4 pint (150 ml) red wine
1 bayleaf
Sprig of parsley
Good pinch mixed dried herbs or a small bunch of fresh herbs
1 level teaspoon salt
Good pinch pepper
1/4 lb (100 g) small onions, peeled
8 oz (227 g) packet puff pastry optional

COOK'S TIP. An ideal opportunity to use an inexpensive cut of beef like thin flank, but remember to remove excess fat and skin first.

Heat the oven to 325 deg.F, 160 deg.C, gas mark 3. Melt the dripping in a frying pan and fry the bacon until it begins to brown. Lift out with a slotted spoon and place in a 3 pint (1.7 l) ovenproof casserole. Fry the meat in the fat remaining in the pan until brown all over, lift out with the spoon and add to the bacon. Pour off all but 2 tablespoons of fat, stir in the flour and cook until browned. Add the stock and wine and bring to the boil, stirring all the time, then simmer for 2 minutes or until thickened. Add the bayleaf, parsley, herbs and seasoning and pour over the meat. Cover and cook in the oven for 1 1/2 hours. Add the onions and cook for a further hour or until the meat is tender. Remove the parsley, bayleaf and bunch of herbs, taste and adjust seasoning. If making a pie, turn the mixture into a 1 1/2 pint (900 ml) pie dish and leave to become quite cold. Roll out the pastry and use to cover the pie, re-roll any trimmings and cut into leaves to decorate the top. Make a small hole in the centre and brush with a little milk or beaten egg. Bake in a hot oven at 425 deg.F, 220 deg.C, gas mark 7 for about 30 minutes until the pastry is golden brown and well risen and the meat is hot through. Serves 4 to 6 for the casserole or 6 to 8 for the pie.

OXTAIL IN BEER

2 oxtails
3 tablespoons dripping
2 oz (50 g) flour
1 pint (600 ml) beer
1/2 pint (300 ml) beef stock
Bouquet garni
Peeled rind of 1 lemon in a spiral
Juice of 1 lemon
2 tablespoons redcurrant jelly
2 tablespoons tomato puree
1/2 teaspoon gravy browning
1 teaspoon salt
Freshly ground pepper
8 oz (225 g) pickling onions, peeled and left whole

COOK'S TIP. Cook this the day before it is needed, skim off surplus fat and reheat on the day.

Cut the oxtail into 2 inch (5 cm) lengths through the vertebrae. Remove the surplus fat and fry gently in an ovenproof dish in the melted dripping for about 30 minutes, or until brown all over.

Heat the oven to 300 deg.F, 150 deg.C, gas mark 2.

Remove the oxtail from the pan and if necessary add more dripping. Stir in the flour and cook for a few minutes. Add the beer and stock and bring to the boil stirring all the time until thick.

Add the remaining ingredients except the onions. Cover with a lid and cook in the oven for 5 hours, adding the onions during the last hour of the cooking time.

Taste and check seasoning and remove the bouquet garni and piece of lemon peel. Serves 6.

BRISTOL BEEF CASSEROLE

1 lb (450 g) stewing steak
3 carrots, peeled
3 onions, peeled
1 small can tomato soup
The small can when emptied filled
  with cold water.
1 oz (25 g) flour
1 beef stock cube
Salt and pepper
Pinch mixed dried herbs

Cut the steak into one inch (2.5 cm) pieces and roughly chop the carrots and onions. Put the meat with the vegetables and soup in an ovenproof casserole. Put the flour in a small bowl and gradually stir in the water and mix to a smooth paste, add the stock cube, seasoning and herbs and stir into the casserole.

Cover and cook at 325 deg.F, 160 deg.C, gas mark 3 for about 3½ hours or until tender. The time will vary with the cut of stewing steak used.

Taste and check seasoning. This is delicious served with potatoes and a green salad. Serves 4.

FRENCH BEEF CASSEROLE

I often make double the quantity of this dish and use the rest as the filling for a pie.

1½ lb (675 g) chuck steak
½ pint (300 ml) red wine
2 tablespoons oil
Bayleaf
Ground black pepper
1 clove garlic, crushed
8 oz (225 g) onions, sliced
8 oz (225 g) carrots, sliced
6 oz (175 g) unsmoked streaky
  bacon
14 oz (397 g) can peeled tomatoes
Salt
4 oz (100 g) mushrooms,
  quartered

Cut the meat into 1 inch (2.5 cm) squares and put in a large china or glass bowl with the wine, oil, bayleaf, pepper, garlic, onions and carrots. Stir well then cover with a piece of cling film or foil and then leave in a cool place to marinate overnight.

Heat the oven to 300 deg.F, 150 deg.C, gas mark 2.

Remove the rind and any bone from the bacon and cut into strips. Put half in a 4 pint (2.3 l) ovenproof dish, then put the meat and marinade on top and cover with the remaining bacon and can of tomatoes. Season with salt and then cover the dish and cook in the oven for 3 hours. Stir in the mushrooms and cook for a further 15 to 30 minutes or until the beef is tender.

Taste and check seasoning and remove the bayleaf. Serves 6.

SWISS STEAK

4 slices topside of beef, each
  weighing about 6 oz (175 g)
1½ oz (40 g) flour
1 level teaspoon salt
¼ level teaspoon pepper
1½ oz (40 g) dripping
2 large onions, finely sliced
2 sticks celery, sliced
8 oz (227 g) can tomatoes
2 level teaspoons tomato purée
1 teaspoon Worcestershire sauce
¼ pint (150 ml) beef stock

Heat the oven to 300 deg.F, 150 deg.C, gas mark 2. Cut each slice of beef in half.

Mix together the flour, salt and pepper. Toss the meat in the seasoned flour, pressing it gently.

Melt the dripping in a pan and fry the meat quickly on all sides until it is browned. Lift out and put in an ovenproof casserole. Add the onion and celery to the dripping remaining in the pan and fry until golden brown. If there should be any seasoned flour left over, stir it into the vegetables and cook for a minute.

Stir in the tomatoes, purée, Worcestershire sauce and stock and pour over the meat. Cover and cook in the oven for about 2½ hours or until the meat is tender.

Serve with creamy mashed potato. Serves 4.

SWEET AND SOUR BRAISED STEAK

3 lb (1.3 kg) piece of chuck steak
½ pint (300 ml) red wine
4 tablespoons malt vinegar
2 bayleaves
3 cloves
6 black peppercorns
2 carrots, sliced
1 onion, sliced
2 sticks celery, sliced
2 tablespoons oil
1 oz (25 g) flour
2 tablespoons tomato puree
2 tablespoons thin honey
2 oz (50 g) raisins
Salt and pepper

Place the piece of chuck steak in a china or glass bowl and add the wine, vinegar, herbs and vegetables. Cover and leave in the refrigerator for 24 hours.

Heat the oven to 325 deg.F, 160 deg.C, gas mark 3.

Put the oil in a frying pan and heat through, then add the meat and quickly brown on both sides. Lift out and place in a large casserole. Stir the flour into the fat remaining in the pan and cook for a minute. Add all the ingredients in the marinade and bring to the boil, stirring. Pour over the meat, cover the casserole with a tight-fitting lid and cook in the oven for 2 to 3 hours, the time will vary with the thickness of the meat. Lift the meat out onto a board, carve in slices and arrange on a serving dish.

Strain the marinade into a small saucepan, add the tomato puree, honey, raisins, salt and pepper and bring to the boil, stirring. Simmer for 2 minutes, taste and check seasoning and then strain over the meat. Serves 8.

—Beef Parcels—

BEEF PARCELS

4 slices silverside

STUFFING:
1 oz (25 g) butter
2 oz (50 g) bacon, chopped
2 oz (50 g) mushrooms, chopped
2 oz (50 g) fresh white
*   breadcrumbs*
1 level tablespoon chopped
*   parsley*
Salt and ground black pepper

SAUCE:
1 oz (25 g) dripping
1 oz (25 g) flour
½ pint (300 ml) beef stock
2 tablespoons sherry
6 sticks celery, sliced

Trim the meat and then place each piece in turn between wetted greaseproof paper and beat flat with a rolling pin. The wet paper helps to stop the meat sticking to the rolling pin.

Prepare the stuffing. Melt the butter in a small pan and fry the bacon and mushrooms gently for 2 to 3 minutes. Stir in the rest of the ingredients and mix well. Divide the stuffing into four and place one portion on each slice of meat, roll up and tie with fine string or fix with wooden cocktail sticks.

Melt the dripping in a large saucepan and fry the beef to brown on all sides, lift out and place on one side. Stir the flour into the dripping remaining in the pan

and cook for two minutes. Add stock and sherry and bring to the boil, stirring until thickened. Add the celery and plenty of salt and pepper.

Return the meat to the pan, cover with a tightly fitting lid and simmer gently for 1½ to 2 hours or until tender.

Taste and check seasoning, arrange the parcels on a warm dish and remove the string or cocktail sticks. Spoon over the sauce. Serves 4.

COOK'S TIP. These parcels may also be cooked in a slow cooker, allowing about 30 minutes on high and then turning down to low for about 6 hours.

CARBONNADE OF BEEF

1½ lb (675 g) chuck steak
1½ oz (40 g) dripping
½ lb (225 g) onions, sliced
2 large carrots, sliced
1½ oz (40 g) flour
½ pint (300 ml) pale ale
¼ pint (150 ml) beef stock
1 rounded tablespoon brown
    sugar
1½ teaspoons mustard
1½ level teaspoons salt
Pepper
1 bayleaf

Cut the meat into ½ inch (1.25 cm) thick strips.
　Melt the dripping in a pan and quickly brown the meat, lift out with a slotted spoon and put on one side. Add the onions and carrots to the dripping remaining in the pan and fry until golden brown. Stir in the flour and cook for a minute, then gradually blend in the pale ale and stock. Bring to the boil stirring until thickened. Add the sugar, mustard, seasoning and bayleaf and return the meat to the pan. Cover and simmer gently for 2 hours or until the meat is tender.
　Taste and check seasoning and remove the bayleaf. Serves 4 to 6.

COOK'S TIP. Once cider or beer is opened and used for cooking, any that is left should be decanted into a small bottle. Keep in the fridge; use within a month.

LIVER IN ONION SAUCE

1 lb (450 g) pig's or lamb's liver
½ lb (225 g) onions
2 oz (50 g) dripping
2 oz (50 g) flour
1 pint (600 ml) beef stock or 1 pint
    (600 ml) water and 1 beef stock
    cube
3 tablespoons tomato ketchup
Pinch dried marjoram
A few drops of Worcester sauce
Salt and pepper

—Carbonnade of Beef—

Cut the liver into long strips about ½ inch (1.25 cm) wide, then soak in milk for 30 minutes; drain off milk and discard.
　Peel and slice the onions. Melt the dripping in a pan, add the onions and fry for 5 to 10 minutes until the onions are golden brown. Stir in the flour and cook for 2 minutes, add the stock and bring to the boil, stirring until thickened. Add ketchup, marjoram, Worcester sauce and seasoning, stir well and cover pan. Reduce heat and simmer for 20 minutes.

Add liver to sauce and cook for about 10 minutes. Serves 5.

COOK'S TIP. If you don't like the stronger flavour of pig's liver but find lamb's liver too dear, then soak it in milk before cooking. This is a moist and flavoursome way of cooking it and your family will find it hard to tell the difference.

DANISH MEATBALLS

8 oz (225 g) lean minced beef
8 oz (225 g) lean minced pork
1 oz (25 g) flour
1 egg, beaten
1 teaspoon salt
Ground black pepper
Pinch grated nutmeg

SAUCE:
1½ oz (40 g) dripping
12 oz (350 g) onions, chopped
1½ oz (40 g) flour
¾ pint (450 ml) dry cider
1 beef stock cube
Salt and pepper
A little browning to colour

Mix the beef, pork, flour, egg, seasoning and nutmeg together thoroughly and shape into 8 even sized balls.

Melt the dripping in a sauce-pan and fry the meat balls quickly until brown all over, lift out with a slotted spoon and keep on one side. Add the onions to the dripping remaining in the pan and fry quickly to brown. Stir in the flour and cook gently until starting to turn brown. Add the cider, stock cube and seasoning and bring to the boil, stirring until thickened. If necessary add a little browning to the sauce. Return the meat balls to the pan, cover and simmer gently for 30 to 45 minutes.

Alternatively, the meat balls may be put in a casserole, covered and cooked in a moderate oven 350°F, 180°C, Gas No. 4 for about 1 to 1¼ hours. Serves 4.

NORFOLK PORK

6 lean pork chops
About 1 tablespoon seasoned
    flour
12 oz (350 g) onions, chopped
12 oz (350 g) Bramley apples,
    peeled, cored and cut in
    chunks
1 level teaspoon salt
Ground black pepper
½ pint (300 ml) cider

Remove the rind and excess fat from the pork chops and keep on one side.

Put the seasoned flour in a bag and drop each chop in one at a time to lightly coat the surface.

Put the pieces of fat in a large frying pan and heat gently until the base of the pan is lightly coated with the fat, then discard them. Add the chops to the pan and brown on both sides, lift out onto a plate.

Add the onion to the pan and fry gently in the remaining fat for five minutes, then add the apple and cook for a couple of minutes, stirring. Add salt and plenty of ground black pepper. Put half the apple and onion in a shallow 2 pint (a good litre) ovenproof dish, lay the chops on top, then cover with the rest of the onion mixture and pour over the cider.

Bake uncovered in the oven at 350 deg.F, 180 deg.C, gas mark 4 for about one hour.

If this dish has been prepared in advance and put in the re-frigerator it will require about 1¼ hours in the oven. Serves 6.

COOK'S TIP. This recipe is a good way of using up windfall apples.

LAMB HOT POT

2 lb (900 g) middle neck or scrag
    end of lamb or 1 lb (450 g) neck
    fillet
2 lamb's kidneys
2 lb (900 g) potatoes, sliced
2 onions, sliced
2 oz (50g) mushrooms, sliced
Salt and pepper
About ¼ pint (150 ml) stock or
    water
Butter

Heat the oven to 350 deg.F, 180 deg.C, gas mark 4.

Trim the meat, removing the spinal cord and any excess fat, and cut into convenient sized pieces. Halve the kidneys and remove the core and skin, then cut into slices.

Layer the potato with the vegetables, lamb and kidneys in a large 4 to 5 pint (2.3 to 2.8 l) casserole, seasoning well and finishing with a layer of potatoes arranged neatly on top.

Pour over the stock or water and dot the potatoes with a little butter. Cover and bake in the oven for 1½ hours, remove the lid and continue baking for a further 30 to 45 minutes to brown the potatoes. Serves 4.

COOK'S TIP. If your family can't cope with bones in their meat use 1 lb (450 g) neck fillet of lamb. This is completely boneless, and you won't need such a large casserole.

MEDITERRANEAN FISH CASSEROLE

Monk fish is inexpensive com-pared with the other firm fleshed fish like halibut and turbot.

1 lb (450 g) monk fish, skinned
1 oz (25 g) butter
8 oz (225 g) onion, chopped
1 fat clove garlic, crushed
14 oz (397 g) can peeled tomatoes
¼ pint (150 ml) dry vermouth
Sprig of lemon thyme
Salt and black pepper
Chopped parsley
Fresh prawns (optional)

Cut the fish into 1 inch (2.5 cm) cubes, removing any filmy tissue with a knife. Melt the butter in a large shallow pan. Add the onion and fry until almost tender, allow-ing it to become a pale golden. Add the garlic, tomatoes, ver-mouth, thyme and seasoning. Boil rapidly (without a lid) for 3 minutes to reduce it slightly. Add the fish and cook for a further 3 to 5 minutes until no longer transparent — it should be firm and white.

Remove the thyme, turn into a warm dish, scatter with chopped parsley and fresh prawns if liked.

Serve either with boiled rice or lots of garlic bread. Serves 4.

FAMILY FAVOURITES

Cooking for a hungry family is a demanding task, and this section provides some recipes that are nourishing, easy to prepare and not too expensive. As well as good old-fashioned cottage pie, there are delicious savoury pancakes and the rich Italian stew osso bucco. From across the Atlantic comes Boston baked beans, guaranteed to go down a treat on a cold winter's night.

STEAK AND KIDNEY PIE

COOK'S TIP. The pastry is my mother's recipe. It is essential to use a hard margarine straight from the fridge. I use this same pastry for fruit pies too.

1 lb (450 g) skirt beef
4 oz (100 g) ox kidney
1 oz (25 g) flour
1 oz (25 g) dripping
1 large onion, chopped
1/2 pint (300 ml) beef stock
1 teaspoon salt
Ground black pepper
4 oz (100 g) mushrooms, sliced

QUICK FAMILY FLAKY PASTRY:
8 oz (225 g) strong plain flour
1/2 teaspoon salt
6 oz (175 g) hard margaine
About 9 tablespoons or a scant 1/4
    pint (150 ml) cold water
A little beaten egg to glaze

Cut the steak and kidney into 1 inch (2.5 cm) pieces, put in a polythene bag with the flour and toss until well coated. Melt the dripping in a saucepan, add the meat and fry with the onion until browned. Stir in the stock and seasoning and bring to the boil. Partially cover the pan and simmer for about 1 1/2 hours, then stir in the mushrooms and continue cooking for a further 30 minutes or until the meat is tender. Taste and check seasoning, turn into a 1 1/2 pint (900 ml) pie dish and allow to become cold. Put a pie funnel or handleless cup in the centre.

For the pastry: Sift the flour and salt into a mixing bowl. Coarsely grate the margarine into the bowl. Stir in just sufficient water to make a firm dough and then roll out on a lightly floured surface to make a strip about 1/2 inch (1.25 cm) thick and 6 inches (15 cm) wide. Fold the pastry in three and give it a quarter turn to the left. Roll out again into a strip and fold in three. Wrap the pastry in foil and chill in the fridge for 30 minutes.

Heat the oven to 425 deg.F, 220 deg.C, gas mark 7.

Roll out the pastry on a lightly floured table and use to cover the pie, seal and crimp the edges and use any pastry trimming to decorate the top with pastry leaves. If there is any leftover pastry this may be used to make a pasty or turnover.

Brush the pie with a little beaten egg and make a small hole in the centre for the steam to escape. Bake in the oven for 40 minutes and if the pastry is browning too much reduce the heat to 350 deg.F, 180 deg.C, gas mark 4 for a further 15 minutes to cook the pastry until it is golden brown and the meat is hot through. Serves 4 to 6.

STEAK AND KIDNEY PUDDING

1 lb (450 g) skirt beef
4 oz (100 g) ox kidney
1 rounded tablespoon flour
1 small onion, finely chopped
4 oz (100 g) mushrooms, sliced
1 level teaspoon salt
1/4 level teaspoon pepper
About 1/4 pint (150 ml) stock

SUET PASTRY:
8 oz (225 g) self-raising flour
1 level teaspoon salt
3 oz (75 g) shredded suet
8 tablespoons (120 ml) cold water

Grease a 1 1/2 or 2 pint (1 l) pudding basin. Cut the steak and kidney into 1/2 inch (1.25 cm) cubes, removing any fat and the core from the kidney. Toss in the flour with the onion, mushrooms and seasoning.

Now prepare the pastry. Put the flour, salt and suet in a bowl and mix with the water to a soft but not sticky dough. Cut off a third of the dough and roll out into a circle the size of the top of the basin for a lid. Roll out the remainder and line the basin.

Fill the basin with the meat mixture and add sufficient stock to

—Steak and Kidney Pie—

and cook for 60 minutes. Then allow the pressure to reduce at room temperature. Serves 4.

SLOW ROAST BRISKET

COOK'S TIP. A good lean piece of brisket slow roasts beautifully. Don't expect the middle to be pink but do expect it to be tender. It makes an economical Sunday roast.

3 lb (1.3 kg) lean brisket, boned and rolled
1 beef stock cube
½-¾ pint (300-450 ml) water
Salt and pepper

Ask your butcher to prepare the brisket for you by removing all the excess fat and bone. Put the meat in a small meat tin, add the stock cube and sufficient water to give a depth of 1 inch (2.5 cm). Season with salt and pepper. Cover the tin with a lid or piece of foil. Put in a hot oven at 425 deg.F, 220 deg.C, gas mark 7 for 30 minutes. Then lower the heat to 300 deg.F, 150 deg.C, gas mark 2 for 50 minutes to the lb (450 g) of meat. Turn the heat up to 400 deg.F, 200 deg.C, gas mark 6 for the last 45 minutes of the cooking time to allow roast potatoes to brown and a Yorkshire pudding to cook.

Make a gravy from the stock and meat juices. Serve with Yorkshire pudding and roast potatoes. Serves 6.

come three quarters of the way up the meat. Damp the edges of the pastry and cover with the lid, sealing firmly. Cover the pudding with a piece of greased greaseproof paper with a pleat in it and a lid of foil.

Cook either by boiling in the normal way for 3½ to 4 hours, topping up with boiling water when necessary, or in a slow cooker on high for 5 hours. The pudding may also be cooked in a pressure cooker: stand the basin on the trivet with 1½ pints (900 ml) boiling water and a spoonful of vinegar. Seal the cooker, wait for a steady flow of steam and then steam gently for 15 minutes. Raise the heat, bring to 5 lb (2.3 kg) pressure

COTTAGE PIE

A little dripping
1 lb (450 g) good raw mince
1 large onion, chopped
2 carrots, peeled and diced
¼ level teaspoon mixed dried
 herbs
2 level tablespoons tomato purée
1 oz (25 g) flour
½ pint (300 ml) beef stock
1 level teaspoon salt
Black pepper
A little gravy browning
1½ lb (675 g) potatoes
1 oz (25 g) butter
A little milk

Melt the dripping in a pan, add the mince, onion and carrots and fry stirring frequently to brown. Stir in the herbs, tomato purée and flour and cook for a minute. Add the stock and seasoning and bring to the boil, stirring until thickened and then add a little gravy browning if liked. Cover the pan and simmer for about 45 minutes or until the meat and vegetables are tender. Turn into a 2½ pint (1.4 l) ovenproof pie dish and leave to cool.

Meanwhile cook the potatoes in boiling salted water until tender. Drain well, mash with the butter and milk and season to taste.

Using a fork, cover the top of the meat with the potato, spreading evenly.

When required bake in the oven at 375 deg.F, 190 deg.C, gas mark 5 for 30-40 minutes or until the pie is hot through. Serves 4.

COOK'S TIP. When using mince buy and cook on the day that it is required. Choose mince that has a good red colour and is made from good quality meat.

LARGE CORNISH PIE

1 lb (450 g) good raw minced beef
6 oz (175 g) potatoes, finely diced
4 oz (100 g) carrots, finely diced
1 large onion, finely chopped
1½ level teaspoons salt
Plenty of pepper

PASTRY:
12 oz (350 g) plain flour
3 oz (75 g) hard margarine
3 oz (75 g) lard
About 4 tablespoons cold water to
 mix
Milk or beaten egg to glaze

Place the beef, potato, carrot, onion, salt and pepper in a bowl and mix thoroughly.

Sieve the flour into a bowl and rub in the fats until the mixture resembles fine breadcrumbs. Add sufficient water to mix to a firm dough. Roll out two-thirds of the pastry on a floured table to an oblong and use to line a deep Swiss roll tin approximately 11 by 7 by 1½ inches (27.5 by 17.5 by 3.75 cm).

Lay the meat mixture in the pastry and press down evenly. Roll out the remaining pastry to form an oblong for the lid. Damp the edges of the pie, position lid and press edges well together. Trim off the surplus pastry, crimp the edge and decorate the top with the pastry trimmings.

Brush the top with milk or beaten egg to glaze and make two small slits in the centre of the pie. Bake in the oven at 425 deg.F, 220 deg.C, gas mark 7 for 20-25 minutes until lightly browned, then reduce the temperature to 350 deg.F, 180 deg.C, gas mark 4 and continue cooking for a further 35-40 minutes. Serve hot. Serves 6

Large Cornish Pie

HOMEMADE BEEFBURGERS WITH BARBECUE SAUCE

¾ lb (350 g) best minced beef
¼ lb (100 g) pork sausagemeat
1 medium onion, grated
1 level teaspoon salt
Ground black pepper

BARBECUE SAUCE:
2 oz (50 g) butter
1 medium onion, finely chopped
8 tablespoons tomato ketchup
4 tablespoons (60 ml) vinegar
4 tablespoons mango chutney,
 chopped
½ level teaspoon French mustard
2 teaspoons caster sugar
2 tablespoons (30 ml)
 Worcestershire sauce

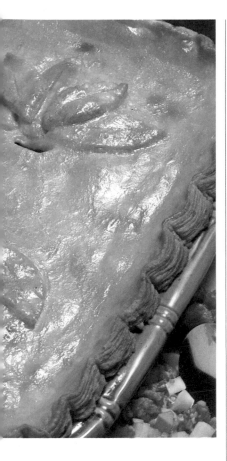

SPICY BEEF CASSOULET

4 oz (100 g) dried red kidney
   beans
2 good pinches bicarbonate of
   soda
1 oz (25 g) flour
1 teaspoon salt
Good pinch pepper
1 teaspoon ground ginger
1½ lb (675 g) shin of beef cut in
   1 inch (2.5 cm) cubes
2 oz (50 g) lard or dripping

SAUCE:
A few drops of Tabasco sauce
8 oz (225 g) can peeled tomatoes
¼ pint (150 ml) stock
2 tablespoons soft brown sugar
¼ lb (100 g) sliced mushrooms
2 tablespoons cider vinegar
2 cloves garlic, crushed
1 bayleaf
1 red pepper

COOK'S TIP. The red beans in this
casserole must be soaked
otherwise they are not soft enough
to eat. The bicarbonate of soda

speeds up the process but is not
essential. If you are in a hurry use a
16 oz (450 g) can of red kidney
beans. This is an excellent dish for
informal entertaining and delicious
with a green salad.

Place the kidney beans in a basin
with bicarbonate of soda, cover
with cold water and leave to stand
overnight, drain. Heat the oven to
325 deg.F, 160 deg.C, gas mark 3.
Mix the flour, seasoning and
ginger together and coat the meat
thoroughly, melt the dripping in a
frying pan and fry the meat quickly
to brown, then place in a 3 pint
(1.7 l) casserole with the beans.
Combine all the sauce ingredients,
except the red pepper, in the pan
and bring to the boil. Pour this over
the meat, cover and cook in the
oven for about 2-3 hours.

Remove the seeds and white
pith from the red pepper and cut
into rings. Add to the casserole,
return to the oven and cook for a
further 30 minutes or until the beef
is tender. Taste, adjust seasoning
and remove the bayleaf. Serves 5.

COOK'S TIP. You could add a
teaspoon of chopped fresh herbs
if liked. These beefburgers freeze
well raw and should be used within
6 weeks if kept in the freezer.

Place the minced beef,
sausagemeat, onion, salt and
plenty of ground black pepper in a
bowl and blend well together. Flour
your hands and roll the mixture into
8 balls and flatten each out to a 3
inch (7.5 cm) beefburger. Grill or
fry in a very little dripping for about
2½ minutes on each side.

To make the sauce: Melt the
butter in a small pan and fry the
onion gently until tender without
colouring. Add the remaining
ingredients and bring to the boil
and simmer for 2 minutes.

Serve the sauce either hot or
cold; if any should be left over it
may be stored in the refrigerator
for up to 3 weeks. Serves 4.

−Spicy Beef Cassoulet−

SAVOURY PANCAKES

FILLING:
2 rashers streaky bacon, chopped
1 lb (450 g) minced beef
1 onion, chopped
1 stick celery, chopped
½ oz (12.5 g) flour
¼ pint (150 ml) beef stock
2 level tablespoons tomato purée
1 level teaspoon salt
Black pepper
A little thyme

SAUCE:
1 oz (25 g) butter
1 oz (25 g) flour
½ pint (300 ml) milk
½ level teaspoon made English
* mustard*
Salt and pepper
4 oz (100 g) grated Cheddar
* cheese*

8 unsugared pancakes (see
* p 106)*

For the filling: Put the bacon, beef, onion and celery in a pan and cook gently for 5 to 10 minutes to allow the fat to run out. Stir in the flour, then add the stock and bring to the boil, stirring. Add the remaining ingredients, cover and simmer for 30 to 40 minutes or until tender.

Spread the pancakes flat and divide the meat mixture between them. Roll up and lay in a single layer in a shallow ovenproof dish and keep warm.

Make the sauce. Melt the butter in a small saucepan, stir in the flour and cook for a minute. Blend in the milk and bring to the boil, stirring until thickened, and simmer for 2 minutes. Add the mustard and seasoning and 3 oz (75 g) cheese. Stir until the cheese has melted.

Spoon over the pancakes and sprinkle with the remaining cheese. Place under a moderate grill until the top is golden brown and bubbling. Serve at once with a green salad and crispy French bread. Serves 4.

If you have made this dish earlier in the day, reheat it in the oven at 375 deg.F, 190 deg.C, gas mark 5 for 20 to 30 minutes.

VARIATION
If desired the pancakes may be stacked. Take a deep round oven-proof dish and put one pancake at the bottom. Cover with a thin layer of meat filling. Add another pancake on top and continue to sandwich the filling and pancakes together, finishing with a pancake. Pour over the cheese sauce, sprinkle with the remaining cheese and bake as above for 25 minutes or until hot through and golden brown and bubbling.

LASAGNE

5 oz (150 g) uncooked lasagne

MEAT SAUCE:
1 tablespoon oil
1 lb (450 g) minced beef
1 oz (25 g) streaky bacon,
* derinded and chopped*
8 oz (225 g) onion, chopped
4 sticks celery, chopped
½ oz (12.5 g) flour
½ pint (300 ml) water
3½ oz (90 g) can tomato purée
2 cloves garlic, crushed
2 teaspoons brown sugar
1 beef stock cube
½ teaspoon salt
Pepper
¼ teaspoon mixed dried herbs

WHITE SAUCE:
1½ oz (40 g) butter
1½ oz (40 g) flour
¼ teaspoon nutmeg
Salt and pepper
1 pint (600 ml) milk
½ teaspoon made mustard
4 oz (100 g) Cheddar cheese,
* grated*
4 oz (100 g) Emmenthal cheese,
* grated*
½ oz (12.5 g) Parmesan cheese,
* grated*

COOK'S TIP. Save time by using this recipe for lasagne. There is no need to cook the pasta first.

For the meat sauce: Heat oil in a pan, add the beef and bacon and fry until browned. Add onions and celery and cook for 5 minutes. Stir in the flour and remaining meat sauce ingredients, stir well and bring to the boil. Cover and simmer for an hour.

For the white sauce: Melt the butter in a large pan, stir in the flour, nutmeg, salt and pepper and cook gently for 2 minutes. Remove the pan from the heat, stir in the milk. Return the pan to the heat and bring to the boil, stirring until thickened. Add mustard and check seasoning.

Combine Cheddar and Emmenthal. In a shallow 3½ pint (2 l) ovenproof dish put a third of the meat sauce, the white sauce and a third of the cheese, followed by half of the uncooked lasagne (lay edge to edge, not overlapping). Then start again with a third of the meat sauce, white sauce and cheese and last half of the lasagne. Repeat, finishing with a final layer of meat sauce, white sauce and cheese and the grated Parmesan. Leave to become cold, then cook at 350 deg.F, 180 deg.C, gas mark 4 for about 45 minutes to an hour or until the top is golden brown and bubbling.

Serve at once or keep hot at 200 deg.F, 100 deg.C, gas mark ¼ for up to one hour if necessary. Serves 6.

—Osso Bucco—

OSSO BUCCO

About 4 lb (2 kg) knuckle veal or
*   1½ lb (675 g) pie veal*
1 tablespoon oil
½ oz (12.5 g) butter
3 carrots, peeled and sliced
2 sticks celery, sliced
1 onion, chopped
1 large fat clove garlic, crushed
½ oz (12.5 g) flour
¼ pint (150 ml) dry white wine
¼ pint (150 ml) chicken stock
14 oz (397 g) can peeled tomatoes
1 sprig parsley
1 bayleaf
Salt and pepper

COOK'S TIP. A rich Italian stew,
ideally made from knuckle of veal,
with the marrow in the bone
carefully preserved. If you have
difficulty in getting knuckle use pie
veal.

GARNISH:
Grated rind of ½ lemon
2 tablespoons chopped parsley
*   and basil*

Heat oven to 325 deg.F, 160 deg.C, gas mark 3.

Ask the butcher to saw the knuckle into 2 inch (5 cm) sized chunks, or if using pie veal cut into 1½ inch (3.75 cm) pieces.

Heat the oil and butter in a large frying pan and fry the meat, half at a time, over a moderate heat, turning once to brown. Lift out with a slotted spoon and place in a large casserole.

Add the vegetables to the pan and fry lightly for 5 minutes. Stir in the flour, then add the wine and stock, tomatoes, parsley, bayleaf, salt and pepper. Bring to the boil and then pour over the meat.

Cover with a lid, put into the oven and cook for about 2½ hours or until the veal is tender.

For the garnish mix together the lemon rind, parsley and basil and when serving the casserole, sprinkle on top. Serves 4.

MOUSSAKA

About 1 lb (450 g) minced lamb
½ lb (225 g) onions, chopped
2 cloves garlic, crushed
1½ oz (40 g) flour
Salt and pepper
1 level teaspoon coriander seeds,
*   crushed*
A little fresh or dried thyme
14 oz (397 g) can tomatoes
4 aubergines

COOK'S TIP. In this recipe the
aubergines are blanched in water
instead of being fried. This makes
the dish healthier and less heavy.

SAUCE:
1½ oz (40 g) butter
1½ oz (40 g) flour
¾ pint (450 ml) milk
1 level teaspoon made English
*   mustard*
Grated nutmeg
Salt and pepper
6 oz (75 g) Cheddar cheese,
*   grated*
1 egg, beaten
Chopped parsley

Heat the oven to 375 deg.F, 190 deg.C, gas mark 5. Butter a large ovenproof dish.

Turn the minced lamb into a large pan, cook over a low heat at first to let the fat run out of the meat and stir to avoid sticking. When the fat has run freely from the meat add the onions and garlic and increase the heat. Fry to brown the meat for about 15 minutes. If there seems to be an excess of fat, spoon off the surplus. Add flour, stir well, then add salt, pepper, coriander, thyme and the contents of the can of tomatoes. Bring to the boil and simmer for 5 minutes. Check seasoning.

Slice the aubergines and blanch in a pan of boiling water for 1 minute. This softens the skin and prevents the aubergines discolouring. Drain, then dry on kitchen paper.

Make the sauce by slowly melting the butter in a pan, add the flour and cook together for a few minutes over a medium heat without colouring. Blend in the milk, slowly at first, and bring to the boil, stirring well. Add mustard, nutmeg, salt, pepper and cheese. Cook to let the cheese melt, then remove from the heat. Cool slightly, then add the egg and mix well.

Now assemble the moussaka. First put a layer of half the meat mixture in the dish, cover with half the aubergines, season, then repeat with the rest of the lamb and aubergines, so that you end up with 4 layers. Pour over the cheese sauce.

Bake uncovered for 45 minutes to an hour until golden brown. Sprinkle with chopped parsley and serve hot. Serves 6-8.

SHOULDER OF LAMB WITH GREEN STUFFING

COOK'S TIP. New Zealand lamb is
ideal cooked in this way. If spinach
is unobtainable use masses of
chopped parsley mixed with a little
thyme. There will be lots of juices in
the meat tin for gravy.

3½ lb (1.5 kg) shoulder of lamb,
*   boned*
Salt and pepper

STUFFING:
8 oz (225 g) packet frozen
*   chopped spinach, thawed*
4 oz (100 g) lamb's liver
1 oz (25 g) butter
1 large onion, chopped
1 clove garlic, crushed
2 oz (50 g) fresh brown bread
*   crumbs*
Seasoning

Heat the oven to 350 deg.F, 180 deg.C, gas mark 4. Open the shoulder out flat and season well.

Cook spinach as directed and drain. Chop the liver into small pieces and then melt the butter in a pan and fry the liver with the onion and garlic for about 3 minutes. Stir in the spinach and breadcrumbs and season very well. Put the stuffing into the cavity in the meat and secure with skewers. Place the meat in a roasting tin and roast in the oven for 1¾-2½ hours or until the meat is tender. Make the gravy from the juices in the pan. Serves 6 to 8

—Moussaka—

—Boston Baked Beans—

OLD ENGLISH RABBIT PIE

2½ oz (62 g) butter
1 lb (450 g) diced boneless rabbit
  meat (or chicken)
8 oz (225 g) onions, chopped
12 oz (350 g) carrots, diced
2 oz (50 g) flour
1 pint (600 ml) milk
Salt and pepper

SUET CRUST:
6 oz (175 g) self-raising flour
3 oz (75 g) shredded suet
A little water to mix

COOK'S TIP. Rabbit is readily available in freezer centres and at some butchers. However, chicken can be used as an alternative.

Heat the oven to 350 deg.F, 180 deg.C, gas mark 4.

Melt the butter in a frying pan and fry the rabbit and onions for 3 to 4 minutes. Add the carrots and cook for a further minute. Stir in the flour and cook for a minute, then add the milk and bring to the boil, stirring until thickened. Season to taste and turn into 3½ pint (2 l) oven-proof casserole. Cover and cook in the centre of the oven for 45 minutes.

Place the flour and suet in a bowl with a little salt and mix to a soft, but not sticky dough with water. Roll out to about ½ inch (1.25 cm) thickness to cover the casserole.

Take the casserole from the oven and increase the heat to 400 deg.F, 200 deg.C, gas mark 6. Remove the lid from the casserole and place the suet crust on top of the rabbit. Return to the oven and bake for a further 30 minutes or until the top is crisp and golden brown. Serves 4.

BOSTON BAKED BEANS

12 oz (350 g) haricot beans
1 tablespoon black treacle
1 tablespoon golden syrup
2 tablespoons dark soft brown
  sugar
2 teaspoons dry mustard
2 tablespoons tomato purée
2 teaspoons salt
Ground black pepper
2 large onions
8 oz (225 g) salt belly pork or
  unsmoked bacon
1 pint (600 ml) water

COOK'S TIP. This dish uses one of the cheapest cuts of pork, but needs really long slow cooking. It is ideal if you have an Aga, Rayburn or Esse cooker.

Wash the beans, put in a bowl and cover with cold water. Leave to soak overnight.

Drain the beans and throw away the water. Rinse beans thoroughly. Put in a saucepan with 1 pint (600 ml) water. Bring to the boil and simmer for 30 minutes. Do not add salt at this stage as it toughens the beans.

Meanwhile take a large 4½ pint (2.5 l) ovenproof casserole and put in the treacle, syrup, sugar, mustard, tomato purée, salt and pepper and stir until well blended. Cut the onions into wedges. Remove the skin from the pork or bacon and cut into ½ inch (1.25 cm) cubes. Add both ingredients to the casserole.

Remove the beans from the heat, do not drain, but add them with the liquid to the casserole. Stir well, cover the casserole and put in a cool oven at 275 deg.F, 140 deg.C, gas mark 1. Cook the beans for 4 to 6 hours, stirring from time to time.

If the dish is too liquid, remove lid towards the end of the cooking time for about 30 minutes. If the dish is too dry add a little extra water.

Serve with garlic bread. Serves 4.

SPANISH CHICKEN

COOK'S TIP. Remember if using a frozen chicken or frozen chicken joints to thaw completely before cooking. The best place to do this is in the refrigerator, slowly overnight.

4 chicken quarters
2 tablespoons oil
3 Spanish onions, sliced
1 clove garlic, crushed
¼ pint (150 ml) chicken stock
1 teaspoon mixed dried herbs
Salt and pepper
1 lb (450 g) ripe tomatoes, peeled and sliced
16 stuffed green olives
1 tablespoon cornflour
1 tablespoon water

Fry the chicken quarters in oil until they are golden brown on both sides. Remove from the pan and set on one side. Add the onions and garlic to the pan and fry for 3 minutes.

Skin the chicken quarters if liked and then return to the pan with the stock, herbs, seasoning and sliced tomatoes. Cover the pan and simmer for 30 minutes or until the chicken is quite tender when pierced with the point of a sharp knife.

Lift out the chicken and place on a warm serving dish. Add the olives to the pan, blend the cornflour with the water and a tablespoon of the hot sauce and stir into the pan. Bring to the boil, stirring until thickened and then simmer for 3 minutes. Taste and check seasoning and then spoon over the chicken joints. Serves 4.

—*Spanish Chicken*—

CHICKEN PAELLA

5 tablespoons (75 ml) oil
1 lb (450 g) raw chicken on the bone, in pieces
8 oz (225 g) streaky bacon pieces, chopped
1 large onion, chopped
2 cloves garlic, crushed
½ lb (225 g) tomatoes, skinned and seeded
1½ pints (1 l) chicken stock
Thimble of saffron powder or ½ level teaspoon turmeric
2 level teaspoons salt
Plenty of ground black pepper
1 lb (450 g) long grain refined rice
4 oz (100 g) peeled prawns
4 oz (100 g) frozen peas
12 whole prawns in shell
8 oz (225 g) green pepper, seeded and sliced
12 stuffed green olives
Wedges of lemon
Mussels if liked

COOK'S TIP. Paella makes a very good party dish. It is traditionally cooked in a round pan with two handles called a paellera, but at home I use an old frying pan with short metal handles or a shallow flameproof dish. If liked add some fresh cooked mussels.

Heat the oil in the paella pan, add the chicken and fry over a medium heat for about 15 minutes, turning until brown on all sides. Add the bacon and onion and fry for a further 5 minutes.

Stir in the garlic, tomatoes, stock and saffron and bring to the boil, add the salt and pepper and stir in the rice, peeled prawns and peas.

Arrange the whole prawns and green pepper slices on top.

Cover with a lid if you have one to fit, or with foil. Transfer to the oven and cook at 350 deg. F. 180 deg. C. gas mark 4 for about 45 minutes or until the rice is tender and the stock is absorbed. Taste and check seasoning and decorate with cooked mussels, stuffed green olives and wedges of lemon if liked. Serves 8.

FISH AND EGG PIE

COOK'S TIP. A great stand-by for Saturday lunch for a crowd. I double up the recipe, make it the day before, or even a couple of weeks ahead, then freeze it. For a large pie I find it best to brown it under the grill first, then to reheat it at 325 deg.F, 170 deg.C, gas mark 3, for about an hour until the dish is piping hot through.

1 lb (450 g) cod
1 pint (600 ml) milk
2 oz (50 g) butter
2 oz (50 g) flour
1 level teaspoon salt
1/4 level teaspoon white pepper
2 level tablespoons chopped
    parsley
Pinch nutmeg
4 hard-boiled eggs, quartered
1 1/2 lb (675g) potatoes, peeled

Wash the fish, put in a saucepan with the milk and simmer gently for 10 minutes or until the fish can be flaked with a fork. Strain the milk from the fish, then skin the fish and flake, removing any bones.

Rinse out the pan, then melt the butter in it and stir in the flour. Cook for 2 minutes, then stir in the milk and cook the sauce for about 2 minutes, stirring until thickened. Add salt, pepper, nutmeg, parsley and the flaked fish, mix well. Taste and check the seasoning and lightly fold in the quartered eggs.

Turn into a shallow 3 pint (1.7 l) ovenproof dish and leave to cool. Boil the potatoes, drain, and mash with milk and butter; taste and season. Spread over the fish and mark the top with a fork.

Reheat when required in a hot oven 425 deg.F, 220 deg.C, gas mark 7 for about 30 to 40 minutes. Serves 6.

QUICK SUPPERS

Here are some tasty quick suppers to prepare for yourself and for your family. They will also prove invaluable if your home is suddenly invaded by a swarm of unannounced and hungry friends.

ITALIAN TUNA BAKE

COOK'S TIP. This is convenient to assemble the day before you bake. Makes a different family supper dish that needs no vegetables, just hot crisp French bread for the hungry ones. If your family is not fond of tuna you could use chopped ham or bacon joint instead.

6 oz (175 g) spaghetti
Salt
2 1/2 oz (65 g) butter
2 oz (50 g) flour
1 pint (600 ml) milk
Freshly ground black pepper
1/2 level teaspoon mustard
4 oz (100 g) Cheddar cheese,
    grated
1 large onion, sliced
7 oz (200 g) can tuna fish, drained
    and roughly flaked
2 hard-boiled eggs, chopped

Cook the spaghetti in boiling salted water until tender, about 10 minutes. Drain and rinse thoroughly.

Melt 2 oz (50 g) butter in a saucepan, add flour and cook for 1 minute. Gradually add the milk and bring to the boil, stirring frequently. Add 1 level teaspoon salt, pepper to taste and mustard and simmer for 2 minutes, remove from the heat and stir in 3 oz (75 g) cheese until melted.

Fry the onion in the remaining butter until golden brown, then drain. Lightly grease a 3 pint (1.7 l) ovenproof casserole and place half the spaghetti in the bottom, pour over half the sauce, cover with the tuna fish, onions, and chopped eggs. Finally lay the remaining spaghetti on top and pour the rest of the sauce over. Sprinkle with the remaining cheese.

Cook in the oven at 400 deg. F. 200 deg. C, gas mark 6 when required for about 1 hour or until hot through and the top is well browned. Serves 4.

—Chilli Con Carne—

CHILLI CON CARNE

6 oz (175 g) mixed red kidney and
  black eyed beans
2 onions
2 cloves garlic
2 green peppers
3 tablespoons oil
1 lb (450 g) good minced beef
14 oz (397 g) can peeled tomatoes
¼ pint (150 ml) beef stock
1 level teaspoon chilli powder, less
  if you like it mild
1 level teaspoon paprika pepper
2 level teaspoons salt

Put the beans in a bowl, cover with
cold water and leave to soak overnight.

Chop the onions and crush
the garlic, remove the seeds from
the green peppers and cut into
chunky pieces. Heat the oil in a
pan, add onions, garlic, green
pepper and beef. Fry for 10 minutes, stirring continuously.

Add tomatoes, stock, chilli
powder, paprika pepper and salt
and bring to the boil, stirring. Drain
the beans and rinse thoroughly,
then stir into the pan. Cover and
simmer for about one hour or until
the beans and mince are tender.
Taste and check seasoning.

Serve with chunky pieces of
bread and a green salad.

If made in advance, this dish
needs to be reheated in a hot oven
for about 30 minutes until piping
hot, or over a moderate heat on a
hob stirring occasionally until hot
through. Serves 6.

*COOK'S TIP. This is best made 12
hours ahead, then the ingredients
blend well and the beans absorb
the spicy flavours.*

SPAGHETTI BOLOGNESE

2 tablespoons oil
8 oz (225 g) onions, chopped
2 sticks celery, sliced
1 lb (450 g) good minced beef
1 good oz (25 g) flour
2 cloves garlic, crushed
2½ oz (62 g) can tomato purée
¼ pint (150 ml) beef stock
¼ pint (150 ml) red wine
14 oz (397 g) can peeled tomatoes
1 tablespoon redcurrant jelly
1 level teaspoon salt
Freshly ground black pepper
12 oz (350 g) spaghetti
Parmesan cheese

Heat the oil in a pan and fry the
onions, celery and beef for 5 minutes. Stir in the flour, garlic and
tomato purée and cook for a minute. Add the stock, wine, toma-

toes, redcurrant jelly and seasoning and bring to the boil, stirring until thickened. Reduce the heat, partially cover the pan and simmer gently for one hour.

Cook the spaghetti in a pan of fast boiling salted water (about two teaspoons salt to every four pints water) until tender. When ready the spaghetti should be slightly firm to bite but not hard in the centre.

Strain through a colander and rinse out the saucepan. Add a little oil or a large knob of butter, return the pasta to the pan and toss gently.

Serve the spaghetti onto plates and ladle the sauce on top. Hand the Parmesan cheese separately. Serves 4 to 6.

MOLS SPAGHETTI

COOK'S TIP. A quick and easy supper dish for when you are on your own.

3 oz (75 g) spaghetti
2 oz (50 g) bacon
½ oz (12.5 g) butter
2 oz (50 g) button mushrooms
1 egg, beaten
Salt and pepper

Cook the spaghetti in plenty of boiling salted water for 12 minutes or until just tender, then drain very well.

Meanwhile cut the rind from the bacon and cut into strips. Melt the butter in a pan and fry the bacon until it is pale golden brown. Slice the mushrooms and add to the pan and cook for 2 minutes, then blend the bacon and mushrooms mixture into the cooked spaghetti.

Stir in the egg, salt and pepper to taste. Cook over a low heat, stirring with a fork until the egg has scrambled. Pile onto a serving dish and if liked sprinkle the top with a little parsley. Serves 1.

—Mols Spaghetti—

WILTSHIRE BACON BAKE

1 lb (450 g) potatoes
8 oz (225 g) cooked ham or bacon
6 oz (175 g) mushrooms
2 oz (50 g) butter
2 oz (50 g) flour
1 pint (600 ml) milk
1 chicken stock cube
3 hardboiled eggs, chopped
Salt and pepper
2 oz (50 g) full flavoured Cheddar cheese, grated
1 oz (25 g) Parmesan cheese, grated (optional)

COOK'S TIP. The last pieces of a joint of ham or bacon are often sold off quite cheaply at delicatessen counters and are ideal for a dish like this. You can also use leftover cooked potatoes.

Boil the potatoes in their skins until cooked, then drain, peel and slice. Cut the ham or bacon into neat cubes and dice the mushrooms.

Melt the butter in a large saucepan, stir in the flour and cook gently for two minutes. Add the milk and stock cube and bring to the boil, stirring until thickened and the stock cube has dissolved.

Add the potato, ham, mushrooms and eggs, mix well and season to taste. Turn into a 3 pint (1.7 l) ovenproof dish and sprinkle with cheese. Place under a moderate grill until golden brown and hot through.

If the pie has been made in advance put it in the oven at 375 deg.F, 190 deg.C, gas mark 5 for 25 to 30 minutes.

Serve hot with French bread and a green salad. Serves 4 to 6.

DEVILLED CHICKEN

COOK'S TIP. For a delicious supper serve devilled chicken with mild spicy rice made by adding ½ level teaspoon turmeric to the boiling salted water when cooking 8 oz (225 g) long grain rice. Cook for about 12 minutes or as instructed on the rice packet.

Salt and ground black pepper
4 thigh roasting joints of chicken

SAUCE:
1 rounded tablespoon apricot jam
1 teaspoon Dijon mustard
Pinch cayenne pepper
Large clove garlic, crushed
1 tablespoon Worcestershire sauce
3 tablespoons tomato ketchup
1 tablespoon soy sauce

Heat the oven to 350 deg.F, 180 deg.C, gas mark 4.

Season the chicken joints well on all sides and put in a shallow ovenproof dish so that they just touch.

Measure the jam into a basin, add mustard, cayenne, garlic and Worcestershire sauce, blend well until smooth. Then add the other ingredients, season with black pepper and a little salt and pour over the chicken, coating evenly.

Bake for about 1 hour at the top of the oven. To test when done prod the thickest part of the thigh with a fine skewer. If the juices run out clear the chicken is done, if pink give the chicken a little longer.

Serve with spicy rice and a green salad. Serves 4.

—Eggs Flamenca—

EGGS FLAMENCA

A colourful dish that makes a tasty informal lunch or supper, This dish can also be cooked in individual dishes in the oven.

1 tablespoon olive oil
2 large onions, sliced
2 large tomatoes
4 oz (100 g) bacon, chopped
Salt and pepper
2 small canned red peppers
4 oz (100 g) chorizo sausage, thinly sliced (optional)
4 eggs
4 oz (100 g) peeled prawns (optional)

Put the oil in a frying pan or heatproof serving dish, add the onions and cook for 10 minutes or until tender.

Put the tomatoes in a pan of boiling water and leave for a minute, then remove with a spoon and carefully peel off the skin and cut each tomato in slices. Add to the onions with the bacon and cook for a further 10 minutes. Season well. Stir in the red pepper and arrange the sausage slices around the edge of the pan.

Make 4 holes in the mixture and break an egg into each. Cook for 3 to 4 minutes or until the whites have set and the yolk is still soft.

Sprinkle over the prawns if used and serve at once from the pan in which it was cooked. Serves 2 or 4.

SUPPER BAKED EGGS

COOK'S TIP. Just the thing for Sunday night supper when you have a crowd and there is no cold meat left from the roast.

6 rashers back bacon
6 tomatoes
12 mushrooms
Butter
6 eggs

Remove the rind and any bone from the bacon and cut each rasher in half. Halve the tomatoes. Place two pieces of bacon and two tomato halves and mushrooms in six small ovenproof dishes. Dot each mushroom with a knob of butter and bake in the centre of the oven heated to 400 deg.F, 200 deg.C, gas mark 6 for about 10 minutes. Crack an egg into the centre of each dish and bake for a further 5 minutes. Serve at once with garlic rolls. Serves 6.

DUTCH CROQUETTES

A tasty supper dish served with a crisp green salad.

2 rashers streaky bacon, chopped
4 oz (100 g) butter
4 oz (100 g) flour
1/2 pint (300 ml) milk
2 eggs, separated
8 oz (225 g) cooked chicken, finely chopped
1 rounded tablespoon chopped chives
Salt and pepper
1/4 teaspoon nutmeg
2 teaspoons Worcestershire sauce
Browned breadcrumbs
Deep fat or oil for frying

Fry the bacon until crisp, lift out with a slotted spoon and drain on kitchen paper.

Melt the butter in a saucepan, add the flour and cook for 1 minute. Add the milk and bring to the boil, stirring to make a very thick sauce. Add the egg yolks, chicken, bacon, chives, seasoning, spice and Worcestershire sauce. Mix well, wrap in foil and chill overnight.

Shape into 12 croquettes, then coat in lightly whisked egg white and browned breadcrumbs. Fry in hot deep fat or oil until golden brown, drain on kitchen paper. Serve hot. Serves 4.

STUFFED GREEN PEPPERS

4 large even-sized green peppers
3 oz (75 g) long grain rice
1 oz (25 g) butter
1 small onion, chopped
4 oz (100 g) button mushrooms, sliced
4 rashers back bacon, chopped
Salt
Freshly ground black pepper
1 rounded teaspoon chopped parsley
1 egg, beaten

CHEESE SAUCE:
1 oz (25 g) butter
1 oz (25 g) flour
1/2 pint (300 ml) milk
1 teaspoon made mustard
A little grated nutmeg
Salt and pepper
4 oz (100 g) Cheddar cheese, grated

COOK'S TIP. A good supper dish served with warm crisp fresh bread. Vary the ingredients with the rice according to what you have at hand, perhaps add a couple of chopped chicken livers or ham instead of bacon. Add shrimps or prawns instead of meat.

Cut a circle from the base of each green pepper to remove the stem and seeds.

Cook the rice in boiling salted water for 10 to 12 minutes or until tender, drain and rinse well. Melt the butter in a pan and fry the onion, mushrooms and bacon for 5 minutes. Stir in the cooked rice, salt, plenty of freshly ground black pepper and parsley, then stir in the egg to bind the rice.

Arrange the peppers fairly close together in an ovenproof dish and spoon in the filling. Heat the oven to 350 deg.F, 180 deg.C, gas mark 4.

Now make the sauce. Melt the butter in a small saucepan and add the flour and cook for a minute. Add the milk and bring to the boil, stirring, simmer until thickened, add mustard, nutmeg and seasoning and stir in 2 oz (50 g) of the grated cheese. Pour this sauce around the stuffed peppers. Sprinkle the top of each pepper with the remaining cheese.

Bake in the oven for 45 to 50 minutes or until the peppers are tender. Serves 4.

BAKED ONIONS

*4 large onions or 8 medium sized
    onions, peeled
A knob of dripping
1 lb (450 g) minced beef
2 large tomatoes, peeled and
    chopped
1 level teaspoon dried thyme
1 level teaspoon salt
Pepper
1/2 teaspoon Worcestershire
    sauce
1 level teaspoon paprika pepper
1 1/2 oz (37.5 g) butter
3 level tablespoons flour
1/2 pint (300 ml) milk*

Place the onions in a saucepan,
barely cover with water and bring
to the boil. Cover the pan and
simmer for 25 minutes. Then drain
the onions and reserve 1/4 pint (150
ml) of the liquor. Remove the
centres of the onions.

Melt the dripping and fry the
mince gently for 5-10 minutes,
stirring frequently. Add the tomatoes, thyme, salt and pepper,
Worcestershire sauce and paprika
and cook for a further 3 to 4
minutes. Spoon the meat mixture
carefully into the onion cavities.

Spoon the remaining meat
mixture into the base of a 4 pint
(2.3 l) casserole or a foil-lined
baking tin. Stand the onions on top.
Cover the casserole or close the
foil and cook in the oven at 350
deg.F, 180 deg.C, gas mark 4 for
1-1 1/2 hours or until the onions are
tender.

Meanwhile melt the butter in a
pan, chop the onion centres and
fry gently for 10 minutes without
colouring. Stir in the flour and cook
for a minute, then gradually add
the onion liquor and milk and bring
to the boil, stirring frequently.
Season well and simmer for 3
minutes.

Serve the onions on a spoonful of meat mixture with the sauce
handed separately. Delicious
served with hot crusty bread.
Serves 4.

GERMAN ONION TART

*Onion tart may sound dull, but you
will see from the photograph that
it's anything but. Serve as a starter,
or as a main course with salad.*

FOR THE DOUGH:
*6 tablespoons lukewarm water
Good pinch sugar
1/2 oz (12.5 g) dried yeast
8 oz (225 g) strong plain flour
2 oz (50 g) butter, melted
1 egg yolk
1/2 level teaspoon salt*

FOR THE FILLING:
*1 1/2 lb (675 g) onions, sliced
1 1/2 oz (40 g) butter
3 eggs
1/4 pint (150 ml) soured cream
1 1/2 oz (40 g) plain flour
1/2 level teaspoon salt
Freshly ground black pepper
1 teaspoon caraway seeds
    (optional)
4 oz (100 g) streaky bacon*

To make the dough: Put the lukewarm water in a bowl, stir in the
sugar, then sprinkle on the yeast
and leave to stand for 10 minutes
or until it is frothy. Stir 4 tablespoons of the flour into the yeast
mixture, cover and set aside in a
warm place for 15 minutes.

Sift the remaining flour into a
bowl, make a well in the centre and
stir in the yeast mixture, cooled
melted butter, egg yolk and salt.
Beat well with a wooden spoon
until the dough is well mixed. Add
a little more milk if the dough looks
very dry. Knead well with floured
hands until the dough leaves the
sides of the bowl clean. Cover the
bowl with a cloth and put in warm
place until dough has doubled in
bulk.

Meanwhile make the filling:
Put the onions and butter in a large
frying pan and sauté gently for
about 20 to 25 minutes until soft
but not brown. Remove the pan
from the heat. Blend the eggs,
soured cream and flour together,
add the salt and plenty of freshly
ground black pepper and caraway seeds if used.

Roll out the yeast dough and
line a 9 inch (22.5 cm), quite deep
flan tin. Pour in the filling and
smooth the top flat. Cut the bacon
into small pieces and sprinkle over
the top.

Bake in the oven at 400 deg.F,
200 deg.C, gas mark 6 for about
35 minutes when the top will be
golden brown and set and the
bread crust crisp. Serve warm.
Serves 6 to 8

POTATO AND ONION LAYER

*COOK'S TIP. An excellent way of
cooking potatoes when you have
friends for supper. They cook by
themselves and need no attention
at all - and you can serve them in
the same dish that they have been
cooked in.*

*2 lb (1 kg) potatoes
1/2 lb (225 g) onions
3 to 4 oz (75 to 100 g) butter
Salt and pepper*

Peel and slice the potatoes and
onions very finely. Melt 2 oz (50 g)

—Baked Onions—

butter in a pan and fry the onions for 3 to 4 minutes. Butter thoroughly a 2½ to 3 pint (1.4 to 1.7 l) ovenproof dish with some of the remaining butter and put in the sliced potato and onion in layers, seasoning well between each layer and finishing with a layer of potato slices neatly arranged on top of the casserole dish.

Put the remaining butter in the pan and when melted pour over the top of the potatoes making sure that they are well coated. Add a little extra butter during cooking if necessary.

Bake at 375 deg.F, 190 deg.C, gas mark 5 for 1¾ to 2 hours. If you are using a shallow dish, the potato and onion layer will probably be cooked in 1½ hours. Serves 6.

RÖSTI

2 lb (900 g) large potatoes
½ level teaspoon salt
Freshly ground black pepper
2 oz (50 g) pork dripping

Scrub the potatoes and boil in salted water for 10 minutes or until the point of a knife can be inserted into the potato for about one inch (2.5 cm) before meeting resistance. Drain and cool and then peel and leave in a cool place overnight or chill for several hours.

Grate the potatoes coarsely into a bowl, add the seasoning and mix well.

Melt half the dripping in a non-stick frying pan and add the grated potato, flattening it with a fish slice. Cook very slowly over a low heat for 20 minutes, when the base will be golden brown. Turn out onto a large plate. Melt the remaining dripping in the pan and slide the potato cake off the plate and back into the pan to brown the second side, very slowly as before.

Turn onto a warm dish and serve. Serves 4-6.

—German Onion Tart—

ENTERTAINING AT HOME

Entertaining at home has taken on a new flavour in recent years, and this section provides a stimulating range of dishes for dinner parties and special occasions. We start with an English classic – glazed roast duckling – and then move on to some equally celebrated Continental favourites, including lamb Boulangère and Kleftico. In addition there is a suggested selection of accompaniments – from suety pudding, a delicious winter time complement to lamb, to tortilla as an accompaniment to Mexican chicken.

GLAZED ROAST DUCKLING WITH ORANGE SAUCE

COOK'S TIP. The glaze is delicious but don't expect it to be as crisp as if you had just open-roasted the bird. You can also roast it as below without the glaze but with the orange sauce.

To reheat the carved duckling, put the joints well spaced out on an uncovered roasting tin and reheat in a preheated oven at 425 deg.F, 220 deg.C, gas mark 7 for about 10-15 minutes.

4½-5 lb (2-2.3 kg) duckling

GLAZE:
1 tablespoon redcurrant jelly
1 teaspoon Soy sauce

SAUCE:
2 oranges
2 tablespoons duck fat
½ oz (12.5 g) flour
About ½ pint (300 ml) giblet stock (see below)
2 tablespoons port or Madeira
1 tablespoon redcurrant jelly
Salt
Ground black pepper

Preheat the oven to 350 deg.F, 180 deg.C, gas mark 4.

For the stock: Take the giblets and put them in a casserole with a little onion, ground black pepper, stock cube and ¾ pint (450 ml) water. Cover and put in the oven on the lower shelf.

Prick the duck all over with a sharp-pronged fork. Rub with plenty of salt and put on a rack or trivet in a roasting tin. Roast without basting for 1½-1¾ hours.

Take the duck out, tip any juices from the inside of it into a measuring jug and put the bird on a board. Mix the redcurrant jelly and the soy sauce together and spread over the top of the duck. Skim off all the fat from the roasting tin and add remaining meat juices to those in the measuring jug. Put the fat aside. Return the bird to the oven for about 15 minutes until the skin is crisp and browned. Test to see if it is done by piercing the thickest part of the leg with a skewer. If the juices run clear and slightly yellow in colour, the duck is done. Save any more juices from the roasting tin to add to the sauce and keep the duck hot.

Meanwhile prepare the sauce. Carefully peel 1 orange, removing the zest only. Chop finely and simmer in a little water for 3 minutes then drain. This is to add to the sauce later. Squeeze the juice out of 1½ of the oranges and finely slice the remaining half for garnish.

Measure 2 tablespoons duck fat into a small pan and add the flour. Cook for a few minutes, allowing to colour a pale brown.

Make the duck juices up to ½ pint (300 ml) with stock, add to the pan and stir until thickened. Add port or Madeira if liked, redcurrant jelly and orange juice. Season with salt and ground black pepper. Add a little gravy browning if you wish.

Lift the duck onto a serving dish and decorate with watercress and orange slices. Serve with the sauce, an orange salad, peas and creamed or new potatoes.

—Classic Turkey Roast—

CLASSIC TURKEY ROAST

Thaw the turkey if frozen.

Check the weight of the bird with stuffing and calculate the cooking time. Preheat the oven.

Put a large piece of foil in the roasting tin. Lift turkey onto the foil and season well. Wrap the foil loosely over the bird with the fold at the top.

Put the turkey on a shelf just below the middle or lower in the oven according to the size of the bird.

To brown the turkey undo the foil and rub the breast and legs with butter. Cook with foil open for the last 1¼ hours of time for a large bird and about 50 minutes for a small bird under 10 lbs (4.5 kg).

Put sausages in a greased roasting tin and cook above the turkey when the foil is opened. Add the bacon rolls on skewers on top of the sausauges 30 minutes before the end of the cooking time.

Roast potatoes may be cooked for the last 1½ to 1¾ hours above the turkey. Bring prepared potatoes to the boil in a pan of water on the stove starting from cold. Drain . Heat oil or fat in a meat tin in the oven, then add potatoes. Turn during roasting.

COOK'S TIP. When cooking a very large bird at a lower temperature, cook sausages, bacon and potatoes for a little longer.

6-7 lb (2.7 kg-3.2 kg) about 3 hours at 350 deg.F, 180 deg.C, gas mark 4.

8-10 lb (3.6 kg-4.5 kg) about 3½ hours at 350 deg.F, 180 deg.C, gas mark 4.

11-15 lb (5.0 kg-6.9 kg) about 4 hours at 350 deg.F, 180 deg.C, gas mark 4.

16-20 lb (7.2 kg-9.0 kg) about 5 hours at 325 deg.F, 160 deg.C, gas mark 3.

CHICKEN WITH ORANGE TARRAGON SAUCE

COOK'S TIP. Frozen concentrated orange juice is excellent for cooking and inexpensive when you think that each 6 fl oz (178 ml) can contains the concentrated juice of 11 oranges.

I find dried tarragon lacking in flavour, so if this is the only thing to hand, I often use fresh chopped chives instead, and the flavour is nearly as good.

1½ oz (37.5 g) butter
2 tablespoons oil
4 chicken joints
1 large onion, chopped
½ can concentrated orange juice, thawed
1 chicken stock cube
¼ pint (150 ml) water
4 sprigs of fresh tarragon, chopped
½ oz (12.5 g) corn flour
2 tablespoons water
5 oz (150 ml) carton soured cream

Melt the butter and heat the oil in a large frying pan and brown the chicken on all sides. Lift out with a slotted spoon and put on one side. If liked the skin may be removed.

Add the onion to the pan and cook for 2-3 minutes. Stir in the orange juice, stock cube and water. Return the chicken joints to the pan and add the tarragon. Cover the pan and simmer for about 30 minutes or until the chicken is tender, basting and turning occasionally.

Lift out the chicken and place on a warm serving dish. Blend the cornflour with the water and stir into the sauce, then bring to the boil, stirring until thickened. Taste and check seasoning, cool slightly and then stir in the soured cream and spoon over the chicken. Garnish with fresh sprigs of tarragon. Serves 4.

—Mexican Chicken with Tortillas—

MEXICAN CHICKEN

This is a colourful dish and looks good served on a large, brightly patterned plate. Rice is a good accompaniment.

4 chicken joints
3 tablespoons olive oil
2 large onions, sliced
2 cloves garlic
14 oz (397 g) can peeled tomatoes
¼ pint (150 ml) chicken stock
1 bouquet garni
Salt and pepper
2 red peppers, sliced
1 oz (25 g) fresh white
    breadcrumbs
12 stuffed green olives (optional)

Heat the oil in a large pan and fry the joints quickly to brown on both sides. Lift out and put on a plate.
    Add the onions and garlic to the pan and fry for 5 minutes. Add tomatoes, stock, bouquet garni and seasoning with most of the red peppers, reserving just a few

slices for garnish.
    Return the chicken joints to the pan, cover and simmer for 30 minutes, or until the chicken is tender.
    Lift out the chicken, place on a serving dish and keep warm. Remove the bouquet garni and stir the breadcrumbs into the pan. Purée the sauce in one or two batches in a blender. Rinse out the saucepan, return the sauce to it and reheat, taste and check seasoning. Stir in the olives and spoon over the chicken, garnish with the remaining rings of red pepper. Serves 4.

CHICKEN IN CIDER WITH MUSHROOMS

COOK'S TIP. For an extra creamy and rich sauce add a couple of tablespoons (30 ml) of soured or thick cream just before serving. Tastes delicious with potato and onion layer (p 72).

3½ lb (1.5 kg) chicken
½ pint (300 ml) dry cider
1 onion, chopped
Ground black pepper
Salt
Milk
2 oz (50 g) butter
2 oz (50 g) button mushrooms
Chopped parsley and croutons to
    garnish

Put the chicken and the giblets in a small roasting tin or casserole, add the cider and chopped onions, season well. Cover with a lid or a piece of foil and cook at 350 deg.F, 180 deg.C, gas mark 4 for 20 minutes to the lb (450 g) and 20 minutes over – i.e. about 1½ hours. Test to see if it is cooked by piercing the thickest part of the leg with a skewer; if the juices come out clear the bird is cooked. Lift the chicken out to cool and strain off the remaining liquid in the tin, skim off the fat and make up to 1¼ pints (750 ml) with milk.
    Keep the liver with the chicken and chop. Remove the meat from the bird and cut into good-sized pieces. Use the carcass and the giblets to make stock for soup on another occasion.
    Melt the butter for the sauce in a pan and add the flour and cook for 2 minutes without colouring. Stir in the stock and the milk, slowly at first and bring to the boil, add the mushrooms and season with lots of black pepper and salt. Stir in the chicken and turn into an ovenproof serving dish, cool, cover and keep in the refrigerator for up to 24 hours.
    To reheat, place in the oven with the potato and onion layer (375 deg.F, 190 deg.C, gas mark

—Chicken Marengo—

PAPRIKA CHICKEN

4 chicken breasts
2 tablespoons salad oil
1 oz (25 g) butter
1 onion, chopped
2 level tablespoons paprika
*   pepper*
1 oz (25 g) flour
¼ pint (150 ml) stock
¼ pint (150 ml) dry cider
5 tablespoons sherry
1 level teaspoon tomato purée
Salt and pepper
6 oz (175 g) small button
*   mushrooms*
¼ pint (150 ml) soured cream
Chopped parsley
Fried sliced mushrooms

COOK'S TIP. A rich creamy chicken dish delicious served with rice, noodles or new potatoes and a green salad or broccoli.

Remove the skin from the chicken breasts. Heat the oil in a large shallow pan, add the butter and then fry the chicken quickly to slightly brown. Remove from the pan and drain on kitchen paper. Add the onion and paprika to the pan and fry for 2 minutes. Blend in the flour and cook for a further minute. Remove from the heat and stir in the stock, cider and sherry Return to the heat and simmer until thick. Add the tomato purée and seasoning to the sauce, stir well and then return the chicken breasts to the pan, cover and simmer gently for 30 minutes, turning once.

Wash the mushrooms, add to the pan and simmer for a further 5 minutes.

When ready to serve, lift the chicken breasts onto a serving dish and stir the soured cream into the sauce, then pour over the chicken. Sprinkle with parsley and garnish the dish with fried sliced mushrooms. Serves 4.

5) for the last 50 minutes of cooking time.

Sprinkle with chopped parsley and serve garnished with fried bread croûtons cut in triangles and a green salad or vegetables. (The croûtons may be made early in the day, drained well and put in the oven to reheat for the last 5 minutes of the cooking time.) Serves 6.

CHICKEN MARENGO

2 tablespoons oil
1 oz (25 g) butter
6 chicken joints
1 oz (25 g) flour
½ pint (300 ml) dry white wine
¼ pint (150 ml) chicken stock
14 oz (397 g) can tomatoes
Salt and pepper
1 clove garlic, crushed
6 oz (175 g) button mushrooms
Croûtons of fried bread

Traditionally this dish is served garnished with fried eggs and croûtons of fried bread. In England we leave out the eggs and just garnish with the croûtons.

Heat the oil and butter in a large frying pan and fry the chicken quickly until brown on both sides. Lift out and put on a plate. Add the flour to the pan and cook for a minute or two, stir in the wine and stock and bring to the boil, stirring until thickened. Add tomatoes, seasoning and garlic and then return the chicken to the pan. Cover and simmer for 30 minutes. Then add the mushrooms left whole and continue cooking for a further 15 minutes or until the chicken is tender. Taste and check seasoning, arrange the chicken on a warm serving dish and spoon the sauce over.

Garnish with the croûtons of fried bread. Serves 6.

LAMB BOULANGERE

Delicious with casseroled carrots cooked in the oven in butter and stock.

1 small leg of lamb
2 cloves garlic
Sprig of fresh rosemary
1½ lb (675 g) potatoes
8 oz (225 g) onions
Salt and pepper
½ pint (300 ml) stock
A little chopped parsley

Heat the oven to 375 deg.F, 190 deg.C, gas mark 5.

Trim any excess fat from the lamb and then peel the garlic, cut into thin slivers and insert into the lamb. Tie the sprig of rosemary over the lamb.

Peel the potatoes and cut into thick slices. Peel and thinly slice the onions, mix with the potatoes and then lay in a shallow ovenproof dish and season well. Place the lamb on top and pour over the stock. Cover with a piece of foil and roast in the oven for 30 minutes to the lb (450 g) and 30 minutes over. After the first hour, remove the foil, baste the meat and vegetables and cook until tender.

When cooked, untie the rosemary and lay a fresh sprig in its place. Sprinkle the vegetables with a little chopped parsley. Serves 6 to 8.

KLEFTICO

A leg of lamb or a lean shoulder
4 cloves garlic, cut in spikes
Tablespoon rosemary or oregano
Juice of ½ lemon
Salt
Ground black pepper
Chopped parsley

Heat the oven to 425 deg.F, 220 deg.C, gas mark 7.

Make incisions into the lamb with a sharp pointed knife and in each hole slip a spike of garlic. Put the lamb in a roasting tin or casserole with herbs, lemon juice and seasoning.

Roast in the oven for 30 minutes to brown then lower the heat to 275 deg.F, 140 deg.C, gas mark 1. Cover the dish and cook for a further 3½ hours until really tender so that when carved the meat falls off the bone. Take all the fat from the juices in the tin. Taste and check seasoning and serve the juices with the lamb.

Carve the lamb and scatter each portion with parsley. Serve with green beans in tomato sauce (p 81) and small potatoes. First blanch the potatoes in boiling-water for a minute and cook in oil and garlic under the meat for at least an hour. Serve scattered with chopped chives. Serves 8.

VEAL ZURICH

A very traditional Swiss dish that I often make when entertaining. The sauce is really heavenly.

12 oz- 1 lb (350-450 g) thinly sliced escalope of veal
1½ oz (40 g) butter
About 1 tablespoon oil
6 oz (175 g) white button mushrooms, sliced
1 medium onion, finely chopped
¼ pint (150 ml) dry white wine
½ pint (300 ml) double cream
Salt and pepper
Chopped parsley

Take each slice of veal and cut into pencil-thin strips.

Melt half the butter in a large shallow pan, add the oil and fry the meat for 2 to 3 minutes over a brisk heat. Lift out with a slotted spoon onto a plate. Add the mushrooms

−Kleftico and Green Beans−

to the pan and toss in the remaining fat for a minute, lift out and add to the meat. Add the remaining butter to the pan with the onions and cook gently until golden brown.

Pour the wine into the pan, scrape off any sediment with a wooden spatula and mix well. Cook quickly until the wine has reduced to about 4 tablespoons.

Stir in the cream with the seasonings, veal and mushrooms and simmer for a minute. Taste and check seasoning.

Serve with Rösti (p 73) scattered with parsley. Serves 4.

FILET DE PORC AUX PRUNEAUX
(Fillet of pork with prune stuffing)

A rather special dish for a dinner party, it can be made in advance, kept in the refrigerator and then just put in the oven to cook the pastry for the last 30 minutes. Serve with young carrots and mange tout if in season. This blend of meat and fruit make the dish one of the classics of French cuisine.

4 oz (100 g) prunes
1 onion, chopped
4 oz (100 g) streaky bacon, chopped
2 oz (50 g) fresh brown breadcrumbs
Salt and pepper
2 rounded tablespoons chopped parsley
2 pork fillets
1 oz (25 g) butter
1 tablespoon oil

SAUCE:
Juices from the pork fillet
4 oz (100 g) mushrooms, chopped
1 oz (25 g) flour
½ pint (300 ml) dry cider
¼ pint (150 ml) chicken stock

14 oz (397 g) packet puff pastry
A little beaten egg

—Veal Zurich with Rösti and Salad—

Cover the prunes with boiling water and leave to stand overnight. Next day, drain and remove all the stones and roughly chop.

Put the onion and bacon in a saucepan and fry over a moderate heat until the fat runs from the bacon. Stir in the prunes, breadcrumbs, seasoning and herbs.

Heat the oven to 400 deg.F, 200 deg.C, gas mark 6.

Carefully slice the fillets almost through to the other side lengthwise and open flat and season. Cover cut side with the stuffing and then cover with the other piece of fillet, cut side down onto the stuffing. Secure with fine string.

Place the fillets in a baking tin with the butter and oil and roast for 45 minutes or until pork fillet is cooked and the juices run clear, basting occasionally. Remove from oven, lift onto a plate and leave to cool.

Strain the juices from the roasting tin into a small saucepan. Add the mushrooms to the pan and cook gently for 5 minutes. Stir in the flour and cook for a minute. Add the cider and stock and bring to the boil, stirring. Simmer for two minutes, then taste and check seasoning and leave on one side until required to re-heat and serve with the pork.

Roll out the pastry to a square 12 inches (30 cm). Place the fillet in the centre and remove the string. Wrap the pastry over the fillet as you would a parcel, sealing the edges with a little beaten egg. Decorate the top with pastry leaves if liked and glaze all over the beaten egg.

Place on a baking tray and bake in the oven at 400 deg.F, 200 deg.C, gas mark 6 for 30 minutes until the pastry is well risen and golden brown. Serves 6.

FONDUE BOURGUIGNONNE

Inviting friends for a fondue party is a fun idea; not only does it make sure that you enjoy yourself, but it keeps your friends busy cooking their own supper!

For each person you will need:
6-8 oz (175-225 g) rump steak or
6-8 oz (175-225 g) leg fillet of lamb
Sufficient vegetable oil for frying
(enough to fill the fondue pot one third full)

Cut the meat into cubes ready to fry in the oil on skewers.

Heat the oil on the hob of the cooker in the kitchen until a faint haze is rising, then transfer it to the fondue stove. Remember that the oil will heat up more quickly with a lid on the pan, but keep an eye on it because it should not become too hot. On no account leave it unattended. Mark the skewers with coloured tape or wool so that each guest will know which is his. Take the meat off the skewers or forks, then spear with a dinner fork. This avoids the chance of burning your lips.

Keep the oil hot by returning it to the cooker at intervals and not cooking more than six portions of meat at a time. Guests can time their own steak cubes as some will like their meat rare.

There is no need for potatoes, just serve crisp French bread with plenty of butter and a green salad. Serve a selection of sauces, that may be made in advance.

CURRIED MAYONNAISE:
Blend 4 tablespoons mayonnaise with a little lemon juice, one teaspoon curry powder and one tablespoon very finely chopped mango chutney.

MUSTARD AND DILL:
Blend 4 tablespoons mayonnaise with one tablespoon Dijon mustard and a little chopped dill.

—Cheese Fondue—

EGG AND PARSLEY:
Blend 4 tablespoons mayonnaise with one finely chopped, hard-boiled egg and one tablespoon chopped fresh parsley. Add a little curry powder if liked.

CHUTNEY:
Blend 4 tablespoons mayonnaise with chopped chunky tomato chutney or just serve tomato chutney on its own.

CHEESE FONDUE

1 clove garlic
Scant ¾ pint (450 ml) dry white
    wine or cider
8 oz (225 g) Swiss Emmenthal
    cheese, grated
8 oz (225 g) Gruyère cheese,
    grated
1 oz (25 g) cornflour
Salt and ground black pepper
1 tablespoon kirsch

Peel and crush the garlic very finely. Pour all but about 4 tablespoons of the wine into a thick enamel or earthenware pan. Add the garlic and grated cheese and heat the mixture very slowly until all the cheese has dissolved. Do not allow to boil.

Blend the cornflour with the remainder of the wine to make a smooth paste. Add a little of the hot cheese mixture to the cornflour then add this to the pan. Carefully bring the fondue to the boil, stirring all the time until the mixture has thickened. Add salt and pepper to taste and lastly stir in the kirsch. Serves 4.

COOK'S TIP. Serve as soon as it is made with plenty of French bread cut into small pieces to dip in the hot fondue.

FENNEL WITH LEMON BUTTER

Such a delicious vegetable. When raw it has a distinct aniseed flavour which is more subtle when cooked.

4 fennel heads
Salt and pepper
Butter
Juice of 1 lemon

Heat the oven to 350 deg.F, 180 deg.C, gas mark 4.

Cut each fennel into six wedges and arrange in an ovenproof serving dish seasoning well between layers. Dot with butter and pour over the lemon juice.

Cover with a lid or piece of foil and bake in the oven for about one hour or until the fennel is tender. Serves 6.

COOK'S TIP. Always buy the whitest bulbs possible, as the green ones taste bitter.

GREEN BEANS IN TOMATO SAUCE

2 lb (900 g) French beans
1 tablespoon oil
1 onion, finely chopped
1 large clove garlic, crushed
14 oz (397 g) can peeled tomatoes
½ teaspoon salt
Freshly ground black pepper
½ teaspoon sugar

COOK'S TIP. This is a classic way of serving beans in Greece. I prefer to cook the whole beans in boiling salted water until al dente - just tender, then serve them with the sauce.

Remove the ends from the beans. Place in a pan of boiling salted water, bring back to the boil and boil for one minute. Drain and put in an ovenproof dish.

Heat the oven to 275 deg.F, 140 deg.C, gas mark 1.

Heat the oil in a saucepan and add the onion, garlic and tomatoes and simmer with the lid off until reduced to a thick consistency. Add all the seasonings and pour over the beans. Cook in the oven for one hour. Serves 8.

RATATOUILLE

1 green pepper
1 red pepper
4 tablespoons oil
2 Spanish onions, sliced
2 courgettes, sliced
8 oz (225 g) tomatoes, skinned,
    quartered and the seeds
    removed
Salt and pepper

Remove the seeds and pith from the green and red peppers and cut into strips. Heat the oil in a thick pan and add the peppers and onions, cover and cook slowly for about 20 minutes, stirring occasionally until the onions are soft.

Add the courgettes and tomatoes with plenty of salt and pepper and cook without the lid for a further 10 to 15 minutes or until the courgettes are tender. Taste and check seasoning and serve piping hot. Serves 4.

COOK'S TIP. Make ratatouille when peppers and courgettes are reasonable priced in the summer. Add garlic as well if you like it. Serve with meat without a sauce such as a roast chicken or grilled fish or chops.

RED CABBAGE

COOK'S TIP. One of the best and most warming vegetables, it also reheats well, should some be left. Reheat in a nonstick pan, stirring until piping hot.

1 medium red cabbage
1 lb (450 g) windfall apples, weight after peeling
¼ pint (150 ml) water
1½ oz (37.5 g) sugar
1 teaspoon salt
4 cloves
6 tablespoons vinegar
2 oz (50 g) butter
1 tablespoon redcurrant jelly

Trim and clean cabbage. Shred finely. Peel, core and slice apples. Place cabbage and apples in a pan with the water, sugar, salt and cloves. Cover and simmer until tender for about ¾ hour. Remove cloves, add vinegar, butter and jelly. Blend well over the heat. Check seasoning and serve hot with meat dishes. Serves 4.

RISOTTO MILANESE

2 oz (50 g) butter
1 small onion, chopped
8 oz (225 g) long grain rice
¼ pint (150 ml) dry white wine
1 pint (600 ml) chicken stock
Salt and pepper
A good pinch powdered saffron
2 teaspoons water
1 oz (25g) Parmesan cheese, grated

COOK'S TIP. If you can't find saffron, add a teaspoon of powdered turmeric to the stock when cooking the rice.

Melt 1 oz (25 g) butter in a sauce-pan and fry the onion over a low heat until soft, but not brown. Add the rice to the pan and continue to cook it for 2 minutes. Pour on the wine and simmer for a few min-utes. Add the stock with lots of salt and pepper. Bring to the boil, cover the saucepan and let the risotto simmer for about 20 min-utes or until the rice is tender and all the liquid has been absorbed.

Blend the saffron with the water and stir into the rice, using a fork. Then add the remaining butter and cheese, taste and serve on a hot dish. Serves 4.

SUETY PUDDING

COOK'S TIP. This pudding goes perfectly with roast lamb in winter. Make it while roasting the joint and use the dripping from the meat tin. The better the flavour of the dripping the nicer the pudding and the further your joint will reach.

2 oz (50 g) lamb dripping from the roasting tin
4 oz (100 g) self-raising flour
1½ oz (37.5 g) prepared shredded suet
½ level teaspoon salt
1 egg
3 tablespoons milk

Heat the oven to 400 deg.F, 200 deg.C, gas mark 6. Place the dripping in a round shallow ovenproof tin or dish and heat until very hot.

Sift the flour into a basin, stir in the suet and salt. Lightly beat the egg, add with the milk to the mixture and mix to a soft but not sticky dough.

Pat out the dough to the size of the dish on a lightly floured table. Put straight into the hot dripping, return to the oven and cook for about 20 minutes or until golden brown. Cut into wedges and serve with roast lamb. Serves 4.

HERB DUMPLINGS

COOK'S TIP. Add these to any casserole in winter for the last 30 minutes of cooking time. They are filling and tasty.

4 oz (100 g) self-raising flour
2 oz (50 g) shredded suet
½ level teaspoon salt
1 level tablespoon freshly chopped herbs
About 5-6 tablespoons water

Sift the flour into a bowl and stir in the suet, salt and herbs and then mix to a soft but not sticky dough with the water. Form into 8 small balls. Place on top of the casserole or stew, cover and simmer for about 30 minutes until well risen. Serve at once. Makes sufficient dumplings for four people.

YORKSHIRE PUDDING

COOK'S TIP. Serve this traditionally with roast beef or use the batter to make a toad-in-the-hole. For a change use beefburgers instead of sausages.

½ oz (12.5 g) beef dripping
4 oz (100 g) flour
1 teaspoon salt
1 egg, lightly beaten
½ pint (300 ml) milk and water mixed

Heat the oven to 425 deg.F, 220 deg.C, gas mark 7. Melt the dripping in a roasting tin 7 by 11 inches (17.5 by 27.5 cm).

Sift the flour and salt into a bowl. Stir in the egg and gradually add the milk and water, mixing to a smooth batter.

Pour into the roasting tin and cook for 35-40 minutes or until the batter is well risen and golden brown and crisp. Serves 4 good portions.

TORTILLAS

1 lb (450 g) strong white flour
2 level teaspoons baking powder
1 level teaspoon salt
About ½ pint (300 ml) less 2 tablespoons warm water

Measure the flour, baking powder and salt into a bowl, make a well in the centre and gradually add the warm water, mixing well to form a firm dough. Add a little extra water if necessary. Turn onto a clean surface and knead until smooth. Place in a polythene bag and leave for 20 minutes.

Divide the dough into 12 pieces and then press each piece

flat and roll out to a very thin round about 10 inches (25 cm) in diameter.

Lightly oil a heavy frying pan and put on quite a high heat, add a tortilla and cook until bubbles appear. Then turn over and cook until a pale golden colour on the other side.

Stack in a folded towel until all the tortillas are cooked and then serve buttered and rolled up. Makes 12 tortillas.

Flatten the tortilla with a fish slice while it is frying.

COOK'S TIP. In Mexico tortillas are served instead of bread or rolls. Any that are left over may be cut in triangles and fried in hot oil until golden brown and crisp.

CRANBERRY, ORANGE AND REDCURRANT SAUCE

8 oz (225 g) cranberries
Grated rind and juice of one small orange
4 tablespoons redcurrant jelly
A little orange liqueur if liked

Put all the ingredients in a saucepan with a tightly fitting lid and cook over a gentle heat until the cranberries are soft, stirring from time to time. Remove from the heat, add a couple of tablespoons of orange liqueur.

Turn into a small dish and serve either hot or cold with Virginia baked ham (p 95).

CHESTNUT STUFFING WITH WATERCRESS

1 lb 15 oz (880 g) can whole chestnuts in water
8 oz (225 g) streaky bacon, chopped
2 oz (50 g) butter
4 oz (100 g) fresh brown breadcrumbs
1 egg, beaten
1 bunch watercress, finely chopped

1 tablespoon caster sugar
2 teaspoons salt
Ground black pepper

Drain the liquid from the chestnuts and turn them into a bowl. Gently mash with a fork to break into small chunky pieces.

Fry the bacon slowly to let the fat run out and then increase the heat and fry quickly until crisp. Lift out with a slotted spoon and add to the chestnuts.

Add the butter to the pan with the bacon fat and allow to melt, then add the breadcrumbs and fry until brown; turn into the bowl. Add the remaining ingredients and mix very thoroughly. Use to stuff the body cavity of the turkey.

SAUSAGE, LEMON AND THYME STUFFING

1 oz (25 g) butter
1 onion chopped
1 lb (450 g) pork sausage meat
4 oz (100 g) fresh white breadcrumbs
Rind and juice of 1 lemon
1 level teaspoon salt
Ground black pepper
2 tablespoons chopped parsley
1 level teaspoon fresh thyme or half teaspoon dried thyme

Melt the butter, add the onion and fry gently until soft, for about 10 minutes. Stir in the remaining ingredients and mix well together. Use to stuff the breast of the turkey.

COOK'S TIP. These are two really good stuffings for turkey. Put the lemon, sausage and thyme stuffing in the breast end, but don't worry if it looks a big bulge: ease the skin a little to get all the stuffing in. Put the chestnut stuffing inside the body cavity of the bird.

Make the stuffings on Christmas Eve, wrap and put in the fridge and then stuff first thing on Christmas morning; the reason for not putting the stuffing in the bird the day before is that often there is not room to get the bird in the

fridge because of all the other Christmas preparations. It is essential to refrigerate the stuffings so that they keep cold and fresh. The stuffings are enough for a 14 to 16 lb bird (6.3 to 7.2 kg).

SAGE AND ONION STUFFING

2 onions
1 oz (25 g) butter
4 oz (100 g) fresh white breadcrumbs
1 teaspoon dried sage
1/2 teaspoon salt
Ground black pepper

Butter well an 8 inch (20 cm) shallow ovenproof dish. Peel the onions. (Add any onion skins and odd pieces of onion to the giblet stock.) Chop the onions roughly and put in a pan. Cover with water and bring to the boil. Simmer until barely tender for about 5 minutes. Drain really well, pressing out all excess liquid. Return the onions to the pan and add butter. Stir to melt the butter, then add breadcrumbs, sage, salt and plenty of black pepper. Spread over the dish and dot with more butter. Bake with the duck for about 30 minutes until pale brown and crispy.

FRENCH CHEESES

Cheese and wine are the solid foundations of much of French regional cuisine. The range of cheeses in France is so great that it is no exaggeration to say that you can sample a different cheese every day of the year, with a choice for high days and holidays. About one hundred of these cheeses are regularly exported. Roquefort, Brie and Camembert are the most famous, and well over 500,000 Camemberts are made daily in the creameries of France. But they represent only the tip of the French cheese mountain.

1 Doux de montagne 2 Tomme au raisin 3 Roquefort 4 Walnut cheese 5 Boursin 6 Hazelnut cheese 7 Neufchâtel 8 Cheese with herbs 9 Brie 10 Port Salut 11 Chèvre 12 Bleu de Bresse 13 Camembert

TOMME: A family of uncooked, pressed cheeses made from cow's milk, which have a velvety-smooth texture and a relatively mild flavour. Tomme au Raisin is increasingly popular in Britain. Tomme cheeses originate in the Savoy region of France

ROQUEFORT: One of the world's most famous blue cheeses and known since Roman times. It comes from Aquitaine where it is matured in cellars whose unique properties give the cheese its strong rich taste.

BOURSIN: Rich, creamy and tangy, it is the product of the lush countryside of Normandy. You can buy it plain, with garlic or parsley, or surrounded by black pepper.

NEUFCHÂTEL: Another Norman cheese, with its characteristic heart shape, is excellent when eaten young. Its coat should be snowy-white and downy with perhaps a hint of red pigmentation. Also look out for Bondon, an unripened Neufchâtel (or Neufchâtel-type cheese shaped like a small barrel bung.)

BRIE: Often said to be the king of cheeses, although Stilton lovers might disagree. Brie has a full, mellow, almost buttery flavour. Farmhouse Brie (Brie de Meaux is the most common) is slightly more tangy, and rather more expensive, than the creamery variety. In a shop, test by pressing your fingers gently on the wrapped cheese; it should be springy to the touch.

PORT SALUT: Originally made by Trappist monks in the 13th century. Commercial versions have a slightly bland flavour. A wedge cut from a whole cheese has a better flavour than a pre-packed wedge.

CHÈVRE: A name for a multitude of goat-cheeses, which have as much variety as cheeses made from cow's milk. The soft blanc illustrated here should have a sharp sweetness; the log of cheese should be firm, a little crumbly and downy. Chèvre cheese is easily digestible and a good introduction to more exciting cheeses.

BLEU DE BRESSE: A blue cheese from the Jura region, made from unskimmed cow's milk. It has a slightly mouldy smell and a thin blue rind. Avoid Bleu de Bresse with a sharp smell and a greyish body colour.

CAMEMBERT: Has a creamier colour than Brie with a flavour varying from milky mellowness to a richer lactic. Genuine farmhouse Camembert made with unpasteurised milk always bears the description 'non pasteurisée' on the chipboard container. Avoid Camembert with a brown rind, which indicates excessive age. Test as for Brie.

STORING: Successful storage depends on avoiding the effects of heat, air and dessication. A cellar or larder is best for storing, otherwise the vegetable container at the bottom of the refrigerator is quite adequate. Always keep soft cheeses wrapped in cling film or aluminium foil. This also applies to goat-cheeses. Blue cheeses should be tightly wrapped in film or foil, or in a damp cloth. Roquefort should also be stored in this way.

ORIENTAL COOKING

The cuisines of India, China and Japan vary greatly. The best of Indian cooking offers a subtle balance of delicate flavours which enhances the taste of natural ingredients. China has a tradition of cooking which goes back thousands of years. Taste and texture are imaginatively contrasted, and opposites – sweet and sour, soft and crisp – cunningly brought together. Seasoning is at the heart of Chinese cooking with soy sauce, ginger, garlic and spring onions all playing their part.

Japanese cooking, which differs greatly from that of China, is the least known in the West. There are no heavy sauces and spices are light. Vegetables are fresh and barely cooked. The presentation of each dish is almost an art form in itself, and sometimes the food literally looks too good to eat.

MILD AUTHENTIC INDIAN CURRY

This recipe was given to me by Fatima Lakhani as a curry that her family has enjoyed for generations. It is not overpoweringly strong, has a superb flavour, a rich deep colour and is surprisingly simple to make. It freezes well so make more than you need. Thaw slowly before reheating.

THE SPICES:
2 rounded tablespoons ground coriander
1 rounded teaspoon ground cumin
1 level teaspoon ground turmeric
1 rounded teaspoon Garam Masala, (ground mixed spices) Or instead of the above use 3 rounded tablespoons curry powder
2 fat cloves garlic, crushed
Piece fresh green ginger, size of a walnut, finely chopped
2 teaspoons salt

3 tablespoons corn oil
2 large onions, chopped
8 oz (225 g) can peeled tomatoes
2 generous tablespoons tomato purée
2 lb (900 g) chuck steak, cut into cubes
1/2 pint (300 ml) water
Fresh mango slices (optional)

First mix the spices together and then add the garlic, ginger and salt.

COOK'S TIP. If you like a really hot curry add chilli powder with the spices. Half a teaspoon of ground chilli is enough for most tastes.

Take a heavy pan, measure in the oil, add the onions and fry until an even golden brown. Take care not to let them catch and brown as this would spoil the flavour. Add all the spice mixture, tomatoes and tomato purée and cook over a medium heat, without a lid, stirring until the oil starts to come through slightly.

Then add the meat, cover with a lid and simmer for 15 minutes. Remove the lid, add water, cover and bring to the boil and simmer gently for about 2½ hours or until the meat is tender.

Garnish with fresh mango slices if you can get them brushed with lemon juice to prevent discolouration. Serves 6.

—Mild Indian Curry and Side Dishes—

ACCOMPANIMENTS FOR CURRY

RICE
Use basmati rice or long grained rice and cook in plenty of salted water until just tender. Drain well and allow about 2 oz (50 g) rice per person.

Indian pilau rice bought in packets is a yellow spiced saffron rice and adds variety.

Poppodums fried in deep fat and served in a stack are also put on the table.

SAMBOLS (side dishes)

CUCUMBER, YOGHURT AND MINT:
Mix a tablespoon chopped mint with 3 inches (7.5 cm) diced cucumber and ¼ pint (150 ml) carton yoghurt. Season well.

BANANA:
2 bananas, sliced and tossed in lemon juice.

ONION AND GREEN PEPPER:
1 mild onion, finely sliced, mixed with chopped green pepper.

MANGO CHUTNEY:
Buy this ready-made.

—Tandoori Chicken—

CURRY POWDER

Buy the spices from an Indian specialist grocer or store. Usually sold in sealed vacuum-packed tins.

Ground coriander 4 parts
Ground cumin 2 parts
Ground turmeric 1 part
Garam Masala 1 part

Add chilli powder to the curry at the cooking time to taste.

Keen curry enthusiasts may make their own Garam Masala from:
Ground cinnamon 2 parts
Ground cloves 1 part
Ground cardamom 1 part

DAHL

8 oz (225 g) green lentils
1 bayleaf
2 tablespoons oil
1 large carrot, chopped
1 large green pepper, chopped
1 large onion, chopped
1 clove garlic, crushed
½ inch (1.25 cm) piece fresh root ginger
½ level teaspoon ground cinnamon
½ level teaspoon ground cumin
½ level teaspoon ground coriander
14 oz (397 g) can peeled tomatoes
Salt and pepper

Soak the lentils overnight in cold water, then drain and discard the water. Put the lentils in a saucepan and add sufficient water to cover. Bring to the boil, add the bayleaf and simmer for 30 minutes or until the lentils are tender. Drain and remove the bayleaf.

Heat the oil in a large pan, add the vegetables and fry for 10 minutes, stirring. Then add the lentils, spices and tomatoes and cook gently for 10 minutes or until the carrots are soft.

Discard the ginger, put the mixture in three batches in the blender and purée quickly for about 30 seconds on top speed. The dahl should not be smooth, retaining some texture.

Rinse out the saucepan, reheat the dahl and taste and check seasoning. Serve hot. Serves 4 with pitta bread or about 8 as an accompaniment to curry.

LAMB CURRY

Take care to wash your hands straight away after handling fresh chillies. I have found that should you rub your eyes with your hands it makes them sting like mad.

1 1/2 inch (3.75 cm) piece fresh root
    ginger, peeled and chopped
3 cloves garlic, peeled
2 green chillies
2 oz (50 g) unsalted cashew nuts
1/4 teaspoon ground cloves
1/4 teaspoon ground cardamom
2 teaspoons ground coriander
1/4 teaspoon ground turmeric
6 tablespoons water
2 oz (50 g) butter
2 onions, finely chopped
2 lb (900 g) lean lamb, cubed
1/2 pint (300 ml) natural yoghurt
1 tablespoon lemon juice
Salt

Put the ginger, garlic, chillies, nuts and all the spices with the water in a blender and purée until smooth.

Melt the butter in a pan, add the onions and lamb and fry for 5 minutes with the yoghurt and mix well, cover the saucepan and simmer gently for one hour.

Stir in the lemon juice and continue cooking for a further 30 minutes or until the lamb is tender. Check seasoning. Serve with plain boiled rice. Serves 6.

PRAWN CURRY

A quick and easy curry that tastes delicious with really fresh giant prawns.

2 oz (50 g) butter
1 large onion, chopped
1 level teaspoon ground coriander
1/2 level teaspoon ground cumin
1/4 level teaspoon ground turmeric
1/4 level teaspoon chilli powder
1/4 pint (150 ml) chicken stock
3 large tomatoes, peeled,
    chopped and the seeds
    removed
Salt
1-2 tablespoons lemon juice

8 oz (225 g) peeled prawns
2 tablespoons plain yoghurt
    (optional)

Heat the butter in a saucepan, add the onion and fry for 5 minutes or until golden brown. Stir in all the spices and cook for a minute. Add the stock, tomatoes and a little salt and bring to the boil, then reduce the heat and simmer for 30 minutes.

Stir in the lemon juice and prawns and heat through, stir in the yoghurt if used and taste and check seasoning. Serves 3.

TANDOORI CHICKEN

4 chicken portions
1 level teaspoon salt
Juice of 1 lemon
1 inch (2.5 cm) piece root ginger
    or 1/2 teaspoon ground ginger
2 cloves garlic
4 green chillies, if available
A few fresh mint leaves
5 oz (150 ml) carton natural
    yoghurt
1 teaspoon chilli powder
1 teaspoon ground black pepper
1/4 teaspoon ground nutmeg
1/4 teaspoon Garam Masala
1/4 teaspoon red food colouring
    (optional)

COOK'S TIP. If liked use a packet of Tandoori Barbecue spice mix and make up as directed on the packet.

Skin the chicken and prick all over with a fork or make small cuts with a sharp knife. Put in a dish and sprinkle with salt and lemon juice. Peel the root ginger and garlic and crush. Finely mince or chop the chillies and mint leaves and add to the ginger and garlic with the remaining ingredients, mix well and pour over the chicken. Cover and leave to marinate overnight.

Remove the rack from the grill pan, lay in the chicken and grill under a hot grill for 5 minutes on each side, then reduce the heat

and cook for a further 10 minutes on each side. Serve with lemon wedges on a bed of lettuce and sliced onion. Serves 4.

SWEET AND SOUR PORK

The contrast of sweet and sour flavours is typically Chinese, but easily reproduced in an English kitchen.

BATTER:
4 oz (100 g) self-raising flour
1/2 teaspoon salt
1/4 pint (150 ml) water

SAUCE:
12 oz (340 g) can pineapple
    chunks
3 tablespoons malt vinegar
1 tablespoon tomato purée
2 teaspoons soft brown sugar
2 teaspoons cornflour
1/4 cucumber, peeled and cut in
    small dice

PORK MIXTURE:
8 oz (225 g) lean pork, cut in 1/2
    inch (1.25 cm) pieces
Salt and pepper
Oil for deep frying

Beat together the batter ingredients and leave on one side.

Drain the pineapple chunks and put 5 tablespoons of the juice in a saucepan with the vinegar, tomato purée, sugar and cornflour. Bring to the boil, stirring until thickened. Add the cucumber and pineapple chunks.

Season the pork well, dip the pieces in the batter and then fry in hot deep fat for about 3 to 4 minutes until crisp and golden brown and the pork is cooked through. Lift out with a slotted spoon and drain on kitchen paper. Serve piled on a hot dish with the sauce poured over or separately if preferred. Serves 4 with other dishes.

—Spring Rolls, Chop Suey, Sweet and Sour Pork with Cashew Nuts—

PORK, SWEET AND SOUR WITH CASHEW NUTS

12 oz (350 g) pork fillet
3 tablespoons oil
2 oz (50 g) cashew nuts
8 oz (225 g) can pineapple cubes
1 level tablespoon cornflour
3 tablespoons malt vinegar
1 tablespoon tomato purée
2 tablespoons brown sugar
Salt and pepper

COOK'S TIP. The Chinese are very partial to nuts. Remember not to buy the salted variety!

Cut the pork into pencil-thin strips.

Put the oil in a pan and stir-fry the nuts until brown. Lift out onto a plate with a slotted spoon. Add the pork to the pan and stir-fry over a high heat turning all the time for about 2 minutes. Lift out with a slotted spoon onto the plate with the nuts.

Drain the pineapple, reserve 6 tablespoons juice and put in a bowl with the cornflour, vinegar, tomato purée and sugar and mix well.

Pour into the pan and stir over a medium heat until thick. Add the pork and nuts with the pineapple cubes and cook for a minute, taste and add seasoning and serve at once. Serves 6 with other dishes.

STIR-FRY PRAWNS

3 spring onions
2 level teaspoons cornflour
2 tablespoons sherry
2 tablespoons corn oil
12 oz (350 g) bean sprouts
1 clove garlic, crushed
1/4 pint (150 ml) chicken stock
2 tablespoons soy sauce
Salt and ground black pepper
8 oz (225 g) peeled prawns

Cut the spring onions into strips lengthwise, then into 2 inch (5 cm) lengths. Slake the cornflour with the sherry.

—Stir-fry Prawns—

Heat the oil in a wok or a large heavy pan until very hot. Add the bean sprouts, spring onions and garlic. Toss well for a few minutes, add the stock and soy sauce with the slaked cornflour and seasoning. Continue cooking and tossing for a further minute and then add the prawns. Heat through for a last minute or until the liquid is creamy and the vegetables still crisp.

Serve with boiled rice or just on its own. Serves 4.

COOK'S TIP. You may want to try this recipe with chicken cut into bite-sized pieces if you can't get prawns.

CHICKEN CHOP SUEY

Chinese egg noodles are tasty and make this dish fairly substantial.

4 oz (100 g) egg noodles
8 oz (225 g) chicken breast
8 oz (225 g) can whole peeled water chestnuts
2 tablespoons oil
1 small onion, finely chopped
1 carrot, cut in fine strips
3/4 inch (2 cm) piece green ginger, very finely chopped
1 tablespoon cornflour
3 tablespoons soy sauce
1/2 pint (300 ml) chicken stock

Cook the noodles as directed on the packet and rinse and drain well.

Cut the meat in pencil strips, drain the water chestnuts and slice.

Heat the oil in a large shallow pan and stir-fry all the chicken and vegetables for 5 minutes, tossing well. Add the noodles.

Blend the cornflour with the soy sauce and chicken stock and stir into the pan until the sauce thickens. Then reduce the heat and simmer for 10 minutes or until chicken and vegetables are tender.

Taste and check seasoning and serve piled on a hot dish. Serves 4 with other dishes.

FRIED RICE

This is a tasty rice dish and a pleasant alternative to plain boiled rice, which you can serve as well.

*6 oz (175 g) long grain rice
2 tablespoons oil
1 onion, finely diced
4 oz (100 g) streaky bacon, diced
1 egg, beaten
1 level teaspoon caster sugar
½ teaspoon salt
1 tablespoon spring onions, cut
    into short lengths
1 tablespoon soy sauce*

Cook the rice in boiling salted water for about 12 minutes or as directed on the packet. Drain and rinse well.

Heat the oil in a frying pan and fry the onion and bacon gently for about 5 minutes so that the fat runs out of the bacon. Stir in the rice and beaten egg and fry for 2 minutes. Add the sugar, salt and the spring onions with the soy sauce and mix thoroughly until hot.

Taste and check seasoning and serve piled on a hot dish. Serves 4 to 6.

SPRING ROLLS

*FILLING:
1 tablespoon oil
1 oz (25 g) sliced almonds
4 oz (100 g) mushrooms, chopped
14 oz (397 g) can beansprouts,
    drained
1 tablespoon soy sauce
1 teaspoon cornflour
2 teaspoons water
Salt and pepper*

*10-12 unsugared pancakes
    (p 106)
1 egg, beaten
Deep oil for frying
Spring onion flowers to decorate*

COOK'S TIP. To make spring onion flowers, cut the onions to about the size of a short cigarette. Cut through the onion to within 1 inch (2.5 cm) of the root in several

places to give a frayed effect. Put in iced water to curl.

For the filling: Heat the oil in a pan and toss the almonds until slightly browned. Add the mushrooms with the beansprouts and soy sauce, toss and cook gently for 2 minutes. Blend the cornflour with the water and stir into the pan and cook for a minute. Season to taste.

Lay the pancakes flat on a work surface and put a tablespoon of the filling in the centre of each. Brush the edges with beaten egg, fold in the sides and then roll up like little parcels.

Deep fat fry for about 3 minutes until golden brown and crisp. Lift out with a slotted spoon and drain on kitchen paper. Makes 10-12 spring rolls.

CRISPY NOODLES

This is something that children will love. The Chinese also serve soft noodles, boiled.

*4 oz (100 g) egg noodles
Corn oil for deep fat frying*

Cook the noodles in boiling salted water for about 5 to 6 minutes, strain and rinse in warm water.

Heat the oil in a deep pan until hot (375 deg.F, 190 deg.C). To test whether the oil is hot enough, drop a small cube of bread into it, which should brown in about 3 seconds.

Place the noodles in a wire basket and lower into the pan, lifting out for a moment if the fat foams up. Lower again and repeat the action until the fat has calmed down. Cook until pale golden, and drain on kitchen paper. Serves 4 with other dishes.

—Sukiyaki—

SUKIYAKI

Sukiyaki can be cooked at the table using a fondue cooker. To eat in the Japanese style each person breaks a raw egg into a bowl beating lightly with chopsticks, then the beef and vegetables are then dipped into the egg and eaten.

1 lb (450 g) rump or sirloin steak
Vegetable oil

SAUCE:
6 tablespoons Japanese soy sauce
4 oz (50 g) granulated sugar
4 tablespoons sake (rice wine)
4 tablespoons chicken stock

VEGETABLES:
8 spring onions, chopped
1 onion, cut in rings
4 oz (100 g) button mushrooms, sliced
4 small carrots, cut in half and then in matchsticks
10 oz (275 g) shirataki noodles
10 oz (275 g) bean sprouts

Freeze the meat for 30 minutes, until it is firm enough to enable you to cut it into wafer thin slices about 1½ inches (3.75 cm) square.

Gently heat a large heavy frying pan or wok and run the oil around the base. Add the meat slices and brown on each side, lift the meat out and arrange on a heatproof dish. Place the sauce ingredients in the frying pan and boil for 5 minutes, to reduce by half. Add the vegetables and cook rapidly for about 5 minutes to lightly cook — they should remain crisp. Taste and add a little more soy sauce if more flavour is needed, or if the liquid in the pan has evaporated add a little more stock and sake.

Arrange the vegetables on the serving dish with the meat, spoon over the small amount of sauce. Serve just with plain boiled rice. Serves 4.

PICNICS AND PARTIES

Picnics, informal buffets and supper parties can cover a wide range of meals eaten under many different circumstances. In the case of picnics, the weather can often take a hand in the proceedings. When going on a picnic remember to take with you a good supply of kitchen paper, paper plates, wide-based mugs (which will stay upright more easily), a damp cloth in a polythene bag and a hand towel.

COLD MEATS

No buffet table is complete without a selection of cold meats, 'the cold collation' beloved of Victorian novelists. It can also prove a handy way of dealing with leftovers. You will find that summer chicken in mayonnaise is an excellent way of using turkey after the Christmas celebrations.

VIRGINIA BAKED HAM

5-6 lb (2.3-2.7 kg) piece of middle gammon, either on or off the bone as preferred
2 pints (1.1 l) cider
4 oz (100 g) brown sugar

COOK'S TIP. I usually find it a good idea to soak the joint overnight to remove any excess saltiness. Ask advice from your butcher, he may suggest a longer soaking period.

GLAZE:
1 teaspoon dry mustard
About 2 oz (50 g) demerara sugar
A little of the cider stock

DECORATION:
A few whole cranberries and half slices of canned pineapple

Soak the gammon overnight in cold water, then throw away the water. Put the joint in a pan just large enough to take it and pour over the cider, topping up with water if necessary to cover the joint. Put on the lid, bring to the boil and simmer for 1½ hours very gently. Then bring to a full rolling boil and at once lift pan onto a thick folded newspaper, then wrap completely in an old thick blanket or sleeping bag and leave for at least 6 hours to continue cooking in a hay box fashion.

Lift out the ham, carefully remove the skin and score the fat with a sharp knife as you would the skin of pork.

To glaze: Measure the mustard into a small bowl, add the sugar and mix to a thin paste with some of the cider stock. Spread over the fat, cover the lean meat with foil and brown the fatty skin in a hot oven at 425 deg.F, 220 deg.C, gas mark 7 for about 10 minutes, but keep an eye on it.

Place on a serving dish and decorate with whole cranberries and slices of canned pineapple. Serve either hot or cold with cranberry, orange and redcurrant sauce (p 83). Serves 10.

SCOTTISH PRESSED BEEF

2½-3 lb (1.1-1.3 kg) salted brisket of beef, boned
1 large onion, roughly chopped
8 cloves
3 bayleaves
2 carrots, sliced
2 sticks celery, sliced
8 peppercorns

Place the brisket in a saucepan just large enough to take it. Add sufficient water just to cover the joint, and add all the remaining ingredients. Bring to the boil very slowly and lift off any scum with a slotted spoon. Cover the pan and simmer very gently for 3-3½ hours until the meat is very tender. It may be necessary to add a little more boiling water to the pan during cooking time.

Lift out the meat carefully from the saucepan and remove any cloves or peppercorns that may be attached to it. Place in a cake tin which is just a little too small for it and cover with a saucer or plate and then several weights or heavy tins. Leave to become quite cold and then chill in the refrigerator for several hours, preferably overnight.

To serve, turn the meat out carefully, cut downwards into thin slices and serve with a selection of salads. Serves 6.

PORK GALANTINE

COOK'S TIP. A true galantine is first boiled in a pudding cloth in the shape of a sausage; this is a rather messy process and I prefer to make it using an oval casserole to get the shape. When cooked, chill it well before turning out and for a very special occasion glaze the galantine with a little aspic or consommé.

4 thin slices ham
8 oz (225 g) pork sausagemeat
1 lb (450 g) finely minced lean
  pork
3 oz (75 g) slice cooked ham,
  diced
3 oz (75 g) slice cooked tongue,
  diced
1 heaped teaspoon salt
Ground black pepper
1 level teaspoon chopped lemon
  thyme
Grated rind of 1 lemon
1 egg
12 whole stuffed green olives

Heat the oven to 325 deg.F, 160 deg.C, gas mark 3 and line an oval 1½ pint (1 l) casserole or terrine with the slices of ham.

Thoroughly blend all the other ingredients together and spread in the dish, cover with a piece of foil and stand in a meat roasting tin half filled with hot water. Bake in the oven for 1½ to 2 hours depending on the depth of the dish – a deep dish will take a little longer. The galantine is cooked when it has shrunk slightly from the sides of the dish and when a skewer inserted in the middle causes the juice to run clear.

Leave to become quite cold then chill overnight in the refrigerator. Turn out and serve sliced with salads. Serves 6.

CHICKEN GALANTINE

3½ lb (1.5 kg) chicken
12 oz (350 g) lean pork, minced
12 oz (350 g) pork sausagemeat
1 small onion, minced
2 cloves garlic, crushed
1½ oz (40 g) fresh breadcrumbs
1 egg
Large pinch dried thyme
1 teaspoon salt
Plenty of ground black pepper
4 oz (100 g) slice cooked ham
1 oz (25 g) green stuffed olives

Bone the chicken. Make a cut along the length of the backbone and with a small sharp knife cut the flesh away from the bones down each side. When you come to the wing knuckle cut it away from the carcass. Scrape the meat off the bone down to the first joint. Cut off there and then repeat with the other side.

With the leg joint, cut away again at the carcass, but scrape the meat away from the two bones of the leg, turning the flesh inside out as you go. Carefully cut the meat away from the rest of the carcass until you can lift it out. Remove any excess lumps of fat and lay the chicken skin-side down on a board, turning the legs back into shape. Use the carcass for making stock or soup.

Heat the oven to 375 deg.F, 190 deg.C, gas mark 5.

Mix together the pork, sausage meat, onion, garlic, bread-

–Chicken Galantine–

crumbs, egg, thyme and salt and pepper. Spread half this mixture down the centre of the chicken.

Cut the ham into ¾ inch (2 cm) strips lengthwise and lay on top of the stuffing interspersed with the olives. Cover with the remaining pork mixture and wrap the chicken over. Turn over and shape to resemble a chicken, place in a meat roasting tin and very lightly spread the breast with a little butter.

Bake in the centre of the oven for 1½ hours, basting occasionally.

Lift out and place on a dish to cool. When quite cold put in the refrigerator until required. Then serve sliced with various salads. Serves 10.

COOK'S TIP. Although this takes time to do it is worth it for a party. If you give your butcher lots of warning he may well bone the chicken for you.

SUMMER CHICKEN IN LEMON MAYONNAISE

COOK'S TIP. This is a very good way of using up turkey after Christmas and makes a delicious special cold supper dish when you have friends in. Canned pineapple may be used if liked but the flavour is rather sweeter than using fresh pineapple. If preparing ahead mix the lemon mayonnaise with the two different coloured meats and put in plastic containers. Prepare the pineapple and then assemble 30 minutes before the meal.

3 lb (1.3 kg) cooked chicken
1 small fresh pineapple
Juice of 1 lemon
½ pint (300 ml) thick home-made
  mayonnaise (see p 103)
Salt
Freshly ground black pepper
1 oz (25 g) walnuts, chopped
Lettuce hearts and watercress to
  garnish

sprinkle with browned, flaked almonds. Garnish the dish with small sprigs of watercress or parsley. Serves 6.

—Summer Chicken in Lemon—

Remove the meat from the chicken. Slice the white meat and cut the dark meat into bite-sized pieces.

Slice the pineapple and remove the skin and centre core. Cut 3 slices in half and reserve for garnish, and chop the remainder. Stir the lemon juice into the mayonnaise and season to taste. Mix 3-4 tablespoons (45-60 ml) mayonnaise with the dark meat and arrange it on a serving dish. Cover with the chopped pineapple and arrange the slices of white meat on top and then coat with the remaining mayonnaise.

Sprinkle over the chopped walnuts and garnish the dish with lettuce hearts, watercress and the halved slices of pineapple. Serves 6.

CELEBRATION TURKEY MAYONNAISE

COOK'S TIP. One of the best ways I know of serving turkey leftovers. This is a good dish for a party, because it is best made the day before with the grapes and almonds added at the last minute. It goes well with most salads and is a good way of using up turkey legs after the roast.

1 small onion, chopped
1/2 clove garlic
1 tablespoon tomato purée
1/2 level teaspoon curry powder
2 tablespoons (30 ml) lemon juice
2 tablespoons (30 ml) apricot jam
1/4 to 1/2 pint (150-300 ml) good mayonnaise
3/4 to 1 lb (350-450 g) cooked chopped turkey
8 oz (225 g) green and black grapes, halved and stoned
1 1/2 oz (37.5 g) browned, flaked almonds
Small sprigs watercress or parsley

Put the onion, garlic, tomato purée, curry powder, 1 tablespoon lemon juice and apricot jam in a small saucepan and bring to the boil, slowly, stirring all the time. Reduce to a purée in a blender or processor. Blend with the mayonnaise in a bowl and stir in the turkey. Chill overnight in the refrigerator.

Toss the grapes in the remaining lemon juice and stir into the turkey mayonnaise, taste and check seasoning.

Pile into a serving dish and

AVOCADO AND CHICKEN MAYONNAISE

COOK'S TIP. To serve, arrange a bed of lettuce hearts on a serving dish, spoon the avocado and chicken mixture into the centre and garnish with sprigs of parsley and tomato slices.

3 1/2 lb (1.5 kg) chicken, roasted
1 large avocado pear
1/4 pint (150 ml) mayonnaise
Salt
Freshly ground black pepper
1 teaspoon lemon juice
Lettuce, tomato slices and parsley to garnish

Cut the chicken into bite-size pieces, removing all skin and bones.

Cut the avocado in half and remove the stone. Scoop out the flesh and chop roughly. Mash half the avocado and mix with the mayonnaise, salt, pepper and lemon juice until smooth. This can be done in a blender. Turn into a bowl and stir in the remaining avocado and the chicken. Serves 4 to 6.

—Avocado Chicken Mayonnaise—

—Raised Derby Pie—

RAISED DERBY PIE

The pastry used in this pie is different from the usual shortcrust. However it is very easy to do and is wonderfully crisp.

FILLING:
3½ lb (1.5 kg) chicken
8 oz (225 g) pork sausagemeat
8 oz (225 g) bacon pieces, finely minced or chopped
1 tablespoon chopped fresh mixed herbs
1 teaspoon ground mace
2 teaspoons salt, according to saltiness of the bacon
Ground black pepper
6 small hard-boiled eggs, shelled
Beaten egg and milk to glaze

PASTRY:
12 oz (350 g) plain flour
1 teaspoon salt
5 oz (150 g) lard
¼ pint and 2 tablespoons water

Grease an 8 inch (20 cm) loose-bottomed cake tin.

First carve off the leg and thigh from the chicken, then remove the skin and bone. Take the meat off the rest of the bird, discard the skin and make stock from all the bones.

Cube all the chicken and put in a bowl with the bacon, herbs, sausagemeat and seasoning.

Now make the pastry. Put flour and salt in a bowl. Put lard and water into a pan and allow the lard to melt and the water to boil. Make a well in the centre of the flour and pour on all the liquid, mixing quickly with a wooden spoon or fork until it becomes a smooth dough.

When cool enough to handle take two thirds of the dough and roll in a circle 3 inches (7.5 cm) larger than the tin. Slip this into the tin and with the hands work it evenly up the sides until it stands about 3 inches (7.5 cm) from the base.

Put half the meat mixture in the tin, level and make six dents in the mixture and arrange the eggs in them. Cover with the remaining meat mixture and flatten.

Brush the inside of the pastry top with beaten egg and milk. Roll out the remaining pastry to a circle just over 8 inches (20 cm) for the lid and lift on top of the pie, press the edges firmly together and flute using the thumb and first finger of the right hand and the index finger of the left hand, or just press with the prongs of a fork. Make four holes in the top of the pie and decorate with pastry leaves if liked. Brush with beaten egg and bake in the oven at 425 deg. F, 220 deg.C, gas mark 7 for 45 minutes. Reduce the heat to 350 deg.F, 180 deg.C, gas mark 4 for a further 30 minutes. Remove from oven and leave to cool in the tin. Chill the pie overnight before turning out and serving sliced in wedges. Serves 8 to 10.

SWEDISH SALAD PLATTER

EGGS INDIAN STYLE:
Halve two hard-boiled eggs lengthwise and lay cut-side down along the edge of a large serving dish. Blend a little mayonnaise with a good pinch of curry powder, squeeze of lemon juice and a little mango chutney juice and spoon over the eggs. Sprinkle each egg with paprika pepper.

CUCUMBER AND DILL:
Toss slices of peeled cucumber in a little French dressing that has had some chopped fresh dill tips added to it and spoon in a line onto the dish alongside the egg mayonnaise. Decorate with dill.

TOMATO AND ONION:
Peel and slice 8 oz (225 g) tomatoes and mix with a very finely sliced onion. Lightly toss in a little French dressing and spoon onto the plate alongside the rolls. Sprinkle with a few finely chopped chives.

HAM ROLLS:
Finely dice a large cooked potato and mix with 2 sticks sliced celery and a chopped eating apple. Add just sufficient mayonnaise to bind well together. Place a spoonful of the mixture on each of the 4 slices of ham and roll up. Place in a line on the dish alongside the cucumber and dill salad.

COOK'S TIP. This is a colourful salad dish which may be served as an hors d'oeuvre. It also makes an attractive addition to any buffet meal. Serves 4.

OPEN SANDWICHES

COOK'S TIP. The joy of open sandwiches is that you can see what you are getting — made well they look and taste good. The ideas below are just a guide. Creamy scrambled egg with added crisply fried bacon pieces is delicious. Thinly sliced meats from the delicatessen go a long way served with a crisp salad and a blob of home-made chutney or mayonnaise.

1. Butter a slice of brown or wholemeal bread and spread with liver pâté. Arrange 2 rashers of crisply fried bacon on top and garnish with a few whole fried button mushrooms and a sprig of parsley or watercress.

2. Butter a slice of brown or wholemeal bread and cover with a slice of cold roast pork. Place a spoonful of apple sauce in the centre and garnish with 2 cooked prunes and a slice of fresh orange.

3. Butter a slice of brown or wholemeal bread and put a lettuce leaf on top. Slice a hard-boiled egg and arrange on the lettuce leaf. Flavour some mayonnaise with a pinch of curry powder and a little mango chutney juice, spoon over the egg and sprinkle with a little paprika pepper.

—Fresh Vegetable Quiche—

SALADS

Here are some appetizing side salads, plus recipes for mayonnaise and French dressing. Recall a holiday in the Aegean with a feta cheese salad, one of the staples of Greek cuisine. Nowadays most of the feta cheese sold in Britain comes from Denmark, the result of the difficulty of importing the authentic Greek version in good condition.

FRENCH VEGETABLE QUICHE

6 oz (175 g) plain flour
4 oz (100 g) butter
1½ oz (40 g) Parmesan cheese
1 tablespoon (15 ml) cold water
1 egg yolk

FILLING:
1 oz (25 g) butter
1 oz (25 g) flour
½ pint (300 ml) milk
1 level teaspoon made mustard
3 oz (75 g) grated Cheddar cheese
Salt and pepper
¾ lb (350 g) cooked mixed vegetables (e.g. leeks, carrots, peas, beans; not cabbage or sprouts)
Chopped parsley

Sift the flour into a bowl. Add the butter cut in small pieces and rub in with the fingertips until the mixture resembles fine breadcrumbs. Stir in the Parmesan cheese. Blend the water with the egg yolk, add to the flour and mix to a firm dough. Roll out on a lightly floured table and line an 9 inch (22.5 cm) flan tin. Chill in the refrigerator for 15 minutes.

Heat the oven to 425 deg.F, 220 deg.C, gas mark 7. Put in a baking sheet to warm. Line the flan with a piece of greaseproof paper and weight down with baking beans. Bake blind for about 20 to 25 minutes until pastry is golden brown at the edges and crisp. Remove paper and beans for last 10 minutes of baking.

Meanwhile melt the butter for the filling in a saucepan and stir in the flour. Cook for 2 minutes. Gradually add the milk and bring to the boil, stirring until thickened. Add the mustard, cheese and seasoning.

Cut the vegetables into even sized pieces and add to the sauce Re-heat thoroughly and then spoon into the flan case. Sprinkle with parsley and serve. Serves 6.

ALL-AMERICAN ICEBERG SALAD

Iceberg lettuces are more expensive than other kinds, but they are crisp and hearty and go a long way.

1 small Iceberg lettuce
1 bunch watercress
2 oz (50 g) button mushrooms, finely sliced
6 spring onions, chopped
1 red pepper

DRESSING:
2 tablespoons mayonnaise
2 tablespoons sour cream
2 tablespoons natural yoghurt
2 tablespoons white wine vinegar
Salt and freshly ground black pepper

Break the lettuce into small pieces and place in a large salad bowl. Break the watercress into small sprigs and add to the bowl with the mushrooms, spring onions and red pepper, which should have the seeds removed and be cut into thin strips. Toss well and then serve with a bowl of dressing. Serves 8.

FETA CHEESE SALAD

Feta is a pure white soft crumbly cheese. It is fairly salty and is the most popular cheese of Greece.

2 oz (50 g) fat black olives
½ crisp lettuce
½ cucumber, thickly sliced
½ green pepper, cubed
5 tablespoons French dressing made with olive oil
4 oz (100 g) Feta cheese
A tablespoon chopped fresh marjoram and parsley

Arrange the salad on individual plates. Cut the Feta cheese in triangles, then put with the salad.
    Spoon over the dressing and sprinkle with herbs. Serves 4.

—Feta Cheese Salad—

—*Mexican Bean Salad*—

TOSSED GREEN SALAD

2 lettuces
2 heads chicory
4 sticks celery, sliced
1 cucumber
Small green pepper
3 spring onions
1 avocado pear
About ⅛ pint (75 ml) French
*   dressing*
2 tablespoons sunflower seeds

Wash and drain the lettuce and break into small pieces. Slice the chicory or break into leaves and put in a large bowl with the celery. Skin the cucumber, cut in half lengthwise and then cut across into slices, add to the bowl. Remove the seeds and white pith from the pepper and cut into thin strips. Chop the spring onions. Peel the avocado pear, remove the stone and roughly chop.

Put the French dressing in a wooden salad bowl, add the avocado pear and toss until well coated.

Just before serving add all the other salad ingredients and toss well. Sprinkle with sunflower seeds. Serves 10 to 12.

COOK'S TIP. Put French dressing in the serving bowl with any snipped chives, herbs or spring onion tops. Add the salad and toss well.

MEXICAN BEAN SALAD

A great change from the usual rice or potato salad. It is essential to soak the beans overnight first.

1 lb (450 g) mixed dried beans;
*   could include haricot, red*
*   kidney, black eye and aduki*
Crushed garlic
A little finely chopped onion
4 sticks celery, finely chopped
French dressing
Chopped parsley

Put the beans in a bowl, cover with cold water and leave to soak overnight.

Drain well and put in a sauce-pan, cover with cold water and bring to the boil. Simmer for one hour or until tender. Rinse under hot water and while they are still warm put in a bowl and add the other ingredients. Toss well, season and then cover. Leave in a cool place to marinate overnight.

Turn into a serving dish, sprinkle with parsley before serving. Serves 4 to 6.

LOW-CALORIE DRESSING

Well worth making if you're trying to decrease the bulges: it cheers up a salad no end.

1 teaspoon Dijon mustard
1 tablespoon lemon juice
1 tablespoon wine or cider vinegar
1 crushed clove garlic
5 oz (140 g) carton plain yogurt
Salt and pepper

Blend the mustard, lemon juice, vinegar and garlic together in a small bowl, whisk in the yogurt and season well.

Keep covered in the refrigerator and use to dress salads. This dressing will keep for up to 10 days.

Variations
Blue cheese dressing: Add about 1 oz (25 gm) crumbled Roquefort cheese to the dressing and use over a plain green salad. This is especially good when served with plain grilled food such as chops or steaks.

Mint dressing: Add a heaped teaspoon of very finely chopped mint to the basic dressing and mix thoroughly. Use this to dress new potatoes or sliced tomatoes.

Tomato cream dressing: Add a tablespoon tomato ketchup and 2 tablespoons double cream to the basic dressing and serve with fish salads.

MAYONNAISE

COOK'S TIP. Should the sauce curdle because the oil has been added too quickly to the egg yolks, take a fresh yolk and start again, adding the curdled mayonnaise very slowly to it in the same way as the oil was added to the original egg yolks.

2 egg yolks
1 level teaspoon made mustard
1 level teaspoon salt
1 level teaspoon caster sugar
Pepper
1 tablespoon white wine or cider
    vinegar
1/2 pint (300 ml) corn or vegetable
    oil
1 tablespoon lemon juice

Stand a bowl on a damp cloth to prevent it slipping on the table. Put yolks, mustard, salt and sugar and pepper into a bowl with the vinegar and mix well. Add the oil drop by drop, beating well with a whisk the whole time until the mixture is smooth and thick. Beat in the lemon juice.

In order that the oil may be added a drop at a time, put into the bottle-neck a cork from which a small wedge has been cut.

Makes 1/2 pint (300 ml) mayonnaise.

VARIATIONS

CURRY MAYONNAISE:
Rub the bowl with a cut clove of garlic before starting and then add 1/2 level teaspoon curry powder to the egg yolk.

ANCHOVY MAYONNAISE:
Stir 4 teaspoons anchovy essence to the finished mayonnaise and use in fish and vegetable salads.

HERB MAYONNAISE:
Add 1 tablespoon finely chopped parsley, 1 tablespoon finely chopped chives and about 2 tablespoons double cream to the basic recipe and serve with fish or meat salads.

TARTARE SAUCE:
To the basic recipe add 1 rounded dessertspoon each chopped gherkins, capers and parsley. Serve with hot fish dishes.

FRENCH DRESSING

1/2 clove garlic, crushed
1/2 teaspoon dry mustard
1/2 teaspoon salt
Pinch freshly ground black
    pepper
1 level teaspoon caster sugar
1/4 pint (150 ml) olive, corn or salad
    oil
4-6 tablespoons cider or white
    wine vinegar

Blend the first five ingredients together in a bowl and then gradually mix in the oil with a whisk or spoon.

Stir in the vinegar, taste and adjust seasoning if necessary. This makes 1/2 pint (300 ml) dressing.

COLESLAW

If you make coleslaw in two stages like this it uses a lot less mayonnaise and the flavours really have a chance to blend overnight in the refrigerator. If white cabbage is not available you can use shredded sprouts. Garnish with parsley sprigs.

1 small, hard white cabbage
    weighing about 1 1/2 lb (675 g)
1/2 pint (300 ml) French dressing
Salt and pepper
1 level teaspoon Dijon mustard
1 small onion, very finely chopped
2 carrots
1/8 pint (75 ml) mayonnaise

Cut the cabbage into four and trim away any hard stalk, then finely slice into strips. Place in a large mixing bowl with the French dressing, seasoning, mustard and onion, toss well, cover and leave in the refrigerator overnight.

Next day grate the carrots coarsely and stir into the bowl with the mayonnaise. Leave to stand for one hour before turning into a serving dish. Serves 6.

—Coleslaw—

PUDDINGS AND DESSERTS

This section provides an array of desserts and puddings to bring almost any meal to a satisfactory conclusion. The recipes cover all the seasons of the year, from Yuletide mince pie to summer pudding. There's tropical Indian fruit salad, a perfect dessert to follow a curry, and a selection of mousses, pancakes and ice creams, including cassata. Traditional English tastes are catered for with syllabub, so simple to make and perfect for summer nights, English custard tart and lemon meringue pie.

HOT DESSERTS

Remember that when making pastry the oven temperature is very important. Opening the door to put in cold trays of food reduces the temperature by up to 30°C, 50°F/2 gas marks. Always set the oven on at least 15°C, 25°F or 1 gas mark higher than you need. For flans, pre-heat a baking sheet in the oven. This gives more even bottom heat than putting the cake or pastry directly to the required temperature when the pastry has been in the oven for a few minutes.

CHOCOLATE SOUFFLÉ

4 oz (100 g) plain chocolate
2 tablespoons water
½ pint (300 ml) milk
1½ oz (40 g) butter
1½ oz (40 g) flour
1 teaspoon vanilla essence
4 large eggs
2 oz (50 g) caster sugar
A little icing sugar

Heat the oven to 375 deg.F, 190 deg.C, gas mark 5 and place a baking sheet in it.

Cut the chocolate into small pieces, put in a pan with the water and 2 tablespoons milk. Stir over a low heat until the chocolate has melted. Add the remaining milk, bring to the boil and remove from the heat.

Melt the butter in a small pan, stir in the flour and cook for 2 minutes without browning. Remove from the heat and stir in the hot milk, return to the heat and bring to the boil, stirring until thickened. Add the vanilla essence and leave to cool.

Separate the eggs and beat the yolks one at a time into the chocolate sauce. Sprinkle on the sugar. Whisk the egg whites using a rotary hand whisk or an electric whisk until stiff but not dry. Stir one tablespoonful into the mixture then carefully fold in the remainder. Pour into a buttered 2 pint (good 1 l) soufflé dish, run a teaspoon around the edge and bake on the hot baking sheet in the centre of the oven for about 40 minutes. Sprinkle with icing sugar and serve at once with whipped cream. Serves 4.

VARIATIONS:
Choose any flavouring and add to the mixture before the egg yolks.
Lemon: Add the finely grated rind of 2 small lemons and the juice of ½ a lemon and increase the sugar to 3 oz (75 g).
Orange: Add the finely grated rind of 2 small oranges and the juice of ½ an orange and increase the sugar to 3 oz (75 g).
Coffee: Add 2 tablespoons coffee essence to the milk.

COOK'S TIP. So good and not a bit difficult to make as long as you have a rotary whisk or an electric beater to whisk the egg whites. Make sure you use the correct size dish because if you choose a larger one the mixture will not rise above the rim. Serve with whipped cream.

LEMON SOUFFLÉ PUDDING

4 oz (100 g) butter or margarine, softened
12 oz (350 g) caster sugar
4 eggs, separated
4 oz (100 g) self-raising flour
Grated rind and juice of 2 large lemons
1 pint (600 ml) milk

Heat the oven to 375 deg.F, 190 deg.C, gas mark 5. Butter well a shallow 3 pint (1.7 l) ovenproof dish.

Beat the butter or margarine with the sugar until smooth. Beat in the egg yolks, then stir in the flour, lemon rind, juice and milk. Don't worry if the mixture looks curdled at this stage; it is quite normal.

Whisk the egg whites using a hand rotary or electric whisk until they form soft peaks and fold into the lemon mixture. Pour into the prepared dish and place in a meat tin half filled with hot water. Bake for about 1 hour or until pale golden brown on top. The pudding will have a light sponge on top with its own lemon sauce underneath. Serves 4 hungry people or 6 average helpings.

COOK'S TIP. This lemon pudding has something to please everyone, for it combines a hot lemon soufflé with its own built-in sauce.

–Soufflé Omelette–

SOUFFLÉ OMELETTE

COOK'S TIP. This is an easy pudding that can quickly be made out of ingredients that most of us have to hand.

2 large eggs
1 dessertspoon caster sugar
2 teaspoons cold water
½ oz (12.5 g) butter
1 rounded tablespoon strawberry
   or black cherry jam
Icing sugar

Separate the eggs and place the yolks in a basin with the sugar and water, beat until pale and creamy.

Whisk the egg whites using a hand rotary or electric whisk until just stiff. Mix 1 tablespoonful into the yolks and carefully fold in the remainder.

Heat the pan and then melt the butter in it over a moderate heat. Spread the mixture into the pan and cook without moving for 3 to 4 minutes until a pale golden brown underneath.

Slip under a medium grill for 2 to 3 minutes to set the top. Make a slight cut across the centre of the omelette, spread one half with warmed jam, fold in half and slide on to a warm serving plate. Dredge with icing sugar and serve at once. Serves 2.

CLASSIC PANCAKES

Caster sugar
4 oz (100 g) plain flour
Good pinch salt
1 egg
½ pint (300 ml) milk and water
   mixed half and half
1 tablespoon vegetable or corn oil
Oil for frying
1 lemon

Sprinkle a little caster sugar onto a sheet of greaseproof paper and put on one side.

Measure the flour and salt into a mixing bowl and make a well in the centre. Add the egg and gradually stir in half the milk and water. Using a whisk, blend in the flour from the sides of the bowl. Beat well until smooth. Stir in the remaining liquid and the oil.

Heat an 8 inch (20 cm) frying pan and a little oil. When it is hot pour off any excess and spoon about two tablespoons of the batter into the pan. Tip and rotate the pan so that the batter spreads out evenly and thinly covers the base. Cook the pancakes for about one minute until pale brown underneath.

Turn over with a palette knife, or wooden spatula if using a non-stick pan, or toss, then cook for another minute until pale golden brown. Invert the pancake onto the sugared paper and roll up. Place on a hot serving dish and put this over a steaming pan to keep warm while you make the remaining pancakes.

Serve with lemon wedges. Makes 8 to 10 pancakes.

COOK'S TIP. To freeze the pancakes leave them until cold. Freeze in stacks, wrapped in clear film, and keep for up to 3 months.

CRÊPES SUZETTE

8 to 10 pancakes

SAUCE:
Juice of 2 oranges
4 oz (100 g) unsalted butter
2 oz (50 g) caster sugar
1 tablespoon orange liqueur
3 tablespoons brandy

Put the orange juice, butter and sugar in a large frying pan and heat gently until the sugar has dissolved. Simmer for about 5 minutes until the sauce is syrupy.

Lay one pancake in the pan and coat with the sauce. Fold in four (to make a triangle) and move to one side of the pan. Repeat with the remaining pancakes. Making sure that the pancakes are piping hot, add the liqueur and brandy. If you wish, light with a match, then arrange on a serving dish and serve at once. Serves 4 to 5.

COOK'S TIP. If you don't have a large enough frying pan, remove the pancakes that you have cooked and keep hot on one side.

Heat a little oil in an 8 inch (20 cm) frying pan. When it is hot pour off any excess oil and spoon about 2 tablespoons (30 ml) of batter into the pan. Tip and rotate the pan so that the batter spreads out and thinly covers the base. Cook for about a minute until pale brown underneath, then turn over with a palette knife and cook for another minute. Slip pancake out of the pan and make about 7 more pancakes with the remaining batter.

For the filling: In a saucepan, gently cook the apples, cinnamon, sugar and 4 oz (100 g) butter for about 20 minutes or until the apples are tender, stirring occasionally.

Spread the pancakes flat, spoon some of the filling on to each and roll them up. In a large frying pan heat the remaining butter with a little oil and fry the pancakes on all sides until golden brown.

Pile on a warm serving dish, sprinkle with sugar and cinnamon and serve with cream or ice cream. Serves 4.

—Cinnamon Apple Pancakes—

CINNAMON APPLE PANCAKES

BATTER:
4 oz (100 g) flour
¼ teaspoon salt
1 egg
½ pint (300 ml) milk
1 tablespoon salad oil
Oil for frying

FILLING:
4 large Bramley apples, peeled, cored and sliced
¼ teaspoon ground cinnamon
6 oz (175 g) demerara sugar
5 oz (150 g) butter

COOK'S TIP. These may be made in advance, then reheated by frying just before serving. Alternatively they may be put in a well buttered tin, brushed with butter and cooked in a very hot oven until brown, for about 20 minutes.

Sift the flour and salt into a bowl and make a well in the centre. Add egg and gradually stir in half the milk. Using a whisk blend in the flour from the sides of the bowl, beat well until mixture is smooth and stir in the remaining milk and oil.

FRESH APRICOT AND ALMOND TART

PASTRY:
6 oz (175 g) plain flour
4 oz (100 g) butter
1 egg yolk
Level tablespoon caster sugar
2 teaspoons cold water

CREME PATISSIERE:
3 egg yolks
3 oz (75 g) vanilla sugar or use
    caster sugar and 1/2 teaspoon
    vanilla essence
1 oz (25 g) flour
1/2 pint (300 ml) milk

TOPPING:
1 1/2 lb (675 g) apricots
Juice of 1/2 lemon
6 tablespoons water
2 oz (50 g) caster sugar
Scant teaspoon arrowroot
1 tablespoon brandy
1/2 oz (12.5 g) toasted flaked
    almonds

First make the pastry. Put the flour in a bowl, add fat cut in small pieces and rub in with the fingertips until the mixture resembles fine breadcrumbs.

Mix the egg yolk, sugar and water, stir into the dry ingredients and bind them together. Roll out the pastry on a floured table, line a 9 inch (22.5 cm) flan tin and chill for 30 minutes.

Heat the oven to 435 deg.F, 225 deg.C, gas mark 7 with a thick baking sheet in it. Line the flan with greaseproof paper and baking beans and bake blind for 10 minutes or until beginning to brown at the edges, Remove the paper and beans and return to the oven for a further 5 minutes to cook the centre through. Cool in the tin and then carefully lift onto a serving plate.

To make the crème patissière: put egg yolks, sugar and flour in a bowl with a little milk and mix to a smooth mixture with a wire whisk. Boil the rest of the milk and pour onto the yolks, whisking well. Rinse out the pan, then return the mixture to the pan and stir over a low heat until thickened. Remove from the heat and leave to cool, stirring occasionally. Spread in the flan case.

Wash the apricots, halve and remove stones. Put lemon juice and water in a large shallow pan. Add apricots cut side down and sprinkle with sugar, then cover with a tight-fitting lid.

Bring to the boil, then simmer very gently for about 5 minutes until the fruit is just soft. Lift out with a slotted spoon and place on top of the crème patissière. Measure the arrowroot into a bowl and mix with brandy, then with the juices in the pan. Return to the pan, bring to the boil and allow to thicken. If it seems too thick to coat the fruit, thin down with a little water. Add the almonds to the glaze then spoon over the tart to give a shiny top. Serves 6 to 8.

LEMON MERINGUE PIE

COOK'S TIP. One of the English classics. Not a simple pudding to make, so the instructions should be followed exactly for success. Ideally make and bake on the same day.

6 oz (175 g) flour
2 oz (50 g) butter
2 oz (50 g) lard
1 egg yolk
1/2 oz (12.5g) caster sugar
2 teaspoons cold water

FILLING:
2 large lemons
1 1/2 oz (37.5 g) cornflour
1/2 pint (300 ml) water
2 egg yolks
3 oz (75 g) caster sugar

MERINGUE TOPPING:
3 egg whites
4 1/2 oz (125 g) caster sugar

—French Apricot and Almond Tart—

First make the pastry. Put the flour in a bowl, add the fats cut in small pieces and rub in with the fingertips until the mixture resembles fine bread crumbs. Mix the egg yolk, sugar and water together, stir into the dry ingredients and bind them together. Roll out the pastry on a floured board, line a 9 inch (22.5 cm) flan tin and chill for 30 minutes.

Heat the oven to 425 deg.F, 220 deg.C, gas mark 7 with a thick baking sheet in it. Line the flan with greaseproof paper, weigh down with baking beans and bake blind for 15 minutes.

Meanwhile prepare the filling. Finely grate the rind and squeeze the juice from the lemons and put in a bowl with the cornflour. Add 2 tablespoons of water and blend to form a smooth paste. Boil the remaining water and pour it onto the cornflour mixture. Return to the pan, bring to the boil and simmer for 3 minutes until thick, stirring continuously. Remove from the heat and add the egg yolks blended with the sugar. Return to the heat for a moment to thicken the sauce and then cool slightly.

Remove the beans and greaseproof paper from the flan and spoon in the filling.

For the topping: Whisk the egg whites with an electric or rotary whisk until they form sitff peaks and add the sugar a teaspoonful at a time, whisking well after each addition. Spoon the meringue over the lemon filling being careful to spread it right up to the edge of the pastry and leaving no air spaces. Return to the oven and reduce the heat to 325 deg.F, 160 deg.C, gas mark 3 for about 30 minutes or until a pale golden brown.

Serve the pie either warm or cold. Serves 6.

—English Custard Tart—

ENGLISH CUSTARD TART

PASTRY:
4 oz (100 g) plain flour
1 oz (25 g) margarine
1 oz (25 g) lard
About 4 teaspoons cold water to mix
CUSTARD:
2 eggs
1 oz (25 g) caster sugar
½ pint (300 ml) milk
A little grated nutmeg

Heat the oven to 425 deg.F, 220 deg.C, gas mark 7 with a baking sheet in it.

Prepare the pastry as usual (see p 60) roll out and line an enamel, tin or foil 7 inch (17.5 cm) flan tin. Fill with baking beans and bake blind for 20 minutes. Remove the beans.

For the custard, beat the eggs and sugar together until blended and then stir in the milk. Pour into the pastry case and sprinkle the top with a little nutmeg. Place in the oven on the hot baking sheet, then reduce the heat to 350 deg.F, 180 deg.C, gas mark 4 and bake for 40-45 minutes or until the filling is set and a pale golden brown. Serve warm on the day that it is made. Serves 4 to 6.

COOK'S TIP. As a variation, add 2 oz (50 g) mixed dried fruit and some freshly grated lemon rind.

BEST BREAD AND BUTTER PUDDING

COOK'S TIP. So good that my children will even go to the fridge and eat it cold if there has been any left! I know that it serves 4 but I must admit that I double up on the amount for my family if it follows a light first course. Use orange instead of lemon if desired.

6 to 8 slices thin bread, well
    buttered and crusts removed
4 oz (100 g) dried fruit
Grated rind of 1 lemon or orange
2 oz (50 g) brown sugar
½ pint (300 ml) milk
1 egg

Butter really well a shallow 1½ pint (900 ml) pie dish. Cut each slice of bread into 3 and arrange half the bread, butter side down, in the dish. Cover with most of the fruit, lemon rind, half the sugar and then top with the remaining bread and butter, butter side uppermost. Sprinkle with the rest of the fruit, lemon rind and sugar.

Blend the milk and egg and strain over the pudding, Leave to soak for at least half an hour, but it is really best to leave it for about 2 hours.

Bake at 350 deg.F, 180 deg.C, gas mark 4 for 40 minutes or until puffy, pale golden brown and set firm. Serve at once. Serves 4.

MINCE PIE

8 oz (225 g) plain flour
Generous pinch salt
3 oz (75 g) margarine, chilled and
    cut in ½ inch (1.25 cm) cubes
3 oz (75 g) lard, chilled and cut in
    ½ inch (1.25 cm) cubes
About ¼ pint (150 ml) cold water
1 lb (450 g) jar of mincemeat
Milk
Caster sugar

Sift the flour and salt into a mixing bowl. Add the cubes of margarine and lard and just enough cold water to mix to a firm pastry, using a sharp knife. On a lightly floured surface roll out the pastry to a strip ½ inch (1.25 cm) thick and 6 inches (15 cm) wide. Fold pastry in 3 and give it a quarter turn to the left. Roll out again into a strip and fold in 3. Wrap the pastry in greaseproof paper and chill in the refrigerator for 30 minutes.

Divide the pastry into 2 portions, one slightly larger than the other. Roll out smaller portion to a ¼ inch (5 mm) thick circle and use it to line a 10 inch (25 cm) pie plate (preferably made of enamel, tin or foil). Spoon the mincemeat into the dish.

Roll out the remaining pastry to a circle ¼ inch (5 mm) thick. Brush the edges of the pastry already on the pie plate with milk and cover the mincemeat filling with the second pastry circle. Press edges together to seal, trim off excess pastry and crimp edges to make a decorative finish. Place in the refrigerator to chill for 10 minutes.

Brush the top of the pie with milk and place in the oven preheated to 425 deg.F, 220 deg.C, gas mark 7. Bake for 25 minutes or until the pastry is golden brown. Sprinkle with caster sugar and serve warm. Serves 8.

COOK'S TIP. Making one large pie means that you have lots of filling and not too much pastry. Use a cheaper hard margarine for the pastry rather than one of the soft more expensive kinds. Delicious served warm with cream or brandy butter.

CHRISTMAS PUDDING

2 oz (50 g) self-raising flour
Good pinch mixed spice
Good pinch grated nutmeg
Good pinch salt
4 oz (100 g) currants
4 oz (100 g) sultanas
4 oz (100 g) stoned raisins
3 oz (75 g) fresh white
    breadcrumbs
3 oz (75 g) shredded suet
1 oz (25 g) chopped mixed peel
1 oz (25 g) almonds, blanched
1 small cooking apple
1 rounded tablespoon marmalade
3 oz (75 g) grated carrot
4 oz (100 g) soft brown sugar
2 eggs

—Best Bread and Butter Pudding—

—Mince Pie—

Grease a 1½ pint (900 ml) pudding basin.

Sift together the flour, spices and salt. Put the currants and sultanas in a large bowl, roughly chop the raisins and add with the breadcrumbs, suet and peel.

Roughly chop the almonds. Peel the apple and coarsely grate, add to the bowl with the almonds, marmalade and carrot. Stir in the spiced flour and sugar. Mix well together. Lightly beat the eggs and stir into the mixture.

Turn into the greased basin, cover the top with greaseproof paper and a foil lid. Simmer gently for 6 hours. Lift out of the pan, leaving the greaseproof and foil in place. Cool, cover with a fresh foil lid and store.

Simmer for about 3 hours on Christmas day. Serves 8.

COOK'S TIP. When the pudding is cooked, cool and then cover with a new piece of foil. Store in a cool place until Christmas day then boil for a further 3 hours or so.

CHRISTMAS PUNCH

COOK'S TIP. It is important not to forget to chill the dry cider and wine as the punch must be served really cold.

1 bottle dry cider
1 bottle dry white wine
Thinly cut lemon peel
1 wine glass sherry
1 wine glass brandy
Thin slices of orange, lemon and
     apple

Chill the dry cider and the white wine.

Place the lemon peel in a large jug or bowl with the sherry and leave to stand for 30 minutes before use.

Add the dry cider, wine and brandy and stir lightly to mix, add the slices of fruit. Serves 16 glasses.

COLD DESSERTS

A tip for preparing the mousses which follow in this section. When folding cream and/or stiffly beaten egg whites into cold mousses, you must ensure that the mousse base is on the point of setting, with the consistency of unbeaten egg white. In hot weather it may be necessary to stir it over ice to reach this stage. If the cream and egg white is folded into the mixture too soon, the mousse will separate out to jelly at the bottom and froth on the top.

—*Apple Jelly with Grapes*—

BARBADOS CREAM

COOK'S TIP. A great favourite with many viewers. Yogurt is the ingredient that gives it its beautifully fresh taste.

½ pint (300 ml) double cream
1 pint (600 ml) plain yoghurt
Soft brown sugar

Lightly whip the cream, blend in the yogurt, turn into a 1½ pint (900 ml) glass dish or 6 small glasses and sprinkle with a ¼ inch (0.60 cm) layer of sugar.
 Put in the refrigerator and chill overnight. Sprinkle again with sugar before serving well chilled. Serves 6.

ORANGE YOGHURT PUDDING

11 oz (300 g) can mandarin
*   oranges*
½ oz (12.5 g) powdered gelatine
2½ oz (62 g) caster sugar
1 lb (450 g) carton natural yoghurt
Finely grated rind and juice of a
*   lemon*
¼ pint (150 ml) double cream

Drain the juice from the mandarins, place in a small bowl with the gelatine and leave to soak for 3 minutes.
 Place the bowl over a pan of hot water and leave until the gelatine dissolves, then stir in the sugar and leave to cool.

Put the yoghurt, lemon rind and juice in a large bowl and stir in the gelatine mixture. Leave until starting to set.

Lightly whip the cream and fold into the mixture with most of the mandarins. Pour into a serving dish and leave to set. Decorate with the remaining mandarin orange segments. Serves 6.

APPLE JELLY WITH GRAPES

COOK'S TIP. To turn out a jelly, first dip the mould quickly into very hot water. Put a plate on top of it and turn sharply upside down. If you have previously wetted the plate you will be able to slide the jelly into a central position should it not land in the middle of the plate. The apple juice can be replaced with cider: both are good. Serve the jelly chilled.

1 packet lime jelly
1/4 pint (150 ml) boiling water
1/2 pint (300 ml) apple juice
8 oz (225 g) large green grapes

Dissolve the jelly in the boiling water. Stir in the apple juice.

Halve the grapes and remove all the pips.

Pour 1/3 of the liquid into the jelly mould and stir in the grapes. Leave to set in the refrigerator, then pour in the remaining jelly. Should this have started to set, heat it slightly so that it melts before pouring it into the mould. Leave until set and thoroughly chill before turning out and serving Serves 4.

SUMMER PUDDING

COOK'S TIP. The very same fruit filling can be served on its own with fresh cream as a rich red fruit salad. If the suggested fruits are not available use loganberries and other currants with either fresh or frozen fruit.

—Summer Pudding—

6-8 large slices of white bread
3/4 lb (350 g) rhubarb
1/2 lb (225 g) blackcurrants
1/2 lb (225 g) granulated sugar
6 tablespoons water
1/2 lb (225 g) strawberries
1/2 lb (225 g) raspberries

Cut the crusts from the bread and put aside one slice for the top. Use the remainder of the bread to line the base and sides of a 2 pint (a good litre) round, fairly shallow dish.

Cut the rhubarb into 1/2 inch (1.25 cm) pieces and put with the blackcurrants in a saucepan. Add the sugar and water and bring to the boil. Simmer until barely tender, stirring: this will only take a few minutes. Add the strawberries and raspberries and cook for a further minute.

Turn the mixture into the dish, reserving a little of the juice. Place a slice of bread on top and bend over the top of the slaced bread at the sides towards the centre. Put a saucer on top pressing down a little until the juice rises to the top of the dish. Spoon the juice remaining in the pan down the side of the dish to make sure that every slice is really well soaked and not left white.

Leave to soak until quite cold and then chill overnight in the refrigerator. Turn out just before serving and serve with lots of cream. Serves 4 to 6.

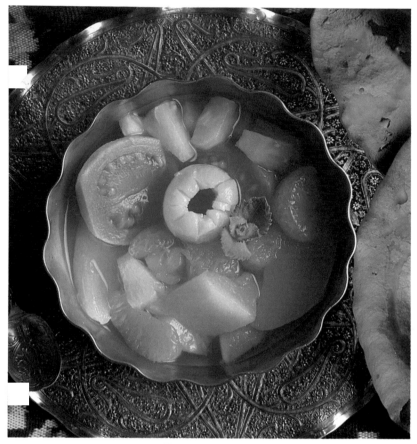

—Tropical Indian Salad—

CHINESE DESSERT FRUITS

Combine the melon and lychees the day before and chill well. Just before serving add the ginger and kiwi fruit.

1 Galia or honeydew melon
1 can lychees
A few pieces of stem ginger in
   syrup
1 kiwi fruit

Cut the melon in half and remove all the seeds. Scoop ball shapes out of the melon with a melon baller. Put in a bowl with the contents of a can of lychees, cover and chill.

Slip the melon cases into a polythene bag and chill ready to use as a container for the fruit.

Next day add a few pieces of chopped stem ginger, about 3 tablespoons. Peel the kiwi fruit and slice and add to the fruit. Blend well and pile into the melon shells.

Serve chilled with no cream. Decorate with a fresh flower if you like. Serves 6.

FRESH FRUIT SORBET

Looks pretty decorated with fresh fruit or sprigs of mint or borage.

1 lb (450 g) raspberries,
   loganberries, blackcurrants,
   gooseberries or blackberries or
   6 large lemons
6 oz (175 g) caster sugar
1/2 pint (300 ml) water
2 egg whites

Prepare your chosen fruit as follows: For raspberries and logan-berries purée the fruit in an electric blender, then sieve to remove all pips.

For blackcurrants, goose-berries and blackberries, cook the fruit in half the water until tender, cool slightly, then purée in an electric blender or sieve and cool.

For lemons, simply squeeze out the juice.

Now make the syrup. Dissolve the sugar in the water, cool and add to the fruit purée or juice. Pour into a flat shallow tray or container and freeze until a mushy consistency. When this stage is reached whisk the egg whites until thick and foamy.

Fold into the mushy fruit mixture. Taste and if liked add lemon juice before freezing until the sorbet is firm. This will take several hours.

Leave to thaw at room temperature for about 15 minutes before scooping out to serve. Serves 8.

MOUSSE AU CITRON

2 large lemons
1/2 oz (12.5 g) gelatine
3 tablespoons water
3 eggs, separated
3-4 oz (75-100 g) caster sugar or
   to taste
1/4 pint (150 ml) double cream,
   whipped

Finely grate the rind and squeeze the juice from the lemons. Place the gelatine and water in a small bowl or cup. Stand for 3 minutes until it becomes spongy, then stand bowl in a pan of simmering water and let the gelatine dissolve. Keep warm.

Put the egg yolks, lemon juice and rind with the sugar in a large bowl, stand over a pan of simmering water and whisk until thick and creamy: this will take about 10 minutes. Remove from the heat and continue whisking until cool, then pour in the gelatine, whisking all the time until well blended.

Whisk the egg whites with an electric or hand rotary whisk until fairly stiff, then fold in first the cream then the lemon mixture until everything is smoothly blended.

Pour into a 2½ pint (1.4 l) dish, smooth the top and leave in a cool place to set. Serves 6.

BLACKBERRY MOUSSE

1 lb (450 g) blackberries
4 oz (100 g) caster sugar
Juice of 1 small lemon
3 tablespoons cold water
½ oz (12.5 g) gelatine
¼ pint (150 ml) double cream
2 egg whites

Wash and pick over the blackberries and put in a saucepan with the sugar and lemon juice. Place over a low heat and simmer gently for about 10 minutes with the lid on until the blackberries are soft and the juice is running out.

Put the water in a small bowl or cup and sprinkle over the gelatine.

Soak for 5 minutes.

Take the fruit from the heat and stir in the soaked gelatine until it has dissolved. Sieve the fruit into a large bowl to make a purée and leave on one side until beginning to thicken and quite cold.

Lightly whisk all but one tablespoon of the cream and whisk the egg whites with a hand or electric whisk until stiff. Fold the whisked cream and egg whites into the purée until blended and turn into a 2 pint (1 l) glass serving dish. Swirl the last spoonful of cream into the centre of the mousse and leave in a cool place until set. Serves 6.

COOK'S TIP. Blackberries will give a superb strong flavour to mousses and team deliciously with apples in pies or crumbles. The best thing about them is that they are free, so make as much use of them as you can, while they last.

ROSY RED FRUIT SALAD

1 large orange
4 cloves
1 lb (450 g) blackcurrants
½ lb (225 g) blackberries
6 oz (175 g) granulated sugar
¼ pint (150 ml) water
8 oz (225 g) raspberries
1 lb (450 g) fresh pears, peeled, cored and sliced

Cut strips of peel from the orange, stick in the cloves and place in a saucepan with the blackcurrants, blackberries, sugar and water, cover and simmer gently for 10 minutes or until tender.

Turn into a bowl, remove and discard the orange peel, cut the orange into segments. Leave to cool, then chill thoroughly.

Stir in the raspberries, pears and orange just before serving. Serves 6.

COOK'S TIP. This uses mostly frozen fruit and is especially good served with lightly whipped cream or ice cream.

TROPICAL INDIAN FRUIT SALAD

A very easy and suitable dessert to follow curry is a chilled fruit salad.

Buy cans of some tropical fruits. Choose a selection from guavas, pineapple, paw paw, lychees, mandarin oranges and mangoes. These are available from Indian food shops and specialist shops. Mix together in a glass bowl and chill for at least 12 hours. Serve with cream.

—Chinese Dessert Fruits—

SPECIAL ICE CREAM

COOK'S TIP. In my previous family recipe books I have included some of the variations of this ice cream, but here are all the combinations together. It is a superb ice cream, very rich and creamy, and needs no whisking during freezing. This means that the water crystals which appear with French custard-based ice cream are prevented from forming. The ice cream goes into the freezer thick and creamy and just needs to be frozen and solidified.

4 eggs, separated
4 oz (100 g) caster sugar
½ pint (300 ml) whipping cream
Vanilla essence (optional)

Whisk the yolks in a small bowl until blended. In a larger bowl whisk the egg whites with a hand rotary or electric whisk until stiff. Then whisk in the sugar a teaspoonful at a time. The whites will get stiffer and stiffer as the sugar is added. Blend in the egg yolks until no streaks of colour remain. Whisk the cream until it forms soft peaks and then fold into the mixture and add vanilla essence if liked.

Turn into a 2½ pint (1.4 l) container, cover, label and freeze until frozen solid. Leave to thaw at room temperature for 5 minutes then serve in scoops in small glasses or dishes.

ORANGE CHOCOLATE CHIP:
Add about 2 oz (50 g) crushed cholate orange sticks to the ice cream before freezing.

LEMON:
Use double cream instead of whipping cream. Whisk this with the grated rind and juice of 2 lemons until it forms soft peaks, then fold into the mixture.

PINEAPPLE:
Use double cream instead of whipping cream. Cut the flesh

—Orange and Chocolate Chip—   *—Lemon—*   *—Pineapple—*

from a small pineapple. Add the juice of a small lemon and 2 oz (50 g) icing sugar. Purée in a blender then freeze until just set. Fold into the ice cream just before freezing.

TUTTI FRUTTI:
Add 4 oz (100 g) chopping glacé cherries, raisins and dried apricots, soaked overnight in 4 tablespoons (60 ml) brandy to plump them up. Fold into the ice cream just before freezing.

FRESH MINT:
Add a handful of finely chopped mint with a little caster sugar to the ice cream before freezing.

AMERICAN MINT:
Add half a bar of crushed seaside rock to the ice cream before freezing. It gives a lovely crunchy taste and speckles the ice cream with pink.

BLACKCURRANT:
Use double cream instead of whipping cream. Add about 6 tablespoons (90 ml) undiluted blackcurrant drink to the cream and fold into the mixture.

COFFEE, RUM AND RAISIN:
Add 2 tablespoons (30 ml) coffee essence and 3 tablespoons (45 ml) rum to about 4 oz (100 g) chopped, stoned raisins and soak overnight. Fold into the ice cream just before freezing.

RASPBERRY, STRAWBERRY OR GOOSEBERRY:
Use double cream instead of whipping cream. Stir in ½ pint (300 ml) fruit purée to the ice cream just before freezing and, if you think it is necessary add a little colouring.

—Tutti Frutti—   —Fresh Mint—   —Toffee Butterscotch—

TOFFEE BUTTERSCOTCH:
Add about 4 oz (100 g) crushed butterscotch to the ice cream before freezing.

CASSATA

A beautiful looking traditional Italian ice cream.

2 oz (50 g) mixed cherries, raisins, angelica and dried apricots, finely chopped
2 tablespoons brandy
4 eggs, separated
4 oz (100 g) caster sugar
½ pint (300 ml) double cream
¼ pint (150 ml) raspberry purée
About 2 tablespoons coffee essence or to taste

Put the finely chopped fruit in a small bowl with the brandy, cover and leave to stand overnight.

Whisk the yolks in a small bowl until blended. In a larger bowl whisk the egg whites with a hand rotary or electric whisk on high speed until stiff then whisk in the sugar a teaspoon at a time; the egg whites will get stiffer and stiffer as the sugar is added.

Whisk the cream until it forms soft peaks and then fold into the meringue mixture with the egg yolks.

Divide the ice cream into three portions of varying size. To the largest portion add the raspberry purée and fold in until thoroughly mixed. Flavour the middle portion with coffee essence to give a good flavour and colour. Finely mix the soaked fruit into the smallest quantity of ice cream.

Put all the bowls in the deep freeze for 30 minutes. Take a 2¼ pint (1.3 l) toughened glass bowl and chill in the freezer with the ice cream.

Take out the bowl and the raspberry ice cream and use this to evenly coat the base and sides of the bowl to within one inch (2.5 cm) of the rim. Return to the freezer for 30 minutes. Then take out with the coffee ice cream and spread this over the raspberry ice cream. Return to the freezer for a further 30 minutes.

Remove the tutti frutti ice cream and stir lightly to mix, then put into the centre of the bowl, cover and return to the freezer. Chill for several hours.

To serve: Remove from the freezer and leave to stand at room temperature for 10 minutes. Wipe the bowl with a warm cloth and then run a knife around the bowl and turn out onto a plate. Serve cut in wedges. Serves 8 to 10

SYLLABUB

COOK'S TIP. Quite the easiest of puddings to make, very rich and best served in small individual dishes or glasses. Another attractive way of serving is in small old-fashioned coffee cups with the spoon in the saucer.

1 large lemon
4 tablespoons fairly sweet sherry
2 tablespoons brandy
2 oz (50 g) caster sugar
½ pint (300 ml) double cream
lemon slices to decorate

Squeeze the juice from the lemon and put in a bowl with the sherry and brandy, add the sugar and stir until dissolved. Pour in the cream and whisk the mixture until it forms soft peaks when the whisk is lifted out. Spoon into individual glasses and leave in a cool place until required. Top each glass with a slice of fresh lemon.

   This syllabub may be made a day in advance as it keeps very well. Serves 4.

CARAMEL CUSTARD

COOK'S TIP. Never turn out the caramel custard until the moment of serving. The caramel loses its gloss and colour with standing when turned out.

CARAMEL:
3 oz (75 g) granulated sugar
3 tablespoons water

CUSTARD:
4 eggs
1½ oz (37.5 g) caster sugar
A few drops of vanilla essence
1 pint (600 ml) milk

To make caramel: Put the sugar and water in a heavy saucepan and dissolve the sugar over a low heat. Bring to the boil and boil until the syrup is pale golden brown. Remove from the heat and quickly pour into the bottom of a 1½ pint (900 ml) charlotte mould or soufflée dish.

—Brown Sugar Meringues—

For the custard: mix together eggs, sugar and vanilla essence. Warm the milk in a saucepan over a low heat until it is hand-hot, then pour it onto the egg mixture, stirring constantly.

   Butter the sides of the mould or dish above the caramel. Strain the custard into it and place in a roasting tin half filled with hot water. Bake in an oven preheated to 300 deg.F, 150 deg.C, gas mark 2 for 1½ hours or until a knife inserted in the centre comes out clean.

   Do not worry if the custard takes longer to cook than the time given; it will set eventually. Don't increase the oven temperature or the custard will have bubbles in it.

   Remove the custard from the oven and leave to cool completely for at least 12 hours or overnight in the refrigerator. Turn out carefully onto a flat serving dish. Serves 4.

BROWN SUGAR MERINGUES

COOK'S TIP. Don't make the mistake of using all brown sugar as often the result will be rather sticky meringues.

4 egg whites
4 oz (100 g) light soft brown sugar
4 oz (100 g) caster sugar
Whipping cream

Heat the oven to 200 deg.F, 100 deg.C, gas mark ¼ or Low. Line two baking sheets with silicone paper.

   Place the egg whites in a large bowl and whisk on high speed with an electric or hand rotary whisk until they form soft peaks.

   Sieve the two sugars together until evenly mixed. Add a teaspoonful at a time to the egg whites, whisking well after each addition until all the sugar has been added.

   Using two dessertspoons, spoon the meringue out onto the

baking sheets, putting ten meringues on each tray.

Bake in the oven for three to four hours until the meringues are firm and dry and will lift easily from the paper. They will be pale brown. Leave to cool.

Whisk the cream until thick and use to sandwich the meringue shells together. Makes ten meringues.

CHOCOLATE MERINGUE GÂTEAU

COOK'S TIP. This is an impressive looking meringue gâteau which can be made the day before it is needed as it improves with keeping for a day.

3 egg whites
6 oz (175 g) caster sugar

CHOCOLATE FILLING:
¼ pint (150 ml) milk
2 oz (50 g) caster sugar
2 oz (50 g) plain chocolate
3 egg yolks
1 level teaspoon cornflour
6 oz (175 g) unsalted butter, softened

TOPPING:
¼ pint (150 ml) double cream, whipped
12 Maltesers

Heat the oven to 300 deg.F, 150 deg.C, gas mark 2 and line 2 large baking sheets with non-stick silicone paper.

Meringue: put the egg whites in a large bowl and whisk with a hand rotary or an electric whisk until stiff. Gradually whisk in the sugar a teaspoonful at a time. Spread the meringue in 2 circles 8 inches (20 cm) in diameter on the baking sheets and bake for 1 hour in the oven, then turn off the heat and leave in the oven to cool.

Chocolate filling: First make the chocolate custard sauce. Put the milk, sugar and chocolate broken into small pieces in a basin

—Chocolate Meringue Gâteau—

and place over a pan of hot water. Heat gently until the chocolate has melted and blended with the milk. Stir a little of the hot liquid onto the egg yolks, blend with the cornflour and then add to the remaining chocolate mixture and stir until thickened. This will take about 5 to 10 minutes and is ready when the sauce will coat the back of the spoon. Remove from the heat and leave to become quite cold.

Cream the butter and beat in the chocolate sauce. If by any chance the butter cream should curdle because the butter and chocolate custard are not at the same temperature, warm the bowl slightly by standing in hot water and then beat well.

Spread half the chocolate cream on one meringue layer then cover with the other meringue. Spread the remaining chocolate cream over this and mark attractively with a palette knife.

Topping: Pipe the double cream in 12 large rosettes around the edge or over the top of the gâteau and press a Malteser into the centre of each rosette. Keep in the refrigerator until required and then allow to stand at room temperature for 2 to 3 hours before serving. Serves 6.

PAVLOVA

3 egg whites
6 oz (175 g) caster sugar
1 teaspoon vinegar
1 level teaspoon cornflour
½ pint (300 ml) whipped whipping
   cream
8 oz (225 g) frozen raspberries,
   just thawed
A little castor sugar to sweeten

Lay a sheet of silicone paper (non-stick vegetable parchment) on a baking tray and mark an 8 inch (20 cm) circle on it. Heat the oven to 325 deg.F, 160 deg.C, gas mark 3.

Whisk the egg whites with a hand rotary or electric whisk until stiff, then whisk in the sugar a spoonful at a time. Blend the vinegar with the cornflour and whisk into the egg whites with the last spoonful of sugar.

Spread the meringue out to cover the circle on the baking tray, building up the sides so that they are higher than the centre.

Put in the centre of the oven, turn the heat down to 300 deg.F, 150 deg.C, gas mark 2 and bake for 1 hour. The pavlova will be a pale creamy colour rather than white. Turn the oven off and leave the pavlova to become quite cold in the oven.

Remove from the baking tray and place on a serving dish .

Fold the cream and raspberries together lightly and sweeten to taste. Pile into the centre of the pavlova and leave to stand for an hour in the refrigerator before serving. Serves 6.

COOK'S TIP. This is very like meringue but the middle is lovely and soft. For a change, fill the centre with tinned cherry pie filling. Use a 15 oz (425 g) can flavoured with a little Kirsch and decorate with whipped cream.

ZABAGLIONE

6 tablespoons Marsala or Madeira
4 oz (100 g) caster sugar
4 egg yolks

COOK'S TIP. Such a simple recipe. It can be made with whole eggs, which gives a very light texture, but is not so firm. If you have neither Marsala nor Madeira use sweet sherry.

Stand an oven glass bowl over a pan of simmering water. Measure the wine and sugar into the bowl, leave to get really warm but not hot. Add the yolks and at once begin whisking until light and foamy. Pour into four large stemmed glasses, preferably with a wide brim.

Serve at once with thin sweet biscuits such as langue de chat. Serves 4.

GRAPEFRUIT CHEESECAKE

COOK'S TIP. If liked this cheesecake may be frozen. Open freeze until solid without crust, overwrap and return to the freezer, use within 3 months. Leave to thaw overnight in the refrigerator, then put on the crust, chill for 1 hour then turn out and decorate with grapefruit segments. The cheesecake is equally delicious made with frozen orange juice, decorated with sliced oranges. You can also use tinned juice, but it is not as nice. A green kiwi fruit (it used to be called Chinese gooseberry) sliced makes a different, more special decoration for a party.

Don't make this in a loose-bottomed cake tin, as the cheesecake mixture could seep out before it has set. The cheesecake is poured into the cake tin and left to set. Then the biscuit crust is put on top, so when you reverse the cheesecake out of the tin the biscuit is underneath.

½ oz (15 g) gelatine
¼ pint (150 ml) cold water
6 fl oz (175 g) can concentrated
   frozen grapefruit juice
12 oz (350 g) rich cream cheese
4 oz (100 g) caster sugar
¼ pint (150 ml) double cream,
   whipped

BISCUIT TOPPING:
2 oz (50 g) ginger biscuits,
   crushed
2 oz (50 g) digestive biscuits,
   crushed
1 oz (25 g) demerara sugar
2 oz (50 g) butter, melted
Fresh grapefruit segments to
   decorate

Soak the gelatine in cold water for about 5 minutes, then stand the bowl in a pan of simmering water and leave until the gelatine has dissolved and become quite clear. Remove from the heat, add the grapefruit juice and leave to become cold and nearly set.

Mix the cream cheese with the sugar and a little of the thick but not set grapefruit juice. Beat well and add the rest of the grapefruit juice mixing well. Lastly fold in the whipped cream.

Turn into an 8 inch (20 cm) cake tin with the base lightly greased then lined with a circle of greaseproof paper. Chill in the refrigerator until set. Mix together the crushed biscuits, demerara sugar and butter. Spread over the cheesecake and chill for a further hour.

Dip the tin in very hot water for a moment to loosen the set cheesecake then turn out and decorate with fresh grapefruit segments. Serves 6 to 8.

BLACK FOREST CHEESECAKE

COOK'S TIP. Black Forest cheesecake is cooked, so expect it to sink slightly in the centre on cooling. For an extra special occasion, fill the dip with cherries in a sauce, laced with a couple of tablespoons (30 ml) kirsch.

6 digestive biscuits, crushed
1 1/2 oz (40 g) butter, melted
3 eggs, separated
4 oz (100 g) caster sugar
1 lb (450 g) cream cheese at room temperature
1/2 teaspoon (2.5 ml) vanilla essence
15 oz (425 g) can black cherries, preferably stoned
1 rounded teaspoon arrowroot

Heat the oven to 350 deg.F, 180 deg.C, gas mark 4. Lightly butter and flour a 7 inch (17.5 cm) round loose-bottomed cake tin.

Blend the biscuits with the melted butter and press firmly over the base of the cake tin.

Whisk the egg yolks and sugar until light and creamy and stir in the cream cheese and vanilla essence until well blended. Whisk the egg whites using a hand, rotary or electric whisk until stiff, fold into the cheese mixture and spoon into the tin. Bake in the oven for about 1 1/2 hours, until well risen and pale golden brown and shrinking slightly away from the sides of the tin, then turn off the heat and leave in the oven for a further 15 to 30 minutes. Remove from the oven and leave to cool in

the tin until quite cold. Then remove the cake from the tin and place on a serving dish.

Drain the cherries and, if necessary, stone. Reserve the juice and blend 1/4 pint (150 ml) with the arrowroot in a small saucepan and then slowly bring to the boil, stirring until thickened. Add the cherries and mix lightly. Spoon over the cheesecake and leave to cool completely. Chill before serving. Serves 6 to 8.

AMERICAN CHEESECAKE

A rich cheesecake that's delicious even without the topping.

FLAN CASE:
3 oz (75 g) butter
1 1/2 oz (40 g) demerara sugar
6 oz (175 g) digestive biscuits, crushed

FILLING:
4 oz (100 g) cream cheese
Juice of 1 1/2 lemons
1/2 pint (300 ml) double cream, lightly whipped with a little sugar to taste

TOPPING:
6 oz (175 g) strawberries
4 tablespoons redcurrant jelly

For the flan case: melt the butter in a saucepan, stir in the sugar and crushed biscuits and mix very well. Press over the base and sides of an 8 inch (20 cm) flan ring on a plate or a loose bottomed flan tin, using a metal spoon.

For the filling: cream the cheese with the lemon juice and a little whipped cream until soft and then fold in the remaining cream. Turn into the flan case and leave in a cool place to set.

Hull and halve the strawberries and arrange on top.

Heat the redcurrant jelly in a small saucepan until it has melted and then spread over the strawberries. Leave to set. Serves 6.

—Pavlova—

THOMAS'S FLAN

FLAN CASE:
2oz (50 g) butter or margarine
1 level tablespoon sugar
8 digestive biscuits, crushed

FILLING:
6 oz (175 g) can condensed milk
1/4 pint (150 ml) double cream
Juice of 2 lemons
Halved grapes to decorate

Melt the butter or margarine in a saucepan, remove from the heat and stir in the sugar and crushed biscuits. Mix well and press the mixture over the base and sides of a 7 inch (17.5 cm) flan ring or loose-bottomed flan tin. Spread evenly using a metal tablespoon.

Put the condensed milk, cream and lemon juice in a bowl and whisk the mixture together until well blended. Pour into the flan case.

Chill for at least 4 hours in the refrigerator. Before serving remove the flan ring and decorate with halved grapes. Serves 4-6.

COOK'S TIP. This is a flan so easy to make that it is ideal for children's cooking. It is named after my elder son who makes it regularly. Delicious after a Sunday roast.

CRÈME BRÛLÉE

COOK'S TIP. This dessert is sheer luxury, and not difficult to make at all. Choose a shallow dish that will withstand being put under the grill. Make the cream custard part a day ahead, then put the sugar topping on 3 hours before serving.

4 egg yolks
1 oz (25 g) caster or vanilla sugar
1 pint (600 ml) single cream
About 2 oz (50 g) demerara sugar

Heat the oven to 325 deg.F, 160 deg.C, gas mark 3. Butter well a shallow 1½ pint (900 ml) ovenproof dish, or 6-8 small individual dishes. Beat the egg yolks with the sugar. (If you haven't any vanilla sugar but like the flavour, then add a little vanilla essence.) Heat the cream to scalding and gradually beat in the egg yolks.

Pour the mixture into the dish or dishes, stand in a baking tin half filled with warm water and bake in the oven for 45 minutes or until set. If using small dishes they will need only 25-30 minutes cooking time. Take out and leave to cool.

Sprinkle the top thickly with demerara sugar and put under a hot grill. Watch carefully until the sugar melts and then caramelizes to a golden brown. Remove and chill before serving for at least 3 hours. This gives time for the hard caramel topping to become less hard and easier to crack and serve. If you leave it considerably longer the caramel will melt and soften, which is not nearly so attractive and doesn't taste so good.

RASPBERRY AND STRAWBERRY BRÛLÉE

8 oz (225 g) strawberries
8 oz (225 g) raspberries
About 2 oz (50 g) icing sugar
3-4 tablespoons brandy
1/2 pint (300 ml) double cream
Light soft brown sugar

Hull the strawberries and if very large cut in half. Place in a bowl with the raspberries and sprinkle with icing sugar. Cover and chill thoroughly for several hours.

Divide the mixture between six individual ovenproof dishes or fill one large overproof dish, capacity about 2½ pints (1.4 l). Leave plenty of room for the cream to bubble up in the cooking.

Sprinkle the brandy over the fruit. Lightly whip the cream until it just forms soft peaks and spread over the top of the fruit. Scatter the sugar quite thickly, but at random, over the top of the cream so that not all the surface is covered. Put under a hot grill until the sugar goes a deep golden brown. Serve at once. Serves 6-8.

CHOCOLATE AND ORANGE MOUSSE

1/2 oz (12.5 g) gelatine
1 tablespoon water
Rind and juice of 1 orange
8 oz (225 g) plain chocolate
5 eggs, separated
4 oz (100 g) caster sugar
1/2 pint (300 ml) whipping cream, whipped

–Helen's Chocolate Layer Pudding–

—Chocolate and Orange Mousse—

Soak the gelatine in the water with the rind and juice of the orange in a small cup or basin and leave until it becomes spongy. Then stand in a pan of simmering water until it has completely dissolved and is runny.

Put another basin containing the chocolate broken into small pieces over the pan of hot water and leave until melted. Add the 5 egg yolks and stir until smooth.

Pour the gelatine into a small mixing bowl and stir in the chocolate mixture and leave for about 5 minutes until cool but not set.

Meanwhile whisk the egg whites using a hand electric or rotary whisk until frothy then add the sugar a teaspoonful at a time whisking all the time until you have the consistency of a meringue. Quickly fold in the chocolate, yolk, orange and gelatine mixture then fold in half the whipped cream. Turn into individual glass dishes, cover with cling film and chill until set. Then decorate with chocolate and swirls remaining whipped cream. Serves 6 to 8.

COOK'S TIP. This is sinfully rich and takes time to make but it is well worth it for a special occasion.

HELEN'S CHOCOLATE LAYER PUDDING

COOK'S TIP. A deliciously rich pudding though not a cheap one. It is also a convenient way of using up leftover bread. Make the bread into crumbs in the blender, but if you haven't got one, use 2-3 day old bread and grate it or rub it through a coarse sieve. Serve in a small glass bowl or 4 individual glasses.

*4 rounded tablespoons drinking chocolate
1 level tablespoon coffee powder
4 oz (100 g) fresh white bread crumbs
4 oz (100 g) demerara sugar
1/2 pint (300 ml) whipping cream chocolate flake bar*

Place the chocolate, coffee powder, breadcrumbs and sugar in a bowl and mix thoroughly. Put the cream in a bowl and whisk with an electric or hand rotary whisk until thick and soft peaks are formed when the whisk is lifted out.

Spread alternate layers of chocolate mixture and cream in a serving dish, starting with the chocolate and finishing with the cream. Leave in a cool place for at least 8-10 hours before serving.

This pudding may be made a day in advance.

Decorate with pieces of chocolate flake before serving. Serves 4.

CHOCOLATE JULIETTE

COOK'S TIP. A very rich confection, so serve in thin slices — they can always come back for more. If I have this for an evening supper party my children are down like lightning next morning to see if there is any left for them!

*8 oz (225 g) milk chocolate
8 oz (225 g) margarine
2 eggs
1 oz caster sugar
8 oz (225 g) 'Nice' biscuits
1/4 pint (150 ml) double cream, whipped
Chocolate buttons or chocolate matchsticks*

Line a small loaf tin 7 1/2 inches (19 cm) by 4 inches (10 cm) by 2 1/2 inches (6 cm) with foil.

Break the chocolate into small pieces and place in a pan with the margarine and heat gently until melted. Beat the eggs and sugar together until blended, then gradually add the chocolate mixture a little at a time. Break the biscuits into 1/2 inch (1.5 cm) pieces and stir into the chocolate mixture. Pack into the tin and smooth the top. Leave to set in the refrigerator for about 6 hours or until firm.

Turn out onto a serving dish and peel off the foil. Cover with the cream and decorate with chocolate buttons or chocolate matchsticks. Serves 8 to 10.

BAKING AND PRESERVING

There are few more pleasant domestic pleasures than that of a kitchen full of the delicious smells of home baking. The bread and cakes you cook in your own oven are always tastier than the ones you buy in a shop. To ensure success, get to know your oven. Buy an oven thermometer to enable you to check the temperature in your oven.

Make sure you have all the equipment you need – enough baking tins in the right sizes, mixing bowls and measuring jugs. Thoroughly grease and line your tins with greaseproof paper to encourage your cakes to leave the tin when they are baked. Before you begin, assemble your ingredients and weigh them out.

FRUIT CAKES

For rich fruit cakes which require long cooking, use a double greaseproof paper and surround the outside of the tin with a double sheet of greaseproof paper, to prevent over-cooking.

— Marmalade Fruitcake —

MARMALADE FRUITCAKE

COOK'S TIP. A first-rate family fruit cake, but don't overdo the marmalade otherwise the fruit will sink to the bottom.

6 oz (175 g) soft margarine
6 oz (175 g) soft brown sugar
12 oz (350 g) mixed dried fruit
3 large eggs, beaten
9 oz (250 g) self-raising flour
2 oz (50 g) glacé cherries,
    quartered
2 level tablespoons chopped
    chunky marmalade

Heat the oven to 325 deg.F, 160 deg.C, gas mark 3. Grease and line an 8 inch (20 cm) round cake tin with greased greaseproof paper.
    Put all the ingredients together in a bowl and mix well until blended. Turn into the tin and spread evenly leaving a slight hollow in the top. Bake just above the centre of the oven for about 2¼ hours; when the cake is pierced with a skewer in the centre it will come out clean. Leave to cool in the tin for 10 minutes, then turn out onto a wire rack and leave until cold.

MINCEMEAT CAKE

COOK'S TIP. As you would expect, this cake is very moist, lightly fruited and, frankly, absolutely delicious. It is a newly invented recipe of mine that I dare not make too often as I enjoy it so much and it is by no means slimming.

5 oz (150 g) soft margarine
5 oz (150 g) caster sugar
2 eggs
8 oz (225 g) self-raising flour
3 oz (75 g) currants
1 lb (450 g) jar mincemeat
1 oz (25 g) flaked almonds

Grease and line with greased greaseproof paper an 8 inch (20 cm) round cake tin. Heat the oven to 325 deg.F, 160 deg.C, gas mark 3.
    Place all the ingredients except the almonds together in a bowl and beat for one minute until blended. Turn into the tin and smooth the top. Arrange the almonds on the top and bake in the oven for about 1¾ hours until golden brown and shrinking away from the sides of the tin. Leave to cool in the tin and then remove the paper and store in an airtight container.

– Special Apple Dessert Cake –

TRADITIONAL CHRISTMAS CAKE

COOK'S TIP. Make this one up to a couple of months before Christmas and keep in a tin. Add the almond paste about 10 days before Christmas, then leave to dry out for 5 to 6 days before covering with royal icing.

4 Eggs.

12 oz (350 g) seedless raisins
12 oz (350 g) sultanas
12 oz (350 g) currants
2 oz (50 g) cut mixed peel
4 oz (100 g) glacé cherries, halved
Grated rind and juice of 1 lemon
2 oz (50 g) blanched almonds,
 chopped
9 oz (250 g) plain flour
Good pinch salt
1 teaspoon mixed spice
8 oz (225 g) butter
8 oz (225 g) soft brown sugar
1 tablespoon black treacle
2 tablespoons brandy

Heat the oven to 300 deg.F, 150 deg.C, gas mark 2. Grease and line with a double thickness of greased greaseproof paper a deep 8 inch (20 cm) round cake tin.

In a bowl mix the dried fruit with the peel, cherries, grated lemon rind and almonds. Sift the flour, salt and spice onto a plate.

In a large bowl cream the butter and sugar until soft and fluffy. Beat in the eggs adding 1 tablespoon flour with each egg. Fold in the remaining flour with the fruit, lemon juice, treacle and brandy.

Turn into the cake tin and smooth the top, leaving a slight hollow in the centre. Bake in the oven for about 3-3½ hours or until cooked and pale golden brown. To test, gently prick with a fine skewer. If it comes out clean, the cake is ready. Leave to cool in the tin, then store in an airtight tin.

SPECIAL APPLE DESSERT CAKE

5 oz (150 g) butter
2 large eggs
8 oz (225 g) caster sugar
1 teaspoon (5 ml) almond essence
8 oz (225 g) self-raising flour
1½ level teaspoons baking
 powder
1½ lb (675 g) cooking apples,
 before peeling
icing sugar

Heat the oven to 325°F, 160°C, gas mark 3. Grease well an 8 inch (20 cm) loose-bottomed cake tin.

Melt the butter in a pan over a medium heat until just runny and pour into a large bowl. Add the eggs, sugar and almond essence and beat well until mixed. Fold in the flour and baking powder. Spread just under two thirds of the mixture in the cake tin. Then straight away peel, core and slice the apples and arrange roughly on top of the mixture. Spread the remaining mixture over the apples. It is difficult to get this last bit of mixture smooth, but don't worry as the blobs even out during cooking.

Bake for about 1½ hours, until the apple is tender when prodded with a skewer. Loosen the sides of the cake with a knife and carefully push the cake out.

Dust over very generously with icing sugar when slightly cooled and serve warm or cold with lots of lightly whipped or thick cream.

Keep covered in the fridge and eat within 4 days. Serves about 12.

CHRISTMAS CAKE WITH PINEAPPLE

COOK'S TIP. This is a really moist, less-rich Christmas cake. It can be made just before Christmas and is best kept fairly cool and used within a month. The pineapple gives a good flavour. Make sure to drain it well and use the juice in a fruit salad or trifle.

2 oz (50 g) glacé cherries
7 oz (200 g) self-raising flour
8 oz (225 g) can pineapple in
    chunks, rings or crushed
    excluding all the juice
5 oz (150 g) butter
4½ oz (112 g) soft brown sugar
2 large eggs, beaten
2 tablespoons milk
12 oz (350 g) mixed dried fruit

Grease an 8 inch (20 cm) round cake tin and line with greased greaseproof paper. Cut cherries in halves and roll in flour. Drain and chop the pineapple very finely.

Cream the butter and sugar together in a mixing bowl. Beat in the eggs, adding a tablespoon of flour with the last amount of egg. Fold in flour, milk and last of all the fruit including the pineapple.

Turn into the prepared tin and place in the centre of the oven preheated to 325 deg.F, 160 deg.C, gas mark 3 and bake for about 2 hours until pale golden brown and shrinking away from the sides of the tin.

Leave to cool in the tin, remove the paper and store in a plastic container in the refrigerator.

SPONGE CAKES

British tea-time would not be the same without the versatile sponge cake. But to show that we are not being completely insular, we include two recipes from the United States: brownies, irresistible for anyone with a sweet-tooth, and Texas she cake, an unusual variation on the traditional brownie recipe.

VICTORIA SANDWICH

COOK'S TIP. One of the classic British cakes. Do not feel you have to use butter. I now use soft margarine for everyday and I find the results excellent.

4 oz (100 g) soft margarine or
    butter
4 oz (100 g) caster sugar
2 large eggs, beaten
4 oz (100 g) self-raising flour
4 tablespoons strawberry jam
2 to 3 teaspoons caster sugar

Heat the oven to 350 deg.F, 180 deg.C, gas mark 4. Grease and line with greased greaseproof paper two 7 inch (17.5 cm) straight-sided sandwich tins.

Cream the margarine and sugar until light and fluffy. Add the egg a little at a time, beating well after each addition. Sieve the flour and add a spoonful with the last amount of egg to prevent it curdling. Fold in the remaining flour with a metal spoon to make a soft drooping consistency. Divide the mixture equally between the tins.

Bake in the oven for 25 to 30 minutes. When the cake is cooked the colour should be a pale golden and the centre of the sponge will spring back into place when lightly pressed with the finger.

Turn the sponges onto a wire rack to cool and remove the paper. When completely cold, sandwich together with strawberry jam and sprinkle with caster sugar.

VARIATIONS
Orange: add the finely grated rind of an orange to the creamed mixture.
Chocolate: replace 1 oz (25 g) of four with 1 oz (25 g) cocoa.
Coffee: dissolve 1 heaped teaspoon instant coffee powder in the beaten eggs before adding to the mixture.

SWISS ROLL

COOK'S TIP. Swiss rolls are traditionally made with plain flour, but I find I always get perfect results with self-raising flour too. Weigh the ingredients very accurately and don't over-whisk the eggs and sugar or you will have difficulty in folding in the flour evenly. Roll up the cake as soon as it comes out of the oven. If it is left to cool it will crack during rolling.

3 eggs, size 2 at room temperature
3 oz (75 g) caster sugar, warmed
3 oz (75 g) self-raising flour

FILLING:
Caster sugar
4 tablespoons raspberry jam

Heat the oven to 425 deg.F, 220 deg.C, gas mark 7 and grease and line a Swiss roll tin 9 by 13 inches (22.5 by 32.5 cm) with greased greaseproof paper.

Whisk the eggs and the sugar together until light and creamy and the whisk leaves a trail when lifted out. Sieve the flour and fold carefully into the mixture with a metal spoon. Turn into the prepared tin and smooth level with the back of the spoon. Bake in the oven for about 10 minutes until the sponge is a golden brown and begins to shrink from the edges of the tin.

While the cake is baking cut a piece of greaseproof paper slightly bigger than the tin and sprinkle with caster sugar. Heat the jam in a small pan until it is just easy to spread: if it is too hot it will soak into the cake.

Invert the Swiss roll onto the sugared paper. Quickly loosen the paper on the bottom of the cake and peel off. Trim all four edges of the sponge and make a score mark an inch (2.5 cm) in from the rolling edge, being careful not to cut right through. This will make the rolling easier. Spread with warm jam, almost to the edges. Fold the narrow strip made by

—*Good Basic Chocolate Cake*—

the score mark down onto the jam and begin rolling, using the paper to keep a firm and even roll. Leave the cake for a few minutes with the paper still around it to allow it to settle, and then lift onto a wire cooling rack. Remove the paper, sprinkle with a little more caster sugar and leave to cool.

FRESH LEMON CAKE

COOK'S TIP. This lemon sponge cake is quick to make and has a crusty lemon topping spooned over it just as it comes out of the oven.

4 oz (100 g) soft margarine
1 level teaspoon baking powder
6 oz (175 g) self-raising flour
6 oz (175 g) caster sugar
2 eggs
4 tablespoons (60 ml) milk
Finely grated rind of 1 lemon

ICING:
Juice of 1 lemon
4 oz (100 g) caster sugar

Heat the oven to 350 deg.F, 180 deg.C, gas mark 4 and grease and line an 8 inch (20 cm) round cake tin with greased greaseproof paper.

Put the margarine, flour, sugar, eggs, milk and lemon rind together in a large bowl and beat well for about 2 minutes. Turn into the tin and bake for 50 to 60 minutes or until the cake has shrunk from the sides of the tin and springs back when pressed with a finger in the centre.

While the cake is baking put

–Lemon Butterfly Cakes–

dust with a little extra icing sugar. Makes 18 butterfly cakes.

GOOD BASIC CHOCOLATE CAKE

1 oz (25 g) cocoa
2 tablespoons hot water
4 oz (100 g) soft margarine
4 oz (100 g) caster sugar
2 large eggs
4 oz (100 g) self-raising flour
1 level teaspoon baking powder

FILLING:
¼ pint (150 ml) whipping cream, whipped

ICING:
1½ oz (40 g) soft margarine
1 oz (25 g) cocoa, sieved
2 tablespoons milk
4 oz (100 g) icing sugar, sieved

Heat the oven to 350 deg.F, 180 deg.C, gas mark 4. Grease and line with greased greaseproof paper two 7 inch (17.5 cm) round sandwich tins.

Blend the cocoa with the hot water in a large bowl and leave to cool. Add the remaining cake ingredients to the bowl and beat with a wooden spoon for 2 to 3 minutes until thoroughly blended.

Turn into the tins and then bake in the oven for 25 to 30 minutes. When cooked the cake will spring back when lightly pressed with the finger.

Turn out, remove the paper and leave to cool on a wire rack. Sandwich the cakes together with cream.

For the icing: Melt the margarine in a small saucepan, stir in the cocoa and cook over a gentle heat for one minute. Remove from the heat and add the milk and icing sugar. Beat well to mix and then leave to cool, stirring occasionally, until the icing has thickened to a spreading consistency. Spread over the top of the cake and swirl attractively with a round bladed knife. Leave to set. Keep covered in the refrigerator.

the lemon juice and sugar in a bowl or cup and stir until blended. When the sponge comes out of the oven, spread the lemon paste over the top while it is still hot. Leave in the tin until quite cold, then turn out, remove the paper and store in an airtight tin.

LEMON BUTTERFLY CAKES

4 oz (100 g) soft margarine
4 oz (100 g) caster sugar
2 large eggs, beaten
Finely grated rind of 1 lemon
4 oz (100 g) self-raising flour
1 level teaspoon baking powder

BUTTER CREAM:
2 oz (50 g) soft margarine
4 oz (100 g) icing sugar
About 2 tablespoons lemon juice

Heat the oven to 400 deg.F, 200 deg.C, gas mark 6. Thoroughly grease 18 deep bun tins.

Place all the cake ingredients together in a bowl and beat well for two minutes until blended and smooth. Divide the mixture equally between the bun tins.

Bake in the oven for 15 to 20 minutes, until a pale golden brown. Turn out and leave to cool on a wire rack.

Now make the butter cream. Beat the margarine in a small bowl until soft and then add the icing sugar and lemon juice and continue to beat until the mixture is light and fluffy. Cut a slice from the top of each cake and cut in half; pipe or spoon a little of the butter cream into the centre of each cake. Arrange the cake wings in the centre of the butter cream and

EXPRESS CHOCOLATE CAKE

6½ oz (187 g) plain flour
2 tablespoons cocoa
1 level teaspoon bicarbonate of
 soda
1 level teaspoon baking powder
5 oz (150 g) caster sugar
2 tablespoons golden syrup
2 eggs, lightly beaten
¼ pint (150 ml) corn oil
¼ pint (150 ml) milk

FUDGE ICING:
3 oz (75 g) butter
2 oz (50 g) cocoa, sieved
About 6 tablespoons milk
8 oz (225 g) icing sugar, sieved

Sieve the flour, cocoa, bicarbonate of soda and baking powder into a large bowl. Make a well in the centre and add the sugar and syrup. Gradually stir in the eggs, oil and milk and beat well to make a smooth batter.

Pour the batter into 2 greased 6 inch (20 cm) sandwich tins lined with greased greaseproof paper. Bake in the oven preheated to 325 deg.F, 160 deg.C, gas mark 3 for 30 to 35 minutes or until the cakes spring back when lightly pressed with a fingertip. Turn cakes out onto a wire rack and leave to cool, removing the paper.

To make the icing: melt the butter in a small pan, stir in the cocoa and cook very gently for 1 minute. Remove the pan from the heat and stir in the milk and icing sugar. Mix well to a spreading consistency. Spread half the icing on one cake, then sandwich the cakes together and spread the remaining icing over the top of the cake. Leave to set. Decorate if liked.

COOK'S TIP. This cake keeps very well when filled with fudge icing. An alternative filling is a layer of apricot jam covered in fresh whipped cream. In this case store covered with clingwrap in the refrigerator and eat within 2 days.

SWISS CHERRY TORTE

4 eggs
4 oz (100 g) caster sugar
3 oz (75 g) self-raising flour
1 oz (25 g) cocoa

FILLING:
15 oz (420 g) can black cherries,
 stoned
1 level tablespoon cornflour
2 tablespoons kirsch or 6
 tablespoons black cherry jam

TOPPING:
½ pint (300 ml) whipping cream,
 whipped
Chocolate curls or grated
 chocolate
A few fresh cherries

Heat the oven to 350 deg.F, 180 deg.C, gas mark 4. Grease and line with greased greaseproof paper two 9 inch (22.5 cm) sandwich tins.

Break the eggs into a mixing bowl, add sugar and either whisk with an electric whisk until thick enough for the whisk to leave a faint trail when lifted out of the bowl, or use a hand balloon whisk in a bowl standing over a pan of hot water. Fold in the sieved flour and cocoa, using a metal spoon. Divide carefully between the tins and bake for about 20 to 25 minutes until well risen and the sponges are beginning to shrink away from the sides of the tin. Turn

onto a wire rack to cool.

Drain the can of cherries and save the juice.

Place the cornflour in a small saucepan and stir in the cherry juice over a moderate heat. Bring to the boil, stirring until thickened, simmer for 2 minutes and then remove from the heat and cool. Add the kirsch and cherries to the sauce. If using jam put in a bowl and stir in the kirsch before adding.

Sandwich the sponges together with a little whipped cream and cherry mixture keeping back some of the sauce for topping. Spread cream thinly around the sides of the cake. Coat with chocolate curls or grated chocolate. Spread the top with the reserved sauce and then pipe rosettes of cream all over.

Decorate with more chocolate curls or grated chocolate and a few fresh black cherries if available. Serves 10 to 12.

BROWNIES

The high proportion of sugar is traditional in this recipe. Americans have a sweet tooth!

1½ oz (40 g) cocoa
About 5 tablespoons water
3 oz (75 g) margarine
2 eggs
8 oz (225 g) caster sugar
3½ oz (87 g) plain flour
½ level teaspoon baking powder
Pinch of salt
2 oz (50 g) walnuts, roughly
 chopped

Heat the oven to 350 deg.F, 180 deg.C, gas mark 4. Line with greased greaseproof paper an oblong tin 11 inches by 7 inches by 1 inch deep (27.5 by 17.5 by 2.5 cm).

Mix the cocoa with the water in a small saucepan till smooth, add the margarine and heat gently until it has melted and the mixture is a thick cream. Remove from the heat.

Whisk the eggs and sugar together until light and then whisk in the cocoa mixture.

Sift the flour with the baking powder and salt and fold into the cake with the nuts. Turn into the tin and bake in the oven for 35 to 40 minutes.

When cooked the Brownies will have shrunk slightly from the sides of the tin and have a pale crust on top.

Leave to cool in the tin and then peel off the paper and cut into 15 pieces. Makes 15 Brownies.

TEXAS SHE CAKE

An interesting regional version of the traditional American brownies.

2 level tablespoons cocoa
1/4 pint (150 ml) less 2 tablespoons water
4 oz (100 g) soft margarine
7 oz (200 g) caster sugar
4 oz (100 g) plain flour
1/4 teaspoon salt
1 egg, beaten
2 rounded tablespoons soured cream
1/2 teaspoon bicarbonate of soda
1/2 teaspoon vanilla essence

ICING:
2 oz (50 g) margarine
2 level tablespoons cocoa
3 tablespoons milk
8 oz (225 g) icing sugar, sieved

Heat the oven to 375 deg.F, 190 deg.C, gas mark 5. Grease and line with greased greaseproof paper a cake tin 11 by 7 by 1 1/2 inches (27.5 by 17.5 by 3.5 cm) deep.

Put the cocoa, water and margarine in a small saucepan. Place over a moderate heat and bring to the boil, stirring, so that the margarine has melted. Remove from the heat and cool.

Put the sugar, flour and salt in a bowl, make a well in the centre and add the chocolate mixture, egg, soured cream, bicarbonate of soda and vanilla essence. Mix well and then turn into the tin and bake for 20 minutes.

Meanwhile prepare the icing. Put the margarine, cocoa and milk in a saucepan and bring to the boil, stirring, so that the margarine melts. Remove from the heat, add the icing sugar and mix well.

As soon as the cake comes out of the oven spread it with the icing so that it soaks into the cake. Leave to cool.

COFFEE AND WALNUT FUDGE CAKES

6 oz (175 g) soft margarine
6 oz (175 g) caster sugar
3 large eggs
2 oz (50 g) chopped walnuts
1 tablespoon coffee essence
6 oz (175 g) self-raising flour
1 1/2 level teaspoons baking powder

COFFEE FUDGE ICING:
3 oz (75 g) soft margarine
8 oz (225 g) icing sugar, sieved
1 tablespoon milk
1 tablespoon coffee essence
2 oz (50 g) chopped walnuts

Heat the oven to 325 deg.F, 160 deg.C, gas mark 3 and grease and line with greased greaseproof a large tin 12 by 9 inches (30 by 22.5 cm).

Measure the margarine, sugar, eggs, walnuts and coffee essence into a large bowl and then sieve in the flour and baking powder. Beat well until smooth and blended.

Turn into the prepared tin, smooth the top and cook for 40 minutes or until well risen and shrinking away from the sides of the tin. The cake will spring back when pressed with the finger tips. Leave to cool in the tin.

For the icing: put the margarine, icing sugar, milk and coffee essence in a bowl and beat until smooth. Spread over the cake and sprinkle with walnuts. Leave to set. Cut into bars.

Texas She Cakes

PASTRIES AND CONFECTIONERY

The art of making pastry is surrounded by much mystery but it is in fact the skill of combining fat, flour and water in the correct proportions according to your recipe; handling lightly but firmly in a cool environment; and baking in a hot oven. To obtain the best results, make sure that the ingredients, working surface and utensils are cold, and where it is possible keep them in the refrigerator before use.

–Apple Strudel–

APPLE STRUDEL

*2 pieces strudel pastry, each 16
  inches (40 cm) square
1½ oz (40 g) butter, melted
2 oz (50 g) white breadcrumbs*

*FILLING:
1½ lb (675 g) cooking apples,
  peeled, cored and finely diced
3 oz (75 g) caster sugar
1 level teaspoon cinnamon
2 oz (50 g) sultanas
Grated rind of 1 lemon
2 oz (50 g) ground almonds*

Heat the oven to 400 deg.F, 200 deg.C, gas mark 6.

Lay the two pieces of strudel pastry flat on the table, brush with melted butter and sprinkle with most of the breadcrumbs.

Mix all the filling ingredients together and divide between the two pieces of strudel pastry leaving a ½ inch (1.25 cm) border. Fold in these borders and then carefully roll up like a Swiss roll.

Place on a baking sheet, brush each with more melted butter and sprinkle with the rest of the breadcrumbs. Bake in the oven for 30 minutes brushing once or twice with more melted butter, until golden brown.

Leave to cool on the baking tray, then cut into slices, and lift onto a serving dish. If liked sprinkle with sieved icing sugar. This makes 2 small strudels and serves 6.

BOTERLETTER

PASTRY:
6 oz (175 g) plain flour
2 oz (50 g) hard margarine, chilled
2 oz (50 g) butter, chilled
About 7 tablespoons cold water

FILLING:
6 oz (175 g) ground almonds
6 oz (175 g) caster sugar
1 egg
Juice of ½ lemon
Almond essence

COOK'S TIP. These ingredients can be bought ready-made, i.e. a large packet of puff pastry and 12 oz (350 g) almond paste.

Put the four into a mixing bowl and grate in the fats. Add just enough cold water to mix to a firm dough, using a sharp knife. On a lightly floured surface roll out the pastry to a strip ½ inch (1.25 cm) thick and 6 inches (15 cm) wide. Fold the pastry in three and give it a quarter turn to the left. Roll out again into a strip and fold in three. Wrap the pastry in greaseproof paper and chill in the refrigerator for 30 minutes.

Heat the oven to 425 deg.F, 220 deg.C, gas mark 7.

Roll out the pastry to a strip 6 by 30 inches (15 by 75 cm). Mix all the filling ingredients together to form a paste, roll into a sausage a little shorter than the pastry and place in the centre. Wrap the pastry around the almond paste, sealing the edges and ends with beaten egg. Form into the shape of a letter of the alphabet.

Glaze with a little beaten egg and bake in the oven for about 30 minutes or until golden brown on top.

Remove from the oven and leave to cool. Serve sliced with coffee.

–Baklava–

BAKLAVA

8 oz (225 g) phyllo pastry (also filo or fillo)
4 oz (100 g) unsalted butter, melted
4 oz (100 g) walnuts, chopped fairly finely
1 oz (25 g) caster sugar

LEMON SYRUP:
¼ pint (150 ml) water
8 oz (225 g) caster sugar
Thinly peeled rind and juice of 1 lemon

Heat the oven to 400 deg.F, 200 deg.C, gas mark 6. Butter a Swiss roll tin 11 by 7 inches (27.5 by 17.5 cm).

Cut the phyllo pastry in half so that it is roughly the size of the tin. Lay one sheet of pastry in the tin, brush with butter and continue until there are 8 layers in the tin. Brush the top layer with butter and sprinkle with nuts and sugar. Finish with a further 8 layers of pastry, brushing with butter between the layers. Brush the top with more butter and cut through to the tin into diamond shapes.

Bake for about 25 to 30 minutes until a pale golden brown and crispy. Cool.

Meanwhile make the lemon syrup. Put the water into a pan, add the sugar and the thinly peeled zest of the lemon, bring to the boil slowly and simmer for 15 minutes without a lid. Remove from the heat and add the lemon juice. Pour over the cold baklava or cool the syrup and pour over hot baklava.

Serve with whipped cream. Serves 8.

GALATOPOUREKO

Make as for baklava (above) and put in a slightly bigger tin, but fill the centre – i.e. when 8 layers are reached – with crème patissière (see apricot tart). Add 1 oz (25 g) sugar to the crème before cooling a little to spread. Top with a further 8 layers of pastry. Cut into squares through the top 4 layers with scissors and a sharp knife. Bake as for baklava but for 35 minutes until pale brown and crisp. Serve warm dusted with icing sugar and cut in squares.

CARROT CAKE

This is gooey and delicious.

8 oz (225 g) self-raising flour
2 level teaspoons baking powder
5 oz (150 g) light soft brown sugar
2 oz (50 g) walnuts, chopped
4 oz (100 g) carrots, washed,
    trimmed and grated
2 ripe bananas, mashed
2 eggs
1/4 pint (150 ml) salad or corn oil

TOPPING:
3 oz (75 g) soft butter or margarine
3 oz (75g) rich cream cheese
6 oz (175 g) icing sugar, sieved
1/2 teaspoon vanilla essence

Heat the oven to 350 deg.F, 180 deg.C, gas mark 4. Grease and line with greased greaseproof paper an 8 inch (20 cm) round cake tin.

Sift together the flour and baking powder into a large bowl and stir in the sugar. Add the nuts, carrots and bananas and mix lightly. Make a well in the centre and add the eggs and oil. Beat well until thoroughly blended.

Turn into the tin and bake in the oven for about 1 1/4 hours until golden brown. When cooked the cake will have shrunk slightly from the sides of the tin and a warm skewer pierced into the centre of it will come out clean. Turn out the cake and remove the paper and then leave to cool on a wire rack.

Topping: Place all the ingredients together in a bowl and beat well until blended and smooth. Spread over the cake and rough up with a fork. Leave in a cool place to harden slightly before serving.

– Chocolate Éclairs –

CHOCOLATE ÉCLAIRS

CHOUX PASTRY:
2 oz (50 g) butter
1/4 pint (150 ml) water
2 1/2 oz (62 g) plain flour
2 eggs, beaten

FILLING:
1/2 pint (300 ml) whipping cream

ICING:
1 1/2 oz (40 g) butter
1 oz (25 g) cocoa
4 oz (100 g) icing sugar, sieved
3-4 tablespoons milk

Heat the oven to 425 deg.F, 220 deg.C, gas mark 7. Grease two baking trays.

Put the butter and water in a small pan and bring to the boil slowly to allow the butter to melt. Remove from the heat, add the flour all at once and beat to form a ball. Gradually beat in the eggs a little at a time to make a smooth paste.

Put the mixture into a piping bag fitted with a 1/2 inch (1.25 cm) nozzle and pipe the mixture into 4 inch (8 cm) lengths on the baking trays. It will make about 14 éclairs.

Bake in the oven for 10 minutes then reduce the heat to 375 deg.F, 190 Deg.C, gas mark 5 and cook for a further 15 to 20 minutes until golden brown, risen and crisp.

Remove from the oven and slit down one side of each éclair to allow the steam to escape, leave to cool on a wire rack.

Whip the cream until it is thick and forms peaks and fill the éclairs.

Make the icing. Melt the butter in a small saucepan, add cocoa and cook for a minute. Remove from the heat and stir in the icing sugar and milk, beat well until starting to thicken and then coat over each éclair.

Leave to set and serve on the same day that they are made. Makes 14 éclairs.

—Chocolate Rum Truffles—

PECAN PIE

PASTRY:
4 oz (100 g) plain flour
2 oz (50 g) butter
1 oz (25 g) lard
1 egg yolk
½ oz (12.5 g) caster sugar
1 teaspoon water

FILLING:
1 oz (25 g) butter
6 oz (175 g) soft brown sugar
3 eggs
*8 oz (225 g) jar maple syrup or 5 oz
  (150 g) golden syrup mixed
  with a tablespoon black treacle
  and made up to 8 oz (225 g)
  with boiling water*
1 teaspoon vanilla essence
¼ teaspoon salt
3 oz (75 g) pecans, halved

Make the pastry. Put the flour in a bowl, add the fats cut in small pieces and rub in with the finger-tips until the mixture resembles fine breadcrumbs. Mix the egg yolk, sugar and water together, stir into the dry ingredients and bind together. Wrap in cling film and chill in the refrigerator for ½ hr.

Heat the oven to 425 deg.F, 220 deg.C, gas mark 7. Roll out the pastry on a floured table and line an 8 inch (20 cm) loose-bottomed deep flan tin. Line the flan with greaseproof paper and baking beans and bake blind for 10 minutes. Remove the paper and beans and return the flan to the oven for a further 5 minutes.

For the filling: Cream butter and sugar together, whisk the eggs and add to the creamed mixture with the maple syrup, vanilla essence and salt. Beat well. Arrange the nuts over the base of the flan flat side down.

Pour in the filling and bake in the oven turned down to 375 deg.F, 190 deg.C, gas mark 5 for about 40 minutes. The pie will have risen but will fall back on cooling.

Leave to cool but serve slightly warm with cream. Serves 6.

CHOCOLATE RUM TRUFFLES

2 oz (50 g) seedless raisins
*2 oz (50 g) glacé cherries,
  chopped*
4 tablespoons rum
*8 oz (225 g) sweet biscuits,
  crushed*
*8 oz (225 g) stale Madeira or
  Victoria sandwich cake,
  crumbled*
5 tablespoons drinking chocolate
2 tablespoons apricot jam, melted
3 oz (75 g) chocolate vermicelli

Put the raisins and cherries in a small bowl with the rum and leave to soak for 2 hours. Mix together the crushed biscuits and cake crumbs in a large mixing bowl. Add the drinking chocolate and soaked fruit and mix well, pounding with the back of a wooden spoon. Alternatively use an electric mixer with a dough hook or the beater on a slow speed.

Stir in the melted jam, adding more if necessary to make a firm dough. Shape the dough into small balls and coat them with the chocolate vermicelli by putting them in a polythene bag together and shaking them up. Leave the truffles on a tray or on flat plates to become firm overnight, then place them in small sweet cases. Makes about 48 truffles.

BISCUITS AND SHORTBREAD

Biscuits are at their best when freshly baked, but can be kept in an airtight tin for a week. Biscuits made from syrup or honey should be left on the baking tray when taken out of the oven to harden before being placed on a wire cooling rack.

TACKY GINGERBREAD

COOK'S TIP. Gingerbread tastes even better if it is kept for 2 to 3 days before cutting.

1 level teaspoon mixed spice
1 level teaspoon bicarbonate of soda
2 level teaspoons ground ginger
8 oz (225 g) plain flour
3 oz (75 g) lard
4 oz (100 g) black treacle
4 oz (100 g) golden syrup
2 oz (50 g) soft brown sugar
2 oz (50 g) chunky marmalade, roughly chopped
2 eggs, beaten
6 tablespoons (90 ml) milk
2 oz (50 g) sultanas
2 oz (50 g) chopped stem ginger, optional

Grease and line with greased greaseproof paper an 8 inch (20 cm) square tin or a 7½ by 9½ inch (19 by 24.5 cm) meat roasting tin. Heat the oven to 325 deg.F, 160 deg.C, gas mark 3.

Sift spices, bicarbonate of soda and flour into a large mixing bowl and make a well in the centre.

Place the lard in a saucepan with the treacle, syrup and sugar and heat until the lard has just melted and the ingredients blended, draw from the heat and cool slightly. Stir the marmalade, eggs, milk, sultanas and stem ginger into the bowl of flour with the lard mixture and beat with a wooden spoon until smooth and glossy.

Pour into the tin and bake in the oven for 1 to 1¼ hours. Leave to cool in the tin for about 30 minutes, then turn out and remove the paper and finish cooling on a wire rack. Store in an airtight tin until required.

GRANTHAM GINGERBREADS

COOK'S TIP. These are very good and well worth making. For a variation, the biscuits can be decorated with lemon glacé icing. To 2 teaspoons strained lemon juice beat in sufficient sieved icing sugar to give a fairly stiff icing. Make a greaseproof paper icing bag and fill with the icing. Cut off just the very tip of the bag and pipe a lacy pattern over the tops of the biscuits.

4 oz (100 g) butter
12 oz (350 g) caster sugar
1 large egg, beaten
9 oz (250 g) self-raising flour
1 to 2 level teaspoons ground ginger

Cream the butter until soft, then beat in the sugar until well blended. Beat in the egg and then add the flour and ginger sieved together (if you like a really gingery taste use 2 teaspoons of ginger) and work to a firm but pliable dough. Knead lightly then roll the dough into balls the size of a walnut. Place well apart on a greased baking sheet. Bake in an oven heated to 300 deg.F, 150 deg.C, gas mark 2 for 20-30 minutes or until well puffed up and lightly browned. Cool on a wire rack.

N.B. Don't be surprised at the first bite, for these biscuits are hollow in the centre. Makes about 30 biscuits.

—Strawberry Shortbread—

BOTERMOPPEN

6 oz (175 g) unsalted butter
Finely grated rind of ½ lemon
4 oz (100 g) caster sugar
8 oz (225 g) plain flour
1 oz (25 g) granulated sugar

COOK'S TIP. No biscuit cutters are needed for this recipe. Make the shortbread into a long sausage shape. Chill, then cut off round slices and bake.

Heat the oven to 325 deg.F, 160 deg.C, gas mark 3, and grease two or three large baking trays.

Cream the butter and lemon rind in a large bowl until soft. Beat in the sugar until light. Blend in the flour and mix until smooth. Using your hands, work the mixture together and divide into two equal portions. Roll both out to form two 6 inch (15 cm) sausages and roll them in the granulated sugar. Wrap in foil and chill in the refrigerator until firm.

Cut each sausage into about 16 slices and place on the baking trays allowing room for the biscuits to spread slightly. Bake in the oven for about 25 minutes or until pale golden brown at the edges. Lift off and leave to cool on a wire rack. Makes 32 biscuits.

JANHAGEL

Using the same basic Botermoppen mixture (see above) omit the lemon rind and instead add one level teaspoon of ground cinnamon. Press the mixture into a shallow 7 by 11 inch (17.5 by 27.5 cm) tin. Flatten with a knife, prick with a fork and then brush with a little beaten egg. Sprinkle the granulated sugar on top and then add approximately 1 oz (25 g) of flaked almonds.

Bake in the oven for about 40 minutes at 325 deg.F, 160 deg.C, gas mark 3.

Leave to cool in the tin for about 15 minutes and then cut into 16 fingers, lift out and finish cooling on a wire rack.

STRAWBERRY SHORTBREAD

COOK'S TIP. To my mind this is far nicer than shortcake which is a glorified scone mixture. This is a crisp thinnish shortbread and stretches ¾ lb (350 g) strawberries to serve six people.

4½ oz (125 g) plain flour
3 oz (75 g) butter
1½ oz (37.5 g) caster sugar
¾ lb (350 g) strawberries
3 tablespoons redcurrant jelly
A little whipped cream

Sift the flour into a bowl, add the butter and sugar and rub in the butter until the mixture resembles fine breadcrumbs, knead together then turn on to a table and knead lightly for 3 minutes until the mixture is smooth. Roll or pat out the shortbread on a baking sheet to a round ¼ inch (½ cm) thick and 8 inches (20 cm) in diameter, crimp the edges and leave to chill in the refrigerator for 20 minutes.

Heat the oven to 325 deg.F, 160 deg.C, gas mark 3 and bake the shortbread for 25 to 30 minutes until a pale golden brown. Leave to cool on the baking sheet.

When quite cold transfer to a serving dish. Hull the strawberries, cut in half and arrange on the shortbread. Heat the redcurrant jelly in a small pan until dissolved and smooth, brush over the strawberries and leave to set.

When quite cold, decorate attractively with whipped cream. Serves 6.

SCOTTISH SHORTBREAD

6 oz (175 g) plain flour
3 oz (75 g) cornflour
6 oz (175 g) butter
3 oz (75 g) caster sugar

Heat the oven to 325 deg.F, 160 deg.C, gas mark 3.

Sift the flour and cornflour together. Cream the butter until soft. Add the sugar and beat until light and fluffy. Work in the flours then knead well together.

Press out the shortbread into a shallow greased baking tin 11 by 7 inches (28 by 17.5 cm) flattening the dough with knuckles. Prick well with a fork and mark into 16 fingers with the back of a knife.

Chill in the refrigerator for 15 minutes, then bake in the oven for about 35 minutes or until a very pale golden brown. Leave to cool in the tin for 15 minutes then cut through where the shortbread is marked and then carefully lift into a wire rack to finish cooling. Makes 16 pieces.

COOK'S TIP. Butter is an absolute must for shortbread because the flavour really does come through. A proportion of cornflour, semolina and ground rice adds a crispy texture. Keep in an airtight tin.

YUM YUMS

COOK'S TIP. These are really good home-made biscuits and ideal for children to make from ingredients that you have in the store cupboard.

8 oz (225 g) soft margarine
6 oz (175 g) caster sugar
1 egg, beaten
10 oz (275 g) self-raising flour
2 oz (50 g) cornflakes, lightly crushed

Heat the oven to 375 deg.F, 190 deg.C, gas mark 5 and grease 3 large baking sheets.

Put the margarine into a large bowl, add sugar and cream together with a wooden spoon until soft. Beat in the egg, then slowly work in the flour until the mixture has come together. If it is a warm day or the kitchen is hot the mixture may be rather soft to handle, so wrap it in cling flim and chill for 10 minutes.

Wet the hands and lightly roll mixture into about 34 balls and roll each one in the crushed cornflakes. Position well spaced on the baking sheets and slightly flatten each with the hand. Bake for about 20 to 25 minutes until turning a very pale brown at the edges. Remove from the oven and leave on the trays for 1 minute before carefuly lifting each biscuit onto a wire rack to cool. When quite cold store in an airtight tin. Makes about 34 Yum yums.

STICKY FLAPJACKS

COOK'S TIP. Whilst the oven is on it is always worth making a couple of tins of these flapjacks, as they keep very well. If you haven't two 7 inch (17.5 cm) square tins, you could put all the mixture into a normal-sized roasting tin about 9 inches (22.5 cm) square, provided that the base of the tin is quite flat. Don't be over generous with the golden syrup otherwise the mixture will be too runny.

8 oz (225 g) margarine
8 oz (225 g) demerara sugar
2 level tablespoons golden syrup
10 oz (275 g) rolled oats

Grease two 7 inch (17.5 cm) square tins that are about 1½ inches (3.75 cm) deep. Heat the oven to 325 deg.F, 160 deg.C, gas mark 3.

Melt the margarine in a saucepan, add the sugar and golden syrup and when blended stir in the oats and mix very thoroughly. Divide the mixture between the tins and press down.

—Yum Yums—

Bake in the oven for 25 minutes until just beginning to brown at the edges. Leave to cook for 10 minutes and then mark each tin into 16 squares. Leave in the tin until quite cold, then lift out and store in an airtight tin. Makes 32 flapjacks.

EASTER BISCUITS

For extra flavour add a little mixed spice to the mixture with the flour. The biscuits can be stored in a tin until they are needed. The egg whites left from this recipe may be used for meringues or Pavlova.

5 oz (150 g) soft butter
4 oz (100 g) caster sugar
Finely grated rind of 1 lemon
2 egg yolks
8 oz (225 g) plain flour
2 oz (50 g) currants
A little egg white

Cream the butter with the sugar and lemon rind until light and fluffy. Beat in the egg yolks and then stir in the sifted flour and currants, knead lightly until smooth and then leave in the refrigerator or a cool place for an hour.

Heat the oven to 350 deg.F, 180 deg.F, gas mark 4 and lightly grease two large baking sheets.

Turn the dough onto a lightly floured table and roll out to an ⅛ inch (0.30 cm) thickness and cut into rounds with a 3 inch (7.5 cm) fluted cutter. Brush with a little lightly beaten egg white, dredge with caster sugar and place on the baking sheets. Bake until just golden brown for about 12 to 15 minutes. Transfer to a wire rack and leave to cool. Store in an airtight tin to keep fresh. Makes 24 biscuits.

—Scottish Shortbread—   *—Sticky Flapjacks—*

BREADS AND TEA BREADS

Bread is the very stuff of life, and professional-looking loaves are well within the scope of even a first-time bread maker. Dough making also has the advantage that it does not require any of the equipment not normally found in a kitchen. A large mixing bowl, a wooden board, or laminated surface, some kitchen scales and a measuring jug make up the basic requirements. Loaf tins help to give good-looking results. A room thermometer is useful and so is one for measuring the temperature of liquids. Scones are made for afternoon tea and spread with butter, jam and cream. Remember to get the consistency of the dough right. Insufficient liquid can produce heavy, badly risen scones; if too little liquid is used the scones lose their shape. Don't overdo the baking powder, as this can impart an acid taste. The first rolling out will produce the best results, but the trimmings can be kneaded together and re-rolled to cut out as many scones as possible.

HOME-MADE WHITE BREAD AND ROLLS

Just under ³⁄₄ pint (450 ml) hand-hot water
1 teaspoon sugar
¹⁄₂ oz (12.5 g) dried yeast (3 level teaspoons
1¹⁄₂ lb (675 g) strong white flour
3 level teaspoons salt
¹⁄₂ oz (12.5 g) lard

Dissolve the sugar in the water, sprinkle on the yeast and leave for 10 to 15 minutes until frothy.

Put the flour and salt into a large bowl and rub in the lard; pour on the yeast liquid and mix well to a dough that will leave the sides of the bowl clean.

Turn onto a floured table and knead until smooth and no longer sticky. This will take about 10 minutes and is done by folding the dough towards you, then pushing down with the palm of the hand. Give the dough a quarter turn, repeat kneading developing a rocking rhythm and continue until the dough feels firm and elastic. Shape into a large ball, place in a large polythene bag greased with a little vegetable oil and leave in a warm place to rise until doubled in bulk. This will take about 1 hour in a warm place, 2 hours at room temperature or it may be left overnight in the refrigerator, in which case the dough must be allowed to return to room temperature before shaping .

Turn the dough onto a lightly floured table and divide in half. Take one half of the dough and flatten with the knuckles to knock out the air, roll up like a Swiss roll and place in a greased loaf tin 7³⁄₄ inches (19.5 cm) by 4 inches (10 cm) by 2¹⁄₄ inches (6 cm). Put inside an oiled polythene bag and leave in a warm place until the dough rises to the top of the tin.

Divide the remaining dough into 9 pieces and shape into rolls. Place evenly spaced on a greased baking sheet, put in a greased polythene bag and leave until

doubled in bulk.

Glaze the loaf and rolls with either salt and water, milk, water or a little beaten egg mixed with water or milk. Bake in a hot oven 450 deg.F, 230 deg.C, gas mark 8 on the centre shelf. The rolls will need about 20 minutes cooking time and the loaf about 30 to 35 minutes. When done, the loaf will have shrunk slightly from the sides of the tin and the crust will be a deep golden brown. To test, tap bread on the base: if ready it will sound hollow.

Cool on wire racks and then store in a polythene bag leaving the ends open. Makes 1 loaf and 9 bread rolls.

COOK'S TIP. For the best results use the same sort of flour that the bakers use: strong plain flour, now available in most grocers and supermarkets. Dried yeast is easier to use than fresh and I find the results equally good. The yeast must froth up with the liquid and if it doesn't, this means the yeast is old and won't make the bread rise. Dried yeast may be stored in a tightly lidded container for up to 6 months.

FRUIT MALT LOAF

COOK'S TIP. Very quick to prepare. Weigh all the ingredients straight into the mixing bowl. I haven't left anything out of the ingredients: this recipe really doesn't contain any fat!

6 oz (175 g) self-raising flour
1 tablespoon malt drink (Ovaltine)
1 oz (25 g) caster sugar
3 oz (75 g) mixed dried fruit
2 level tablespoons (2 oz or 50 g)
    golden syrup
1/3 pint (200 ml) milk

Mix all the ingredients to a thick batter and put in a 1 lb (450 g) loaf tin that is well greased. Then bake at 325 deg.F, 160 deg.C, gas mark 3 for about 1¼ hours until cooked through in the centre. Turn out and leave to cool on a wire rack. Serve sliced with butter.

SPECIAL SCONES

COOK'S TIP. The secret of good scones is not to have the mixture too dry – it should feel a bit sticky. Don't handle the dough too much, cut out quickly and bake. Wrap the scones in a tea towel after baking to keep them moist.

8 oz (225 g) self-raising flour
Pinch salt
2 oz (50 g) butter, softened
1 oz (25 g) caster sugar
1 egg
Milk

Heat the oven to 425 deg.F, 220 deg.C, gas mark 7 and lightly grease a baking sheet.

Sift the flour and salt into a bowl, add the butter and rub in with the fingertips until the mixture resembles fine breadcrumbs. Stir in the sugar.

Crack the egg into a measure and lightly beat, then make up to ¼ pint (150 ml) with milk. Stir into the flour and mix to a soft dough. Turn onto a lightly floured table,

knead gently and roll out to ½ inch (1.25 cm) thick. Cut into rounds with a 2½ inch (6.25 cm) fluted cutter to make 10 or 12 scones.

Place on the baking sheet so that the scones touch, brush the tops with a little milk and bake for 10 minutes or until pale golden brown. Remove from the baking sheet and leave to cool on a wire tray. Makes 10 to 12 scones.

HOT CROSS BUNS

Scant ½ pint (300 ml) milk
1 level teaspoon caster sugar
Scant ½ oz (12.5 g) dried yeast
1 lb (450 g) strong bread flour
1 level teaspoon salt
Pinch mixed spice
Pinch cinnamon
Pinch nutmeg
2 oz (50 g) caster sugar
4 oz (100 g) currants
1 oz (25 g) mixed chopped peel
1 egg, beaten
1 oz (25 g) butter, melted
Shortcrust pastry trimmings

Heat the milk to hand hot and pour into a 1 pint (600 ml) measure. Add the level teaspoon caster sugar and yeast and whisk with a fork; leave for about 5 to 10 minutes until frothy.

Sift the flour with the salt and spices into a large bowl. Add the sugar and fruit. Stir the egg and butter into the yeast mixture, add the flour and mix well. This will make a soft dough.

Turn the dough onto a floured table and knead for about 10 minutes until smooth and no longer sticky, place in a lightly oiled polythene bag and leave to rise at room temperature for 1½ to 2 hours or until double in bulk.

Divide the dough into 12 pieces and shape into buns by using the palm of the hand, pressing down hard and then easing up. Place well spaced on a floured baking sheet. Put inside the oiled polythene bag and leave to rise at room temperature for

about 1 hour until doubled in bulk.

Remove the bag. Roll out the pastry trimmings and cut into 24 strips about 4 inches (10 cm) long and ¼ inch (5 mm) wide, place two in a cross on each bun dampening the underside with water to make them stick. Bake in a hot oven 425 deg.F, 220 deg.C, gas mark 7 for 15 to 20 minutes until golden brown.

Make a glaze by bringing 2 tablespoons water and 2 tablespoons milk to the boil, stirring in 1½ oz (40 g) caster sugar and then boiling for 2 minutes. Remove the buns from the oven and glaze at once. Makes 12 buns.

COOK'S TIP. For oven-fresh breakfast buns, cover the tray of shaped dough with a polythene bag and store in the fridge overnight. Remove and leave in a warm place until double the original size before baking.

SMASHING BARABRITH

COOK'S TIP. A mouth-watering idea for family tea. This is beautifully moist and fruity and doesn't crumble one bit when sliced, however thinly you choose to cut it.

6 oz (175 g) (1 cup) currants
6 oz (175 g) (1 cup) sultanas
8 oz (225 g) (1 cup) dark soft brown
  sugar
½ pint (300 ml) (1 cup) hot tea
10 oz (275 g) (2 cups) self-raising
  flour
1 egg, beaten

Put the fruit and sugar in a bowl and pour over the hot tea, stir well, cover and leave to stand overnight.

Grease and line with greaseproof paper a large loaf tin 9 inches (22.5 cm) by 5 inches (12.5 cm) by 3 inches (7.5 cm). Heat the oven to 300 deg.F, 150 deg.C, gas mark 2. Stir the flour and egg into the fruit, mix thoroughly and turn into the tin.

Bake in the oven for about 1¾ hours or until it has risen and has shrunk away from the sides of the tin. Turn out and leave to cool on a wire rack. Serve sliced either with butter or just as it is.

BANANA LOAF

4 oz (100 g) butter, softened
6 oz (75 g) caster sugar
2 eggs, beaten
2 ripe bananas, mashed
8 oz (225 g) plain flour
1 level teaspoon baking powder
1 level teaspoon bicarbonate of
  soda
2 tablespoons boiling milk

Heat the oven to 350 deg.F, 180 deg.C, gas mark 4, and grease and line a 2 lb (900 g) loaf tin with greased greaseproof paper.

Cream the butter and sugar until light and fluffy and beat in the eggs and mashed bananas.

—Smashing Barabrith—

Sift the flour and baking powder together and stir the bicarbonate of soda into the milk. Then fold both into the creamed mixture. Turn into the tin and bake in the centre of the oven for 1 hour or until well risen and golden brown. Turn out and leave to cool on a wire rack with the paper removed. Serve just as it is or sliced and spread with butter.

COOK'S TIP. The last two bananas left in the fruit bowl often get over-ripe so that no one fancies them. At this stage they are perfect for this cake.

PRESERVING

The ancient art of preserving has come a long way since the Romans introduced orchards and vegetable and herb gardens to Britain. Modern technology now produces the means to preserve an ever-increasing range of fruit, vegetables and herbs which provide a wide variety of flavours and tasty additions to meals during the months when the fresh items are not available. Preserving is one of the most simple and satisfying of home skills – it takes little more than time and patience to produce a delicious range of jams, chutneys and pickles

Setting test for preserves: Use a thermometer to 220 deg.F, 100 deg.C, or by spooning a small amount onto a cold saucer. When it has cooled the skin that forms should wrinkle when pushed with the finger.

APRICOT AND ORANGE MARMALADE

COOK'S TIP. This marmalade is unusual, rather like the apricot conserve they have on the Continent for breakfast, but even nicer with the sharpness of Seville oranges. The fruits need to be soaked overnight or longer – no need to buy the best quality dried apricots, you can often get broken pieces or uneven shapes. If you prefer large pieces of apricot don't cut them up at all, just leave them whole.

*1½ lb (675 g) Seville oranges
1 lemon
1 lb (450 g) dried apricots
5½ pints (3 l) water
6 lb (2.5 kg) granulated sugar*

Wash the oranges and lemon, cut in half, squeeze out the juice and pour into a large bowl. Scrape the pith from the fruit with a teaspoon and put it with the pips in a smaller bowl.

Shred the orange and lemon skins finely and cut the dried apricots in halves, quarters or if preferred leave whole and put in the large bowl with the juice. Add 4½ pints (2.5 l) water and put the other 1 pint (500 ml) water over the pips and pith. Cover both containers and leave for at least 24 hours, 36 is better, to soak. This process softens the peel and swells the apricots.

Put the pith and pips in a piece of muslin and tie with string to form a bag, then tie the ends of the string to the handle of a large saucepan. Add any water remaining from the pips to the pan with the large container of fruit and water, bring to the boil and simmer without a lid for about 45 minutes or until tender and the contents have reduced by about a third.

Remove the muslin bag, add the sugar to the pan and stir until dissolved, then boil rapidly until setting point is reached. Remove from the heat and leave to stand for 20 minutes to suspend the fruit evenly, skim, then pot in clean warm jars, cover and label. Makes 10 lb (4.5 kg.)

QUICK DARK MATURED MARMALADE

COOK'S TIP. If each year you make a large quantity of marmalade this method speeds the process up. If you like a lighter marmalade add white sugar instead of brown and no treacle.

*3 lb (1.5 kg) Seville oranges
2 lemons
5 pints (3 l) water
5 lb (2.5 kg) granulated sugar
1 lb (450 g) dark soft brown sugar
1 level tablespoon black treacle*

Wash the fruit, then cut in halves and squeeze out the juice into a large saucepan.

Cut the fruit skin in quarters, put the pips in a piece of muslin and tie with string to form a bag. Using a coarse blade mince the peel and add to the pan with the juice. Add the water and tie the muslin bag to the handle of the pan.

Bring slowly to the boil and simmer gently without a lid for about 2 hours or until the peel is tender and the contents of the pan have reduced by half. Remove the bag of pips and discard.

Add the sugars and black treacle to the pan, stir over a low heat until the sugar has dissolved, then boil rapidly until setting point is reached.

Skim and pour into clean warm jars, cover and label. Makes 10 lb (5 k.)

GINGER MARMALADE

COOK'S TIP. A very good way of using any stem ginger that you have been given for Christmas. Use the syrup from the jar to serve over ice cream or in a trifle.

1½ lb (675 g) Seville oranges
1½ pints (900 ml) water
Juice of 1 lemon
3 lb (1.5 kg) granulated sugar
8 oz (225 g) stem ginger, chopped

Wash the oranges and put in the pressure cooker with the water, cover and bring to 15 lb (7 kg) pressure for 20 minutes. Cool the pan in water to release the lid. Test the oranges by pricking the skin with a pin, and if it goes in easily the oranges are done.

Lift out the fruit into a colander, catch any juice from the oranges in a bowl underneath and return to the pan. Cool the fruit enough to handle, then cut oranges in half and remove all the pips with a teaspoon and put back into the pressure cooker, cover and bring back to 15 lb (7 kg) pressure for a further 5 minutes.

Meanwhile slice the orange peel shells using a knife and fork on a wooden board. Put this peel with the lemon juice and sugar in a large pan and strain in the water and juice from the pressure cooker, discarding all the pips.

Stir over the heat until the sugar has dissolved, then boil quickly until setting point is reached, which will take about 10 minutes. Remove from the heat, stir in the ginger and leave to stand for 10 minutes, skim, and pour into clean warm jars, cover and label. Makes 5 lb (2.3 kg).

WHOLE STRAWBERRY JAM

2¼ lb (1 kg) small strawberries
3 tablespoons (45 ml) lemon juice
3 lb (1.3 kg) sugar
Butter or margarine
½ bottle Certo (commercial pectin)

Hull the fruit and put in a pan with the lemon juice and sugar. Leave to stand for one hour stirring from time to time. Place the pan over a low heat stirring occasionally until the sugar has dissolved. Add a small knob of butter or margarine to reduce foaming. Bring to a full rolling boil and boil rapidly for 4 minutes, stirring occasionally. Remove from the heat and stir in the Certo.

Leave to cool for at least 20 minutes to prevent the fruit floating. Then pour into clean warm jars and cover with a disc of waxed paper. Put the tops on the jars when the jam is quite cold. Label. Makes 5 lb (2.3 kg) jam.

APPLE AND BLACKBERRY JELLY

COOK'S TIP. To test for setting take a scant teaspoon of the jelly and put in a cold saucer. After a few minutes the surface should begin to set and crinkle when pushed with a finger. Do not boil the jelly rapidly while the test is going on, otherwise setting point may be lost. A very good home-made concentrated drink can be made by boiling up the fruit pulp from the bag with 3 pints (1.7 l) of water and 12 oz (350 g) sugar. Strain and keep in bottles in the refrigerator and dilute to taste with water and ice cubes.

4 lb (1.8 kg) cooking apples
2 lb (900 g) blackberries
2 pints (1.1 l) water
Sugar

Wash and cut up the apples, removing any bad portions. Wash the blackberries and drain, place in a large pan with the apples and water, cover and simmer until the fruit is a soft pulp. The time will vary with the variety of apples used but will probably be about 30 minutes.

Strain the fruit through a scalded jelly bag and leave overnight. Measure the juice and place in a large pan and bring to the boil. Add the sugar, allowing 1 lb (450 g) to each pint of juice.

Allow the sugar to dissolve and then boil rapidly for 10 minutes. Remove the pan from the heat and test for setting. Skim the jelly, pour at once into warmed jars and cover with waxed circles. Leave to cool. Seal the jars and label and then store in a cool dark place away from strong light. Makes about 3 lb jelly.

GREEN GOOSEBERRY JAM

COOK'S TIP. Quite the most favourite jam with us, the children prefer it to marmalade at breakfast. Pectin is a gum-like substance in fruit which when combined with sugar in jam-making helps the jam to set. Fruits high in pectin such as gooseberries and blackcurrants can take more sugar per lb (450 g) of fruit. You then get more jam for the amount of fruit used. Fruits low in pectin such as fresh apricots, greengages, plums and raspberries need equal quanties of fruit and sugar. Always choose good quality fruit. It should be under-ripe rather than over-ripe.

Using a copper or brass pan gives the jam a brighter green colour.

I find it best to add commerical pectin, i.e. Certo, to get a good colour, flavour and set to strawberry jam, as strawberries are very low in pectin.

2¼ lb (1 kg) gooseberries
¾ pint (450 ml) water
3 lb (1.3 kg) granulated sugar

Top and tail the gooseberries. Place them in a large pan with ¾ pint (450 ml) water and bring to the boil. Simmer gently without a lid for about 30 minutes until the mixture is reduced to a pulp and the fruit is soft. At this stage the contents of the pan will weigh about 2 lb 6 oz (a good kg)

Add the sugar to the pan and stir over a low heat until it has dissolved, then boil rapidly until setting point is reached. This will take about 8 to 10 minutes and can be tested by allowing a teaspoonful to cool on a saucer in the fridge. When pushed with the finger it should ripple.

Pour into clean warm jars and cover with discs of waxed paper. You should either put the tops on the jars when the jam is still hot or

—Lemon Curd—

when it is quite cold, then label.

For a variation of the gooseberry jam recipe put 10 heads of elderflowers in a piece of muslin and tie with a string to form a bag. Put this with gooseberries while they are simmering. Before adding the sugar remove the bag (you will find this easier if you have tied it to the handle of the pan) and squeeze gently using rubber gloves to extract the pectin juice. Makes 5 lb (2.3 kg) jam.

LEMON CURD

2 oz (50 g) butter
7 oz (200 g) caster sugar
2 lemons
4 egg yolks, beaten

Place the butter and sugar in the top of a double saucepan with simmering water in the lower part. If you do not have a double saucepan, use a basin over a pan of water. Stir well until the butter has melted.

Stir the finely grated rind and the juice from the lemons into the pan together with the egg yolks. Continue to stir over the simmering water until the curd thickens: this will take about 20 to 25 minutes. Remove from the heat and pour the lemon curd into clean warm jars, cover and seal while hot and label when cold.

Keep in a cool larder for 4 weeks or in the refrigerator for 3 months. Makes a 1 lb (450 g) or two ½ lb (225 g) jars.

MINCEMEAT

COOK'S TIP. It is worth getting stoned raisins for mincemeat as they have a much better flavour than the stoneless ones. I remember as a child our small grocer had a machine that took the stones out rather like a huge mechanical parsley mincer – you turned a handle and the pips dropped out underneath and rather squashy seeded raisins came out at the other end. At Christmas the machine had to work overtime.

1½ lb (675 g) stoned raisins
¼ lb (100 g) candied peel
1 lb (450 g) cooking apples
¾ lb (350 g) currants
½ lb (225 g) sultanas
6 oz (175 g) shredded suet
½ level teaspoon mixed spice
2 lemons
1 lb (450 g) soft brown sugar
6 tablespoons rum, brandy or
    sherry

Finely chop or mince the raisins and peel. Peel, core and mince or chop the apples. Place in a large bowl with the other fruit, suet and spice. Grate the rind and squeeze the juice from the lemons, add with the sugar and rum, brandy or sherry to the fruit and mix very well.

Cover the bowl with a cloth and leave to stand overnight. Next day turn into clean jars, cover and label. Makes about 5½ lb (2.5 kg).

CHUTNEYS AND RELISHES

Home-made chutney is a delicious addition to any store cupboard. Chutneys are made from fruits and vegetables, or a mixture of the two, with vinegar, salt and spices acting as preserving agents.

Cooked slowly and gently, chutneys acquire a smooth texture and mellow flavour which represents a successful blending of all the ingredients. Always use a good quality vinegar with an acetic acid content of at least 5%. Brown sugar gives a better colour to chutney than other sugars. And, if you can, use whole spices when making chutney, as ground spices can give a muddy appearance to a finished chutney. The whole spice should be gently bruised, tied in a muslin bag and cooked with the other ingredients. Never use metal spoons, knives or forks in making chutney as they can impart a metallic taste.

MIRANDA'S RHUBARB AND APPLE CHUTNEY

COOK'S TIP. You can use all apples if you have no rhubarb in the garden. This is a good way of using up the last of the rhubarb and wind-fall apples at the end of the season and makes a very reasonably priced chutney if the fruit is free. It is essential to use a covering to the jars that is moisture-proof. Clean screw-topped honey jars are ideal, but otherwise use plastic snap-on lids or seal with melted paraffin wax.

3 lb (1.3 kg) apples
1½ pint (900 ml) malt vinegar
1 lb (450 g) rhubarb
2 lb (900 g) soft brown sugar
8 oz (225 g) chopped dates
8 oz (225 g) sultanas
1 small red pepper
1 tablespoon ginger powder
2 tablespoons pickling spice,
    ground
1 teaspoon mixed spice
1 dessertspoon cumin seed
1 teaspoon cayenne pepper
2 tablespoons salt

Peel, core and roughly chop the apples, place in a pan with half the vinegar and cook to a pulp. Slice the rhubarb into small pieces, place in a large pan with the remaining vinegar and bring to the boil. Simmer for 5 minutes, then add the apple purée, sugar, dates and sultanas. Seed and chop the red pepper and add to the pan with the spices and salt. Bring to the boil and simmer gently for 15-20 minutes until fairly thick and clear looking.

Pour into jars and cover. Store for 2 to 3 months before using. Makes about 8 lb (3.6 kg).

GREEN TOMATO CHUTNEY

COOK'S TIP: Make with the last of the home-grown tomatoes.

3 lb (1.3 kg) green tomatoes,
    skinned and sliced
1 red pepper, seeded and
chopped
12 oz (350 g) onions, sliced
12 oz (350 g) cooking apples,
    weighed when peeled, cored
    and chopped
6 oz (175 g) raisins
¾ oz (19 g) salt
One inch (20 cm) piece, peeled
    root ginger
A little cayenne pepper
12 oz (350 g) brown sugar
1 pint (600 ml) malt vinegar

Place all the ingredients in a preserving pan and simmer gently, stirring occasionally for 2 to 3 hours. The mixture will be of a thick consistency and all the liquid absorbed.

Remove the piece of root ginger and pot in clean warm jars. Seal with plastic or vinegar proof lids. Makes about 5 lb (2.3 kg).

CHUTNEY IN THE RAW

1 marrow, peeled, seeded and
    finely diced
1 cucumber, finely diced
3 carrots, grated
3 onions, grated
1 cauliflower, broken into tiny
    pieces
10 oz (275 g) salt
5 pints (2.8 l) water

SAUCE:
3 oz (75 g) flour
½ oz (12.5 g) curry powder
½ oz (12.5 g) turmeric
1½ oz (40 g) mustard powder
2 pints (a good litre) malt vinegar
1¼ lb (550 g) granulated sugar

Place all the prepared vegetables in a large bowl or plastic bucket and add the salt and water and leave to soak for 24 hours.

Next day rinse the vegetables and drain very thoroughly.

Put the flour and spices in a preserving pan and gradually blend in the vinegar to make a smooth paste. Add the sugar and bring to the boil, stirring until thickened.

Add the vegetables, bring back to the boil and boil for 5 minutes. Remove from the heat and pot in clean warm jars and seal with plastic or vinegar proof lids. Makes about 9 lb (4 kg).

APPLE AND PEPPER RELISH

Windfall apples are perfect for this recipe as the fruit is prepared first and weighed afterwards.

2 lb (900 g) cooking apples,
    peeled and cored and weighed
    after preparation
2 onions, quartered
6 tablespoons malt vinegar
12 oz (350 g) demerara sugar
1 rounded teaspoon mustard
    powder
Grated rind and juice of one lemon
2 bay leaves
6 oz (175 g) sultanas
1 level tablespoon salt
½ level teaspoon mild chilli
powder
2 level teaspoon ground ginger
2 cloves garlic, crushed

Mince the apples and onions and place in a thick-based saucepan with the vinegar, sugar, mustard, lemon rind and juice. Simmer for 20 minutes and then add the remaining ingredients, stir well.

Bring to the boil and then reduce the heat and simmer, stirring occasionally until the mixture is fairly thick with a chutney consistency. This will take about 45 minutes.

Remove the bay leaves and then pot the relish in clean warm jars. Seal with plastic or vinegar proof lids. Label. Makes a good 3 lb (1.4 kg).

A Selection of Relishes

VINEGAR

One hundred years ago vinegars flavoured with fruit, vegetables or herbs were a familiar sight in most kitchens. Today they are making a come-back. They are both easy to make and inexpensive and provide an interesting addition to salad dressings, cold meats, drinks and grilled meat and fish. This is the equipment you will need: A large earthenware or glass bowl, wooden spoons, scales, knives and bottles. You can use both screw-top and corked bottles, but remember to boil the screw-tops for ten minutes before use.

TARRAGON VINEGAR

Sprays of tarragon
White wine vinegar

Half-fill a 1 pint (600 ml) jar or bowl with fresh tarragon leaves previously washed and drained. Cover with wine vinegar and leave covered for four weeks, occasionally stirring. Strain and bottle, adding a fresh spray of tarragon to each bottle before corking.

You can also use other herbs — such as marjoram or thyme for this recipe.

CHILLI VINEGAR

Makes approximately 1 litre
(2 pints)
2-3 oz (50-75 gm) red chillis
2 pints (1 litre) malt vinegar

Split the chillis in half and place in a jar or bowl. Cover with vinegar. Leave, covered, for 4 weeks stirring occasionally, strain and bottle.

CUCUMBER VINEGAR

Makes approximately 2 pints
(1 litre)
4 large cucumbers
3 medium onions
2 pints (1 litre) wine vinegar

Peel and finely chop the onions and cucumbers. Place in a large bowl or jar and cover with vinegar. Leave, covered tightly, for a week stirring occasionally. Strain and bottle.

FRUIT IN SEASON

● Months when of best quality ○ Available all time

	J	F	M	A	M	J	J	A	S	O	N	D
HOME-PRODUCED FRUITS												
Apples	●	●	●	●	●	●	●	●	●	●	●	●
Crab apples									●	●		
Apricots	●	●		●	●	●	●					●
Cherries						●	●	●				
Pears	●	●	○	○	○	○	○	○	●	●	●	●
Plums								●	●			
Quinces										●	●	
HOME-PRODUCED SOFT FRUITS												
Bilberries							●	●	●			
Blackberries								●	●	●	●	
Blackcurrants							●	●				
Blueberries							●	●	●			
Gooseberries				●	●	●	●					
Loganberries							●	●				
Raspberries							●	●				
Redcurrants							●	●				
Rhubarb			●	●								
Strawberries						●	●					
White currants							●	●				
IMPORTED CITRUS FRUITS												
Clementine	●	●									●	●
Grapefruit	●	●	●	●	●	●	●	●			●	●
Lemon	●	●	●	●	●	●	●	●	●	●	●	●
Lime	●	●	●	●	●	●	●	●	●	●	●	●
Mandarin	●	●	●	●	●	●	●	●		●	●	●
Orange	●	●	●	●				●		●	●	●
Ortanique	●	●	●							●	●	●
Satsuma	●	●								●	●	●
Tangerine	●	●	●							●	●	●
Ugli	●	●									●	●
IMPORTED FRUITS												
Bananas	●	●	●	●	●		●	●	●	●	●	●
Cape gooseberries	●	●	●	●	●	●	●	●	●	●	●	●
Chinese gooseberries	●	●					●	●	●	●	●	●
Coconuts	○	○	○	○	○	○	○	○	○	○	○	○
Cranberries	●	●								●	●	●
Dates	●	●	●						●	●	●	●
Figs								●	●	●	●	●
Grapes	●	●	●	●	●		●	●	●	●	●	●
Lychees	●	●										●
Mangoes	●											●
Melons	○	○	○	○						○	○	○
Nectarines							●	●	●			
Water Melon					●	●	●	●				
Pawpaws						●	●	●	●		●	●
Peaches					●	●	●	●		●		
Persimmon	●									●	●	●
Pineapple	●	●	●	●	●	●	●	●	●	●	●	●
Pomegranates	●								●	●	●	●

NUTS	J	F	M	A	M	J	J	A	S	O	N	D
Chestnuts										●	●	●
Hazel or cob nuts	○	○	○	○	○	○	○	○	○	●	●	●
Walnuts	○	○	○	○	○	○	○	○	○	○	○	○
Almonds	○	○	○	○	○	○	○	○	○	○	○	○
Brazil nuts	○	○	○	○	○	○	○	○	○	○	○	○

VEGETABLES IN SEASON

	J	F	M	A	M	J	J	A	S	O	N	D
Artichoke, globe	○	○	○	○	○	●	●	●	●	○	○	○
Artichoke, Jerusalem	●	●	●							●	●	●
Asparagus	○	○	○	○	●	●	○	○	○	○	○	○
Aubergine	○	○	○	○	○	○	○	○	○	○	○	○
Avocado	○	○	○	○	○	○	○	○	○	○	○	○
Beans, broad				●	●	●	●	●	●			
Beans, French	○	○	○	○	○	●	●	●		○	○	○
Beans, runner							●	●	●	●		
Beetroot	●	●	●	●	●	●	●	●	●	●	●	●
Broccoli	●	●	●	●	●	●	●	●	●	●	●	●
Brussels sprouts	●	●	●							●	●	●
Cabbage	●	●	●	●	●	●	●	●	●	●	●	●
Carrots	●	●	●	●	●	●	●	●	●	●	●	●
Cauliflower	●	●	●	●	●	●	●	●	●	●	●	●
Celeriac	●	●	●							●	●	●
Celery	●	●				●	●	●	●	●	●	●
Chicory	○	○	○	○	○				○	○	○	○
Corn							●	●	●	●		
Courgette	○	○	○	○	○	●	●	●	○	○	○	○
Cucumber	○	○	●	●	●	●	●	●	●	●	○	○
Endive	○	○	○	○	●	●	●	●	○	○	○	○
Fennel	○	○	○	○	○	○	○	○	○	○	○	○
Kale	●	●	●	●	●						●	●
Kohlrabi	○	○	○	○			○	○	○	○	○	○
Leeks	●	●	●	●	●			●	●	●	●	●
Lettuce	●	●	●	●	●	●	●	●	●	●	●	●
Marrow							●	●	●	●		
Mushroom	●	●	●	●	●	●	●	●	●	●	●	●
Mustard and cress	●	●	●	●	●	●	●	●	●	●	●	●
Okra	○	○	○	○	○	○						○
Onions	●	●	●	○	○	○	○	○		●	●	●
Parsnip	●	●	●	●						●	●	●
Pea						●	●	●	●	●		
Pepper	○	○	○	○	○	○	○	○	○	○	○	○
Potato	●	●	●	●	●	●	●	●	●	●	●	●
Pumpkin									●	●	●	●
Radish	○	○	○	●	●	●	●	●	●	●	○	○
Salsify	○	○	○	○	○					○	○	●
Sea Kale	●	●	●					●	●	●	●	●
Shallot	●	●	●						●	●	●	○
Spinach	○	○	●	●	●	●		●	●			○
Swede	●	●	●	●	●				●	●	●	●
Sweet potato	○	○	○							○	○	○
Tomato	○	○	●	●	●	●		●	●	●	●	●
Turnip	●	●	●	●	●	●	●	●	●	●	●	●
Watercress	●	●	●					●	●	●	●	

FISH IN SEASON

● Months when of best quality   ○ Available all time

White Fish in Season

	J	F	M	A	M	J	J	A	S	O	N	D
Bass					●	●	●	●				
Bream, sea						●	●	●	●	●	●	●
Cod	●	●	●		○	○	●	●	●	●	●	●
Coley, saithe	○	○	○			○	○	○	○	○	○	○
Dogfish (huss, rig, flake)	●	●	●	●	●	○	○	○	●	●	●	●
Flounder	●	●			○	○	○		●	●	●	●
Haddock	●	●	○		○	○			●	●	●	●
Hake	●	●	●				●	●	●	●	●	●
Halibut	●	●	●	●			●	●	●	●	●	●
Mock Halibut	●	●	○	○	○	○	○	●	●	●	●	●
Plaice	●	●	●		○	○	○	○	○	○	○	○
Skate	●	●	●							●	●	●
Dover Sole	●	●	○	○	●	●	●	●	●	●	●	●
Lemon Sole	●	●	●	○	○	●	●	●	●	●	●	●
Turbot	○	○	○	●	●	●	●	●	○	○	○	○
Whiting	●	●	○	○	○	○	○	○	○	●	●	●

Oily Fish in Season

	J	F	M	A	M	J	J	A	S	O	N	D
Carp	●	●	●			●	●	●	●	●	●	●
Conger eel	○	○	○	○							○	○
Herring	●	●				●	●	●	●	●	●	●
Mackerel	●	●	●	○			○	●	●	●	●	●
Mullet, grey	●	●	●			●	●	●	●	●	●	●
Mullet, red					●	●	●	●	●			
Perch	●	●	●			●	●	●	●	●	●	●
Pike	●	●	●			●	●	●	●	●	●	●
Pilchard	●	●	●	○	○	○	○	○	○	○	○	●
Salmon						●	●	●				
Sardine			●	●	●	●	●	●				
Smelt or Sparling	●	●	●									
Sprat	●	●	●							○	○	○
Trout, rainbow	○	○	○	○	○	○	○	○	○	○	○	○
Trout, river or brown			●	●	●	●	●	●	●			
Trout, sea or salmon			●	●	●	●	●					
Whitebait			●	●	●	●	●					

Shellfish in Season

	J	F	M	A	M	J	J	A	S	O	N	D
Clams	○	○	○	○	○	○	○	○	●	●	●	○
Cockles	●	●	●	●	○	○	○	○	●	●	●	●
Crab	○	○	○	●	●	●	●	●	○	○	○	○
Lobster	○	○	○	●	●	●	●	●	○	○	○	○
Mussels	●	●	●						●	●	●	●
Oysters	●	●	●	●					●	●	●	●
Prawns & Shrimps	○	○	○	○	○	○	○	○	○	○	○	○
Scallops	●	●	●						●	●	●	●
Whelks	●	●	○	○	○	●	●	●	●	●	●	●
Winkles	●	●	●	●	●	●	●	●	○	●	●	●

CALORIE CHART

Calorie values are given in
Calories per ounce.

	CALORIES
Almonds	165
Apple, fresh eating, (medium about 4 oz)	15
Apricot, tinned	30
Apricots, dried	50
Asparagus, fresh	5
Bacon, lean, fried	125
Bacon, lean, grilled	90
Bananas, fresh, peeled	20
Barley, pearl	105
Beans, broad, fresh	20
Beans, butter, boiled	25
Beans, green, runner	5
Beef, corned	60
Beef, roast, lean & fat	100
Beef, roast, lean	65
Beer, bottled, pale or brown	10
Beer, draught, bitter or mild	10
Beetroot, boiled	10
Beverages	
Chocolate, drinking	115
Cocoa powder	130
Coffee	0
Tea	0
Biscuits, plain	120
chocolate	140
Blackberries	10
Bread	70
Broccoli, boiled	5
Brussels sprouts, boiled	5
Butter	205
Cabbage, boiled	5
Cakes	
plain sponge	130
fruit	100
jam tarts	105
Carrots, fresh, boiled, raw, tinned	5
Cauliflower, boiled	5
Celery, fresh, raw	5
Cereal, breakfast (varies from about 90-115)	
Cheese, Cheddar	115
Cheshire	115
Cottage	30
Cream	120
Danish Blue	100

	CALORIES
Cherries, fresh,	15
Chicken, roast	40
Chips, potato, fried	70
Chocolate, milk	160
Chocolate, plain	150
Cooking fat, lard	255
Cooking oil	250
Corn on the cob	35
Cream, fresh, single	60
Cream, fresh, double	130
Cress, fresh, raw	5
Crisps, potato	150
Cucumber, raw	5
Damsons, fresh, raw or stewed	10
Dates,	60
Doughnuts, jam	100
Egg, boiled or poached	45
Egg, fried	70
Egg, raw	45
Fish, white	20
fried in batter	55
herrings	65
kipper fillets	60
Fish, canned	
pilchards in tomato	40
salmon	40
sardines in oil	60
shrimps, drained	35
tuna in oil	75
Fish fingers, grilled	50
Flour, white or wholemeal	100
Fruit, dried	
sultanas	70
raisins	70
Gherkins	0
Grapes, white	15
Grapefruit, fresh	5
Grapefruit, canned	15
Ham	75
Ice cream	55
Lamb chop, grilled	75
Leek, boiled	5
Lemon, fresh	5
Lemon barley water	30
Lentils, boiled	25
Lettuce, raw	0

	CALORIES
Liver sausage, cooked	65
Margarine	205
Marmalade	75
Marrow, boiled	0
Melon, yellow, fresh	5
Milk, fresh, dairy	20
Milk, evaporated	50
Milk, dried, whole	140
Mushrooms, raw	0
Olive oil	255
Olives	30
Onion, fried	100
Onion, raw	5
Orange, sweet, fresh	10
Orange, juice, fresh	10
Orange squash, concentrate	30
Parsley, raw, fresh	5
Parsnip, boiled or raw	15
Pasta	
dry weight	105
Peaches, canned	25
Peanuts, shelled	170
Peanut butter	175
Pear, fresh, raw, eating or fresh, cooking, stewed	10
Peas, frozen	20
Peas, fresh, boiled	15
Peppers, red or green	5
Pineapple, fresh, raw	10
Pineapple, canned	20
Plums, dessert, fresh	10
Potatoes, boiled	25
Potatoes, roast	35
Prawns	10
Prunes, canned	25
Rabbit, stewed	50
Raspberries	5
Rhubarb, stewed	0
Rice, boiled	35
Salad cream	90
Sauce, Worcestershire	5
Sausages, pork, fried	95
grilled	90
Spinach, fresh, boiled	5
Spirits, alcoholic, average	60-70
Sugar, white	115
brown	115
Sweet Pickle	40

QUANTITIES OF FOOD TO BUY FOR AVERAGE PORTIONS

FISH	AMOUNT PER PERSON
Crabs	1 small
Cutlets	½ lb (250 g)
Fillets	6-8 oz (250 g)
Fish, whole	½-¾ lb (250 g)
Lobster	½-¾ lb (250 g)
Mussels	1 pt (½ l)
Prawns	½ pt (¼ l)

FRUIT FOR COOKING	4-8 oz (125-250 g)

MEAT	
Cooked	2-3 oz (50 g)
With bone	½-¾ lb (250 g)
Without bone	4-6 oz (125 g)

VEGETABLES	
Artichokes, globe	1
Artichokes, Jerusalem	½ lb (250 g)
Asparagus	6-8 pieces
Beans, broad	¾-1 lb (500 g)
Beans, dried	2-4 oz (50-125 g)
Beans, French or runner	6-8 oz (250 g)
Beetroot	6-8 oz (250 g)
Brussels Sprouts, Cabbage, Savoy	6-8 oz (250 g)
Carrots	6-8 oz (250 g)
Celery	½ head
Celeriac	6-8 oz (250 g)
Chicory	4 oz (125 g)
Kale	½ lb (250 g)

VEGETABLES	AMOUNT PER PERSON
Leeks	½-¾ lb (250 g)
Marrow	½-¾ lb (250 g)
Mushrooms	2-4 oz (50-125 g)
Parsnips	6-8 oz (250 g)
Peas	½ lb (250 g)
Peas, dried	2-4 oz (50-125 g)
Potatoes	½ lb (250 g)
Spinach	½ lb (250 g)
Swedes and Turnips	6-8 oz (250 g)
Tomatoes	4-6 oz (125 g)
Watercress	1-2 oz (25-50 g)

QUANTITIES OF COOKED DISHES TO ALLOW

	AMOUNT PER PERSON
Custards	¼ pt milk (125 ml)
Jellies	¼-⅓ pt (125 ml)
Milk Puddings	¼-⅓ pt milk (125 ml)
Pastry	2 oz flour (50 g)
Sauces	⅛-¼ pt liquid (125 ml)
Soups	⅓-½ pt (250 ml)
Steamed Puddings	2 oz flour (50 g)

WEIGHTS AND MEASURES CONVERSION TABLES

WEIGHT	
1 lb	0.4536 kg
1 kg	2.205 lb
½ oz	14 g
1 oz	28 g
2 oz	57 g
3 oz	85 g
4 oz	113 g
8 oz	227 g
1 lb	454 g
2 lb	907 g
3 lb	1.36 kg
4 lb	1.81 kg
7 lb	3.17 kg
1 st	6.35 kg
2 st	12.69 kg
4 st	25.38 kg
1 cwt	50.76 kg
1 ton	1015.26 kg
10 g	0.4 oz
25 g	0.9 oz
50 g	1.8 oz
100 g	3.5 oz
200 g	7.1 oz
500 g	1 lb 2 oz
1 kg	2 lb 3 oz
2 kg	4 lb 7 oz
3 kg	6 lb 10 oz
4 kg	8 lb 13 oz
5 kg	11 lb
10 kg	22 lb
100 kg	221 lb
1 t	2205 lb

LIQUID

1 pint	0.568 litre
1 litre	1.760 pints
1 fl oz	28 ml
2 fl oz	57 ml
3 fl oz	85 ml
4 fl oz	114 ml
5 fl oz	142 ml
10 fl oz	284 ml
1 pint	568 ml
2 pint	1.137 l
3 pint	1.705 l
4 pint	2.273 l
6 pint	3.408 l
1 gal	4.546 l
50 ml	2 fl oz
100 ml	4 fl oz
200 ml	7 fl oz
300 ml	11 fl oz
400 ml	14 fl oz
500 ml	18 fl oz
1 l	1 pint 15 fl oz
2 l	3 pints 10 fl oz
5 l	8 pints 16 fl oz
10 l	17 pints 12 fl oz

APPROPRIATE MAXIMUM STORAGE TIMES FOR MEAT IN THE HOME

	Days in meat safe	Days in refrigerator	Months in freezer −17°C (0°F)
UNCOOKED MEAT			
Beef	2	3-5	12
Pork	2	2-4	6
Lamb	2	3-5	9
Bacon rashers	4	7	1
Bacon vacuum-packed rashers	5	10	3
Mince	same day	1	3
Offal	same day	1-2	3
Sausages	1	3	3
COOKED MEATS			
Casseroles with bacon	1	2	3
Casseroles without bacon	1	3	6
Ham	same day	2-3	2
Meat pies	1	1	3
Sliced meat with gravy	1-2	2-3	3
Sliced meat without gravy	1-2	2-4	2
Pâté	1	2	1
Stock	same day	4	6

OVEN TEMPERATURES

	ELECTRIC (°F)	(°C)	GAS MARK
Very slow oven	250-275	120-140	¼-½
Slow	300-325	150-160	1-2
Moderate	350-375	180-190	3-5
Moderately hot	375-400	190-200	5-6
Hot	400-425	200-220	6-7
Very hot	450-475	230-250	8-9

Index